Economic Systems of Northern Thailand

STRUCTURE AND CHANGE

Economic Systems of Northern Thailand

STRUCTURE AND CHANGE

****

Edward Van Roy

Cornell University Press

ITHACA AND LONDON

First published 1971

International Standard Book Number 0-8014-0607-2
Library of Congress Catalog Card Number 70-137394

PRINTED IN THE UNITED STATES OF AMERICA
BY VAIL-BALLOU PRESS, INC.

ACKNOWLEDGMENTS

The field work on which this study is largely based was conducted during 1963–1964 under the sponsorship of the Bennington-Cornell Anthropological Survey of Hill Tribes in Thailand. Further opportunities for observation were provided in 1966–1967 during an appointment with the Research and Planning Division of the United Nations Economic Commission for Asia and the Far East.

In North Thailand, I received generous assistance from a number of people, among whom I must single out for special thanks Prasit Phumxusri, Kraisri Nimmanahaeminda, Chak Kalayanamit, Chamnian Chaimano, and my research assistant, Yongyoot Rudchusuntikul. A great debt is owed the many upland peasant families who provided me hospitality, friendship, cooperation, and information. In Bangkok, I was aided beyond the call of duty by staff members of a number of government agencies, who must here remain nameless, and by various scholars and friends with firsthand knowledge of the Northern hills, including Khrui Bunyasingh, Hans Manndorff, and Richard Paw U.

The approach employed here is the outgrowth of my studies under F. Eugene Melder at Clark University and later under Clarence E. Ayres, Walter C. Neale, and Benjamin Higgins at the University of Texas. I owe my initial interest in Southeast Asian studies to my wife's encouragement and to the opportunities and guidance offered by Walter Neale, Lucien M. Hanks, and Jane Richardson Hanks.

Various chapters were read in draft form by my colleagues in the departments of Economics and Anthropology at Stony Brook, as well as by Lucien and Jane Hanks, Delmos Jones, Maivan Lam, Frank LeBar, Walter Neale, Ralph Van Roy, Harold Ware, and Jeanne Zammataro. A number of ideas developed in the following chapters would have been less coherent or would have been overlooked entirely but for the trenchant comments of these friendly critics. Financial support to complete the writing of the study was furnished by the American Council of Learned Societies and the Social Science Research Council during 1968–1969.

I am grateful to the editors of several publications for permission to incorporate material from my articles: "The Introduction of Plantation Economy to North Thailand," *Explorations in Entrepreneurial History*, second series, V (1968), 36–57; "An Interpretation of Northern Thai Peasant Economy," *Journal of Asian Studies*, XXVI (1967), 421–432; "Economic Dualism and Economic Change among the Hill Tribes of Thailand," *Pacific Viewpoint*, VII (1966), 151–168; "Structure of the Miang Economy," in *Ethnographic Notes on Northern Thailand*, Cornell University Southeast Asia Program, Data Paper Number 58 (1965), pages 21–30.

Three generations of my family, both in America and in Thailand, have made many sacrifices so that this book might see the light of day. The following pages are a testimony to their patience and love.

EDWARD VAN ROY

Stony Brook, New York
November 1970

CONTENTS

MAPS

CHARTS

TABLES

Economic Systems of
Northern Thailand

STRUCTURE AND CHANGE

PROBLEMS AND
PARAMETERS

This book seeks to interpret in interdisciplinary terms the
organizational patterns and developmental processes of three
economic systems located in the Northern Thai uplands. It
is directed primarily at two audiences: students of Southeast
Asian economics and anthropology, and students of economic
development, comparative economic systems, and economic
anthropology. The former are presented a description and
analysis of certain types of economic systems found in the
upland areas of North Thailand and neighboring countries,
based on a survey of the scattered literature and on the observations of a year's field work.[1] The latter are provided a
case study in the application of the so-called institutional or
substantive approach to the analysis of economic issues in a
culturally pluralistic setting.[2]

[1] The field work on which this study is based was conducted
during the year 1963–1964, six months of which were spent in residence at Nikhom Chiengdao, Chiengmai Province. Unless otherwise
noted, all descriptive materials included in this study refer to conditions as observed in 1963–1964.

[2] The institutional, or substantive, approach to economic anthropology is discussed in detail in Dalton, 1969; Firth, ed., 1967; and
Kaplan, 1968. Additional references to the topic may be found in
the excellent bibliographies included in these works. Recent discussions of institutionalism among economists include Gordon, 1963;
Thompson, ed., 1967; and Kapp, 1968.

Basically, this study attempts to develop general models of three interacting economic systems. It seeks to explain their individual "structures" and the processes of economic change which result from the interaction of these "structures." [3] Model-building in economics, as in the social sciences generally, inevitably generates controversy, for no model can include all possible variables; to do so would be to duplicate the very reality from which the model seeks to abstract. Each model must select from the vast array of everyday practices only those elements considered most significant in determining the conditions of human existence (in economics, the level and composition of material well-being). Only the factual persuasiveness, or explanatory power, of a model as an interpretation of the logic of human affairs can serve as a defense of the particular variables selected as significant.

Model-building, in other words, must be discriminatory; it collapses under the weight of encyclopedic fact-gathering. [4] As understanding of the economic systems of the Northern Thai uplands increases, improved models will inevitably be forthcoming, for more intensive examination of the various aspects of economic affairs in this setting will permit clearer evaluation of their relative degrees of structural significance.

[3] The multiple meanings of "structure" are critically reviewed in Machlup, 1967. Synthesizing various of these meanings which he considers "clear," I define structure as the relatively permanent, invariant conditions or relationships within a system which are outcome-determining but not outcome-determined.

[4] On the other hand, model-building must, if it is to have explanatory value, not abstract to the extent that it becomes empirically impotent (that is, irrelevant to factual circumstances). While anthropology has historically been guilty of the vice of overindulging in data collection, economics has tended to move so far in the direction of abstractionist analytics as to result in models of great sophistication and refinement but of little real-world problem-solving value.

Thus, the interpretation of economic structure and change in the Northern Thai uplands presented here may be expected to have a limited life span; its obsolescence can only mean improved understanding, and thus the more indigenously oriented, or culture-conscious, economic development of North Thailand.

The Substantive Economy

In this study of economic systems the economist's conventional methodological orientation, which focuses on the individual's "rational" or "economizing" behavior, is replaced by the approach commonly employed in the other social sciences and known in economics as institutionalism or substantivism. From this perspective, the economy is analyzed as a system of collective behavior governed by rules of social organization, a system which forms an indissociable part of the cultural whole and the development of which is but one aspect of cultural evolution. Specifically, the economy is defined as that realm of collective behavior, or social action, concerned with the provision and disposition of the material means of human want satisfaction.

The substantive economic process can be divided conceptually into two dimensions of collective behavior: technology and institutions. Technology refers to the application of man's fund of knowledge concerning environmental control, his utilization of artifacts and implements, craftmen's skills, engineering concepts, and operating procedures, all of which permit him to alter material conditions to fit socially defined schemes of production, distribution, and consumption. Economic institutions, on the other hand, constitute networks of continuing human interaction supported by rules, conventions, myths, and mores which regulate interpersonal dealings associated with the technological process.

3 ✕

Technology

Economists concerned with questions of growth and development have generally stressed the importance of technology, though they have ordinarily not defined its scope as broadly as is done here. In fact, the entire realm of conventional economic analysis falls within the province of technology as here defined. Conventional economic theory is concerned at heart with the efficient allocation and utilization of scarce factors of production and the proceeds of their employment, but, as increasing numbers of economists have come to realize in recent years, factor endowments and allocative patterns are themselves functions of existing technologies.[5] In historical investigations, particularly, the fact that each system's level of material welfare is fundamentally determined by its technological capacity ordinarily goes unquestioned.[6] Furthermore, the import of studies dealing specifically with the causes and consequences of invention, innovation, and diffusion of technology is that technological progress constitutes the key variable in the process of economic development.[7]

The basic generalizations emerging from past work may be

[5] See, for examples of this emerging view, American Economic Association, 1966, which is entirely devoted to the economic analysis of technological change, technology nowhere in the volume being carefully defined. (Note, however, the exploratory discussion of the subject in Boulding, 1966.)

[6] For instance, Supple, ed., 1963, pp. 27-31; and Lynn White, 1962, *passim*.

[7] Work has proceeded along diverse lines in the various social sciences: Representative of the line taken in sociology are Allen *et al.*, 1957; Gilfillan, 1935; and Rogers, 1962. Representative of anthropology are Barnett, 1953; Erasmus, 1961; Steward, 1955; and Leslie White, 1959. Recent work in economics is surveyed in Lave, 1966; Mansfield, 1968; and Schmookler, 1966.

summarized as follows: Technology progresses in evolution-ary fashion from the simple to the complex, from lesser to greater effectiveness as an environmental control. Its progress features increasing variety in resource inputs, increasing functional specialization of labor, increasing employment of machine processes and nonhuman energy sources, increasing numbers of stages in the production process, and increasing economies of scale in the efficient organization of productive activities. The pace of technological change tends to accelerate as the complexity of technology increases. Technology transcends cultural boundaries through diffusion from the relatively complex to the relatively simple.

Although the broad sweep of history confirms the universality and exponential continuity of technological progress, close inspection of particular cultural life-histories does not. If, as has been proposed, a determinate set of principles governs technological progress, the following questions may well be asked: Why have some economies deteriorated while their neighbors have thrived? Why have some stagnated during certain periods of their histories and developed rapidly during others? Why have some achieved levels of material well-being undreamed of by others? Why is the fundamental reality of international affairs today a marked and apparently rising inequality among the world's economic systems rather than the equality implicit in the universal applicability of man's technological stock? Such questions cannot be solved by an investigation of technology. Their answers lie in the institutional dimension of the substantive economy.

Institutions

Technology relates man to his environment; institutions relate men to one another. They constitute the regularities of interpersonal dealings, the fabric of social organization. To the sociologist, "institutions are the 'ways in which the value patterns of the common culture of a social system are integrated in the concrete action of its units in their interaction with each other through the definition of role expectations and the organization of motivation.' " [8] Institutions exist on the levels of both thought and action; it is in the latter realm that they are open to empirical investigation by the economist. They are normative in the sense of forming patterns, regularities, or configurations of collective action while taking into account the inevitable range of individual behavioral variation.

The continuing performance of tasks, or functions, necessary for the preservation of the established order is promoted by institutions carrying appropriate rewards and punishments. "Success" in this effort is ordinarily reflected in institutional stability and persistence; "failure" is manifested in cultural change.[9] The economy is no exception: "The instituting of the economic process vests that process with unity and stability; it produces a structure with a definite function in society; it shifts the place of the process in society, thus adding significance to its history; it centers interest on values, motives and policy." [10]

In institutionalizing means toward the fulfillment of its participants' aspirations, the economic system inevitably creates pressures that favor the established order. To the

[8] Parsons and Smelser, 1956, p. 102. Cf. Walton Hamilton, 1930.

[9] The body of theory which seeks to explain man's survival in terms of his ability to systematize social events is known as functionalism. Most work along this line has been done by anthropologists and sociologists; few economists have followed in their tracks. A broad-based evaluation of functionalism is provided in Martindale, ed., 1965. On the methodological problems involved in functional analysis see Hempel, 1959; Buckley, 1959; and Martindale, ed., 1965.

[10] Polanyi, 1957b, pp. 249–250.

degree that the system tends to satisfy the preponderance of its members' material aspirations, deviations from accepted norms generate popular reaction, for they threaten the very stability that provides an acceptable way of life.[11] The economy featuring the closer coincidence between its production and distribution mechanisms on the one hand and its members' material aspirations on the other will, other things being equal, tend to be the more stable; it will be relatively more functionally integrated in the sense that the institutional framework and economic incentives will be mutually supportive or reinforcing.[12] In systems institutionally less coherent, more participants find themselves more frequently frustrated in their efforts to realize their ambitions. Where economic security and opportunity, as defined by the ideals of the community, elude their grasp, participants tend to have a smaller stake in the preservation of the established order. Accordingly, deviation carries smaller opportunity costs as well as smaller risks of social disapprobation and political reprisal; the system is said to be relatively dysfunctional.

One of the primary tasks of comparative institutional analysis is to spell out the economic substance of different types of institutional configurations. This task is complicated by the "embeddedness" of the economy within "non-Western" cultures.[13] Participants within non-Western sys-

[11] Coser, 1956, pp. 96–103.

[12] This point is frequently made in sociopsychological studies of such systems. See, for instance, Hagen, 1962, pp. 161–199; and McClelland, 1963.

[13] The terms "embedded" and "non-Western" require brief clarification here because they appear superficially ambiguous and frequently carry connotations which raise the hackles of anthropologists. [continued on page 8]

tems do not perceive clear distinctions between economy, society, and polity. Economic *activity* exists, of course, insofar as individuals strive to manipulate their environment for material gain. But such activity is not functionally compartmentalized in the indigenous *mind*, as empirically reflected in the institutional structure.

To the individual [in the non-Western community] his emotions fail to convey any experience that he could identify as "economic." He is simply not aware of any pervading interest

"Economic embeddedness" is a term used in Polanyi *et al.*, eds., 1957, to refer to the place of the economy within the broader realm of human affairs. The concept, though not the descriptive term, has been refined in Nash, 1964, into a tripartite classification of ways in which the economy fits into other categories of social action: "normative integration" (meaning that the ends sought in the economy are mutually supportive of goals in other spheres of social action); "functional interdependence" (meaning that the economic roles played by individuals are consistent with their roles in other spheres of social action); and "causal interaction" (meaning that the quantity and composition of economic output is partly determined by and in turn determines social action in other spheres). Despite the dislike of many anthropologists and sociologists for "embeddedness" as a descriptive term for this cluster of associated concepts, none better has been proffered, and so it will be employed here.

"Non-Western cultures" are those which, from the perspective of economics, possess relatively backward (or preindustrial) technologies and noncommerical (or deeply embedded) economic institutions. Western culture is characterized as possessing a unique synthesis of industrial technology and commercial institutions; thus, the commercial-industrial economy. Geographically, Western culture covers Europe (including the Socialist camp, which in this view has merely centralized its commercial institutions) and North America, as well as various underpopulated lands colonized by Western emigres and numerous metropolitan enclaves in non-Western cultures. Non-Western culture, on the other hand survives in rural enclaves in many areas of the West. Despite the term's openness to criticism because of its simplistic cultural classification and neglect of marginal cases, it will be employed here because of its essential descriptive value and brevity.

in regard to his livelihood which he could recognize as such. Yet the lack of such a concept does not appear to hamper him in the performance of his everyday tasks.[14]

In the non-Western setting, then, "economic action, indeed the substantive economy itself, is defined and demarcated by sets of rules, values, and goals largely extrinsic to the economy itself." [15]

This peculiarly non-Western—or, according to the ethnocentric view of the Western economist, "irrational"—variety of economic institutionalization results in a certain fuzziness when conventional economic analysis, fitted to the Western economic model, is indiscriminately employed to identify such systems' problems and prospects. For example, the lack of careful evaluation of pecuniary costs and benefits in daily decision-making in such systems, accompanied by the absence of pervasive price formation and record keeping, gives economic activity the appearance of gross inefficiency by conventional economic criteria. It also leaves the conventional economist in the frustrating position of investigating systems for which the statistical data required for standard analysis are lacking, reinforcing his prejudices against "primitivism" and preordaining his development policy prescriptions.[16]

In sum, institutions form self-perpetuating patterns of thought and action and are therefore functional in the technical sense of the term. Consequently, institutions exhibit pressures against nonconformity with established norms and

[14] Polanyi, 1957a, p. 70.   [15] Nash, 1966, p. 91.

[16] Frankel, 1953, pp. 56–81. Cf. Stolper, 1966, *passim*, esp. pp. 6–16. The conventional economist's biases are nowhere better demonstrated than in Fei and Ranis, 1964, especially in their ethnocentric value premises as reflected in their discussion of economic dualism and subsistence wages and the policy implications deriving from their two-sector growth model, which seeks to commercialize economic life.

thus inhibit culture change. The strength of institutions in preserving the status quo is a product of their "success" in providing the organizational means whereby cultural ideals can be pursued; stated differently, institutions are structurally conservative to the degree that they generate a broad-based vested interest in the established order. Lastly, in non-Western cultures economic institutions are embedded in the broader realm of collective behavior.

Institutional-Technological Interaction

The concept of institutional-technological conflict derives from the dual propositions that whereas technology is of its own accord developmental the institutional dimension of human affairs is static, resistant to, and inhibitory of structural change. Institutional configurations are transformed in response to the strains generated by technological progress. However, just as institutions may crumble in the face of technological advance, so may technological progress be stultified by rigid institutional configurations.[17]

The most important source of economic innovation in any non-Western culture, particularly in such an institutionally and technologically pluralistic environment as the Northern Thai uplands, is external to itself.[18] Intercultural relations bring the adventurous or disenchanted into direct contact with goods and services, institutions, and technologies that are strange but frequently attractive. However, diffusion of

[17] Among the many modern studies which have come to similar conclusions let me cite just five, three in economics and one each in anthropology and sociology, respectively: Ayres, 1962; Lowe, 1965; Myrdal, 1968; Foster, 1962; and Udy, 1959.
[18] This statement touches on the broad and controversial theory of invention and innovation, neatly summarized in Murdock, 1956, and extensively documented in Rogers, 1962.

alien objects and ideas into one's own economy tends to promote evolutionary sequences of technological change and institutional accommodation destructive of the established order.[19] Therefore, to the extent that the preponderance of participants in the economic system have a stake in the status quo—that is, to the degree that their system is functionally integrated—intercultural relations are discouraged. To them, cultural diffusion appears a distinct threat rather than an opportunity, with the innovator, the key catalytic agent in the process, taking the guise of economic dissident, political revolutionary, or social renegade.

The importance of the conjunction of economic development and technological diffusion in the non-Western setting is underscored by a comparison between the process of innovation here and in the West. The idea of progress is very modern, and very Western.[20] This does not mean that the *fact* of progress is peculiar to the West, but merely that, because of its faster pace, only there has it in the past few centuries entered into the public consciousness. Progress, in the guise of science, has caught the imagination of Western man, and he has enshrined it as his god. Increased mastery of his physical environment has become his overwhelming concern. To what purposes his ever increasing technological capacity will be directed has been left to *ad hoc* consideration; he has concerned himself with the means of environmental control rather than with its ends.[21]

The commercial-industrial economy is a major element in Western man's pursuit of progress. The Western economic system is uniquely geared to technological change. The in-

[19] A number of examples are provided in Erasmus, 1961, *passim.*

[20] The uniqueness and recency of the conscious recognition of progress as the direction of history is nowhere more persuasively documented than in Bury, 1932.

[21] Ellul, 1964; Mishan, 1967.

11 *

novator, in the guise of the entrepreneur (or, in the public sector, the economic planner), has been institutionalized as a respected and handsomely rewarded community leader whose function it is to promulgate ever higher standards of material prosperity by introducing into the economy the latest fruits of scientific investigation and discovery.

Outside the commercial-industrial system and its enclaves in the underdeveloped world the idea of progress remains nascent. The absence of the scientific imagination and thus of controlled experimentation in a determined search for technological improvements means that fresh ideas are slow in coming. Through generations of cautious trial and error (in which the germ of the scientific method can be perceived by the alien observer), through the survival of the fittest in the ecological struggle, and through rare strokes of genius, technological evolution does occur, but at a snail's pace, so slow as to go unrecognized by the affected populations. The quest for security and opportunity typically resolves here into submission to one's assigned role within the established order; the vision of the good life is limited by the absence of the idea of progress itself.[22]

We are thus brought back to the theoretical foundations of the preceding discussion: With the spirit of free inquiry and constant experimentation absent from the non-Western scene, the most significant potential source of technological progress becomes contact with alien cultures, which permits the cross-cultural diffusion of ideas instrumental in raising the level of material well-being. However, the cross-cultural flow of technology is disruptive of institutional configurations geared to the pursuit of given ends with given means. To the degree that such systems are functionally integrated—tantamount to the degree to which they approximate what conventional

[22] Foster, 1965.

economics calls static equilibrium—they not only discourage indigenous innovations but invoke sanctions against those nonconformists who, through intercultural relations, may introduce them.[23]

The functional integrity of the preindustrial economy is thus promoted by its repulsion of intercultural relations which give rise to innovations. The absence of innovation, furthermore, preserves the economy's functional integrity. Such a causal sequence is widely referred to as the vicious circle, a self-perpetuating, low-level equilibrium that results in economic stagnation. On the other hand, to the degree that dysfunctions, or elements of institutional stress, are generated by technological change, the system is opened to heightened culture contact, technological diffusion, and innovation, generating further disharmonies in the institutional fabric and increased openness to change in a cumulative growth process which has been called the virtuous circle.[24]

One important question that emerges from this view of the development process is whether or to what extent an immutable sequence of institutional-technological correlatives underlies economic history. Every social scientist is aware of the venerable but largely unproductive disciplinary tradition of "stages" theories of development. Examination of the historical record in an effort to discern some unilinear order of economic stages in the evolutionary interaction of technology and institutions continues today, but with no more success than in the past. Yet, the conventional wisdom among economists continues to hold that the development process is at heart an inexorable drift along lines parallel with those previously traveled by the West, constituting

[23] Hoselitz, 1963, pp. 25–29.
[24] Note the value premises implicit in the terms "vicious," "virtuous," "stagnation," and "growth."

industrialization through the adaptation of increasingly complex, capital-intensive technologies to local resource bases and *commercialization* through the adoption of the self-equilibrating market mechanism as traditional, "inefficient" institutional configurations are abandoned—thus making "them" more like "us."[25]

Industrial technology can, however, be accommodated to a wider range of institutional forms than is thought possible by those who emphasize the inevitability of commercial industrialism. Underdeveloped economies can, with enlightened planning, industrialize without suffering the serious social dislocations and physical deprivations which ordinarily afflict peoples forced to discard indigenous institutional configurations for the rigors of the alien market system. By selectively adapting industrial processes to indigenous institutions, sophisticated planning can preserve cultural identities while fostering economic development and permitting gradual adjustment to the West, but this will be possible only when the structures of non-Western economies are understood and appreciated in terms of their own logic.

This outline of an "institutional" approach to the study of economic structure and change has dichotomized not only the concept of the substantive economy but also the methodology employed in its analysis. It has suggested that in-

[25] Most standard surveys of the subject focus on the industrializational aspect of development, making only passing reference, at most, to the interrelated problem of commercialization. See, for instance, Bauer and Yamey, 1957; and Bruton, 1965. An important segment of orthodox opinion goes even further, entirely dismissing the question of commercialization by assuming that economizing behavior in all settings guarantees efficient allocation of the factors of production, thus making development solely a matter of technological progress. See, for example, Schultz, 1964.

stitutional configurations can be fruitfully studied as functionally integrated systems transformed through cultural revolution, whereas technology, inherently dysfunctional (that is, destructive of the established order) because of its progressive character, can best be analyzed in an evolutionary context. These simplifications are useful because they provide an analytic framework and a set of working hypotheses which permit a more comprehensive explanation of economic conditions in the Northern Thai uplands than is allowed by alternative appreaches; that is, I consider this approach to be of superior relevance in a development context because it appears to fit more of the facts more of the time.

The following study of economic systems in the Northern Thai uplands does not attempt to "prove" the concepts discussed here but seeks to work within their frame of reference. Attention will be focused primarily on the institutional dimension of economic structure and on the institutional aspects of economic change under the impact of intercultural economic relations and technological diffusion.

Chapter 1 introduces the place and the people, providing geographical, cultural, political, and economic background information on the nation, region, and Research Area in which the study is set.

Chapters 2, 3, and 4 define the structural models of three economic systems found in the Northern Thai uplands—the hill tribe peasant economy, the upland Thai peasant economy, and the tea plantation economy. These chapters are divided into sections that deal individually with each system's technology and institutions in macrocosm and are followed by discussions of the interplay of institutions and technology in the microcosm of the Research Area. In each chapter the macrocosmic analysis, based on a survey of the literature, the field notes and personal communications of experts, and personal observation, is supplemented in the microcosmic discussion by the more detailed information gathered during my field work.

Chapter 5 explores the relationships between indigenous political institutions and the intervening national bureaucracy on the one hand and economic structure and development in the uplands on the other. The inseparability of "economic" institutions from "political" institutions (and, by extension, "social" institutions) in the non-Western setting is here empirically observed.

Chapter 6 takes a cross-cultural view of developmental and counterdevelopmental forces impinging upon and working within the upland economies. It analyzes the connection between the relative degree of functional integration of the indigenous institutional configurations, the concomitant scope of intercultural economic relations, and the resultant prospects for economic development in the Northern Thai uplands.

In the Afterword I suggest a development strategy for the Northern Thai uplands based on the structural interpretations of this study.

Chapter 1

SETTING

Nation and Region

Thailand is considered one of the most unified countries of Southeast Asia. To the casual observer its population appears remarkably homogeneous except at the geographic fringes and in isolated urban pockets. The Thai speak a single language, practice a single religion, produce a single crop complex with a single technology, subsist on a single staple, are uniformly aligned with Bangkok as their political hub, subscribe to a single mode of social organization, and harbor a single world view. This is the popular understanding, and as far as it goes it is not incorrect.

Careful investigation, however, has revealed that important regional variations underlie these nationwide regularities. For instance, the national language breaks down into distinct regional dialects; the intensity, sophistication, and social connotations of religious practice differ regionally; methods of agricultural production vary, as do patterns of economic exchange; the types of rice and supplementary food stuffs consumed, as well as their modes of preparation, vary; degrees of political sophistication and interest in regional autonomy differ; and regional differences appear in the underlying matrix of economic and social institutions, in the definition of the good life, and in the intensity and direction of individual aspirations.

Whether Thailand is regarded as a homogeneous entity or as a cluster of distinct regions remains largely a matter of interpretation. The nation includes elements of both uniformity and diversity. Each view provides unique insights, but neither can stand alone. The usual approach, which accepts the nation as a consolidated whole, tends to dismiss the very real and difficult regional disparities that divide the nation; only in the last few years, in fact, have problems of regionalism begun to find their way into discussions of national development and security. Regional analysis acts as a healthy counterweight to the centralist bias, though care must always be taken that it does not divorce itself from the wider national frame by accentuating particularistic problems and espousing special regional interests over the paramount task of nation-building.

The major regions of Thailand are the Central Plain, the South, the Northeast, and the North. The centripetal forces that have evolved during the past several centuries to bind these regions together as the Thai nation have been widely discussed and will not be reviewed here. The centrifugal forces making for regionalism have been generally neglected. They may be grouped under the following headings, each of which will be briefly explored here with particular reference to the North: geography, culture, polity, and economy.[1]

[1] The North comprises different portions of Thailand depending on one's disciplinary focus. From the ecological viewpoint the region stretches north from the foothills of the Central Plain. The cultural view distinguishes it as the zone predominantly occupied by the Tai Yuan peoples. The political view regards it as the seven northernmost provinces of the Thai nation. All these definitions include the seven provinces of Maehongsorn, Chiengmai, Lamphun, Chiengrai, Lampang, Nan, and Prae. Opinion is divided as to the the inclusion of the regional border provinces of Tak, Sukhothai, Kampaengphet, Uttaradit, Phitsanulok, and Loei. To resort to specific delineations of regional boundaries here would be futile; at any rate, the various ap-

This discussion of the North as a distinct region will identify the general setting in which the following study of economic systems is located.

Geography

Thailand's topography constitutes the nation's most obvious decentralizing influence.[2] The nation's heartland, the great alluvial basin formed by the Chao Phraya River, stretches some 300 miles north from the Gulf of Siam to Uttaradit, where it encounters the sharply convoluted hill country of the North. This mountainous land stretches further north into Burma and Laos and beyond them into mainland China's southern provinces. Running through this country, Thailand's northern border cuts through the midst of a geographically distinct region rather than roughly following its boundaries, as is the case to the south, east, and west.

To the west of the Central Plain rises the Tenasserim mountain range, which forms a physical barrier separating Thailand from Burma. To the east of the plain rises the Khorat escarpment, behind which lies the northeastern plateau, whose poor soils, low rainfall, and unpredictable flood conditions make it agriculturally inferior to the Central Plain. To the south the Chao Phraya delta meets the sea and fades into the Chanthaburi hills on one side and the peninsular mountains on the other. This ring of natural barriers shelters the Central Plain and the civilization it supports, but such shelter works two ways: it promotes unity among those within, and it distinguishes and isolates them from those without.

proaches to defining the region all cover the area and populations with which this book is primarily concerned; see Map 1.

[2] Extensive geographical treatments of the nation and the North are provided in Credner, 1935, and Pendleton, 1962.

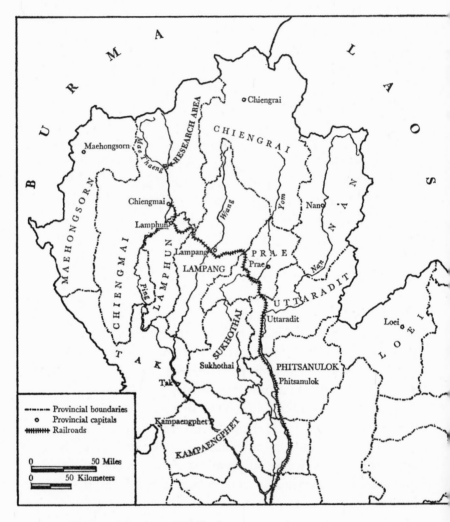

Map 1. Northern Thailand

The pan of alluvial soils which distinguishes the Central Plain from the surrounding regions rises at its rim to little more than a few hundred feet above sea level. There is a marked contrast between this vast arable flatland of perhaps 40,000 square miles and the roughly 66,000 square miles of rugged hill country which covers the North. The physical pattern of the mountainous region is set by the four major rivers (the Nan, Yom, Wang, and Ping) which flow south through it to form the Chao Phraya; the terrain, too, generally follows a north-south course. These rivers are a most important interregional link. Not only have they provided historic routes of southward migration, but the sediments they carry down from the northern mountains provide the soils on which is grown the rice which supports the population of the Central Plain.

Not all the alluvium finds its way to the delta, however. Some lodges in the cavities carved out by the torrential courses of the northern rivers, forming small riverine basins suitable for irrigated rice cultivation. Of varying size but invariable fertility, these valleys dot the courses of each northern river like beads on a shimmering thread, each strand stretching southward toward the Central Plain and Bangkok.

These valleys are inhabited by the Northern Thai (the Tai Yuan, or Khaun Myang).[3] Each basin is dominated by

[3] Ethnic identification throughout this book will follow the taxonomy employed in LeBar et al., eds., 1964, with one exception. In that gazetteer the term "Tai" refers to an ethnic group, while "Thai" is reserved for a political group. Because the present study is concerned as much with political as with ethnic distinctions, the Tai Yuan peoples and related groups such as the Tai Lue and Lao of North Thailand will be referred to as the Northern Thai (see *ibid.*, pp. 214–215) and the Tai of Thailand's Central Plain will be identified as the Central Thai (rather than as the Siamese, as employed in *ibid.*, pp. 197–205). The term "Tai" will be reserved for references to these and related ethnic subgroups as a whole.

its own population center, the larger the plain the more "urbanized" the town. Some valleys thus support no more than a handful of villages, of which the largest may contain a population of less than 1,000. Other valleys are far larger, the largest supporting the town of Chiengmai (with a population of about 100,000) and numerous neighboring villages. In many respects—both physically and culturally—these riverine plains and their margins of luxurious tropical forest are miniature replicas of the Central Plain. Historical analysis suggests that centuries ago they provided the laboratory conditions under which were developed the techniques which were later turned to the successful exploitation of the vast delta lands.[4]

The riverine valleys, generally lying between 1,000 and 1,200 feet above sea level, form but one of the several ecological zones which mark the topography of the North. At altitudes above 1,200 feet, the fertility of the valley jungles fades into the dry, porous soil of the deciduous forests, which is unsuitable for intensive agriculture. This forest belt contains the nation's primary timber reserves; throughout the past century extensive forestry concessions were granted to foreign loggers, who sacrificed these tracts to quick profits and left much scrub land in their wake.[5] Along the lower margins of these hill forests Thai peasants have here and there tried their hand at dry-rice cultivation using slash-and-burn methods.[6] With these exceptions the deciduous ecological zone has been little used by the valley dwellers.

The deciduous zone gives way to more fertile soils and evergreen forests at altitudes approaching 3,000 feet, with

[4] See, for instance, Nimmanahaeminda, 1965.
[5] LeMay, 1926, pp. 58–64, recognized at an early date what has come to be a major problem in the Northern economy. Also see Pendleton, 1962, pp. 224–231.
[6] Judd, 1964.

the peaks rising to an average of over 5,200 feet. Despite their fertility, these mountain heights are rarely frequented by the Northern Thai. To travel so far into the hills would ordinarily necessitate several days' journey to and from the valley. To practice slash-and-burn dry-rice agriculture there would require a physical effort, a variety of risks, and a degree of discomfort and isolation from the lowland community which the Northern Thai have not appeared willing to accept. The relatively infertile deciduous belt thus insulates the Northern Thai in the valleys and leaves the fertile highlands free of their domination. Into these no-man's lands have migrated various non-Tai "tribal" peoples, who are themselves limited to the higher mountain reaches and thus insulated from the Northern Thai in part because of the inferior productivity of the deciduous forests below them.

Culture

The cultural uniformity so often remarked of Thailand actually far transcends the nation's boundaries. Though the estimate that some 80 per cent of Thailand's population is Tai in the ethnolinguistic sense seems reasonable,[7] Tai culture does not stop at the borders: it encompasses populations far to the west, east, and north, including among a number of ethnic subgroups the Shan of Burma and China, the Lao of Laos, the Tho of Vietnam, and the Chuang and Chung-chia of China's southern provinces. The estimate that the total Tai-speaking population numbers some thirty million (including the abovementioned 80 per cent of Thailand's population) appears extremely conservative, especially when the Tai population of China alone is considered to amount to about nine million.[8]

[7] Kunstadter, 1967a, pp. 4, 15.
[8] LeBar et al., eds., 1964, pp. 187, 189.

The Tai peoples are not only a linguistically definable group but also feature a "well known propensity . . . for forming complex sociopolitical structures," [9] concentrated valley settlement as wet-rice cultivators, a widespread intermixture of animism and Hinayana Buddhism (except among the Sinicized), matrifocal tendencies, a common store of customs and myths, and, perhaps most important, a sense of Tai uniqueness.[10] Like other Southeast Asian cultures the Tai have tended to fragment into ethnic subgroups of which the Tai Yuan of North Thailand are but one. Their tendency to splinter is accentuated by their ability to assimilate superior cultural traits from their non-Tai neighbors, particularly the Chinese, the Burmese, and the Khmer. In terms of these wider cultural affiliations, the Northern Thai appear no closer to the Central Thai than they do to their "foreign" fellows, the Lao, the Shan, the Lue, and others.

At the lower end of Thailand's social hierarchy—that is, among the peasantry—cultural filiations tend to take precedence over national political ties. Largely because of their lack of formal education, Thai peasants are but dimly aware of the nation-state, its political implications, and their role within it; they are better informed on their cultural heritage. Thus, in 1954 in one village some three miles from Chiengmai, Thailand's second largest urban area, only 44 per cent of the adults questioned knew the name of the prime minister, 50 per cent knew the name of the king, and 61 per cent recalled the name of Thailand's capital city.[11] But the peasantry at large appears better schooled in the history and traditions of the North, and many a village scholar can trace

[9] *Ibid.*, p. 187.
[10] See the various descriptions of Tai subcultures in *Ibid.*, pp. 190–239, and Moerman, 1965.
[11] Kingshill, 1960, pp. 273–282.

⋇ 24

major events (as recorded in popular folklore) back to the first Tai incursion. Among the lower strata of Northern Thai society, recollections of a common past and feelings of fellowship and solidarity appear to be as strong within the group calling itself Khaun Myang as is their sense of Thai citizenship. Their feelings of fellowship for "foreign" groups such as the Lao and Shan seem to rival their regard for Central Thailand and Bangkok.

The regionalism that distinguishes the North from the Central Plain thus results in part from the fact that the Thai nation as a political unit is geographically subordinate to and somewhat arbitrarily imprinted upon one corner of the Tai culture zone. To those who regard cultural affinities as more important than the rewards and responsibilities of citizenship, the boundaries of the Thai state have relatively small significance. And so it seems among a wide swath of the Northern Thai peasantry, though among the young, the better educated, the "citified," the more southerly located, and the wealthier, the balance between cultural and national affiliation is today changing rapidly.

The towns of the North are in a multiple sense culturally discrete from the agrarian hinterlands—or rather, the Central Thai and Chinese minorities concentrated in the commercial centers form a distinct subculture within the towns themselves.[12] Thai government officials, who form a large part of the urban elite, appear to the Northern Thai peasant population as representatives of a far-removed dominant group. Similarly, town-dwelling Chinese merchants are perceived as aliens representing a distinct and incomprehensible economic world. Both groups are intruders who do not fit legitimately into the indigenous Northern Thai milieu but

[12] The culture gap between the commercial community and the bulk of the Thai population is analyzed in Van Roy, 1970.

must be considered regional extensions from the Center.

The Northern highlands are also culturally distinct from the Tai civilization of the valleys. The hills contain elements of at least ten non-Tai hill tribes (the number of tribes represented varies with the interpretation of what factors indicate tribal autonomy).[13] Estimates of the region's tribal population range from 50,000 to 400,000; a published "conservative" estimate of 217,000 (c. 1960) is generally considered the most authoritative.[14] All available estimates are based on cursory data which, no matter how accurate, are liable to rapid obsolescence due to the constant international migration of these seminomadic peoples. Because the main migratory flow has historically been southward through the Southeast Asian highlands, it may be assumed that Thailand's hill tribe population is expanding, with current political turmoil in neighboring countries acting to accelerate the rate of increase.[15]

The non-Tai upland peoples of North Thailand may be divided into two ethnolinguistic categories, the Sino-Tibetan and the Austroasiatic.[16] The latter category (including in North Thailand the Khmu, Lawa, T'in, and Yumbri) has a history tracing back to the initial Tai filtration into the North

[13] The label "tribe" is a misleading term in reference to mainland Southeast Asian upland peoples. The term suggests, among other culture traits, discrete, homogeneous, isolated, and primitive communities. It also implies that such groups are distinguishable from peasants. Leach, 1954, has argued persuasively against this usage in the mainland Southeast Asian setting, as have Lehman, 1967; and Kunstadter, 1967a, pp. 37–47. Because no superior alternative term has been suggested to designate the culture of these upland peoples, however, the term will nevertheless be used in this book.

[14] Young, 1962, p. 85.   [15] Bennington-Cornell, 1964, pp. 6–8, 14.

[16] As previously mentioned, ethnic classification here follows LeBar et al., eds. 1964.

during the ninth century A.D. and represents remnants of indigenous peoples who were displaced by the Tai conquest of their valley habitat. Their lowland roots are evident in their cultural affinities with the present riverine civilization, by the relatively low elevations of their village sites, and by their technologies, which remain hybrid varieties of the generic form of lowland agriculture. The Karen, a tribe linguistically related to the Sino-Tibetans, is in other cultural characteristics more readily identifiable with the Austroasiatics and will be so considered here.

The Sino-Tibetans (including in North Thailand the Akha, Lahu, Lisu, Meo, and Yao) are relatively recent immigrants to Thailand, most having filtered across the Chinese and Burmese frontiers within the past 100 to 150 years as a result of political and demographic pressures. Often classified with these tribes are the Haw, Yunnanese Chinese who act as economic intermediaries between tribal villages and the lowland peoples. In this study all references to "hill tribes" will be limited to the Sino-Tibetan tribes; none of the description, analysis, or conclusions should be taken as referring to the Austroasiatic group, though similarities do appear.

The regional significance of the tribal peoples far outweighs their relative numbers. They have little understanding of or interest in the Thai polity; nor has the Thai nation recognized them as citizens or legal residents. In fact, relations between these peoples and the Tai have historically not been particularly cordial, the lowlanders looking upon them as inferiors and occasionally having raided them for slaves. Today the government is becoming concerned over the presence of these peoples, primarily because they represent a potential threat to the integrity of the nation's northern borders and are being influenced by political propaganda from mainland China. Their command of the Northern high-lands constitutes but another centrifugal influence working within the Thai nation.

Polity

The political ascendency of Bangkok and the formation of the present-day Thai nation were unusual developments in the cultural history of the Tai peoples. Historically, the Tai political pattern has been one of fragmentation into petty states (loosely called "kingdoms") of constantly shifting alliances.[17] The larger towns of Thailand today are almost without exception descendants of "city-states" which once forcibly drew their sustenance from the agrarian hinterlands which they controlled and for whose dominance they competed. Rarely did any of these states achieve firm control of a realm more than 100 miles in radius. This was as true of the Tai peoples of present-day Laos, northern Burma, mainland China, and North Vietnam as it was of those of North Thailand.

The southward drift of the Tai principalities eventually brought them onto the Chao Phraya delta. The seemingly boundless territories and incomparable fertility of the delta provided those petty kingdoms which had staked claims to it with the economic power to consolidate far wider realms than had been the traditional case. Gradually the delta inhabitants were brought under the aegis of Ayutthaya and later Bangkok, which pressed ever further south, east, and north, integrating ever more principalities under its direct control or indirect suzerainty. This process of political expansion and consolidation ground to a halt only in the closing decades of the nineteenth century because of colonialist pressures exerted by the British from the Burmese side and

[17] LeMay, 1954, pp. 154–183; and Hall, 1964, pp. 158–172, 238–246.

the French along the Indochinese border. Otherwise it might eventually have absorbed and thus eliminated most of what today remains mainland Southeast Asia's troublesome political "buffer" areas.

Until the 1870's the region today referred to as North Thailand was dominated by the principality of Chiengmai, which controlled the subsidiary states of Lamphun, Lampang, Nan, and Prae, among others. In turn, Chiengmai was a vassal state of Siam (Central Thailand). To understand the North's regionalism, its heritage of political independence and the recency of its inclusion into the Thai nation must not be underplayed. Chiengmai's history has been traced back to 1296, with the founding of the city as the capital of the kingdom of Lannathai. In 1558 the kingdom was invaded and subjugated by the Burmese, a situation from which it was relieved in 1774 by a Siamese invasion, into whose sphere of interest the kingdom then gravitated. Renewed attacks from Burma in 1848 prompted the Siamese to send an expedition to the North which succeeded in once again "rescuing" the vassal kingdom.[18] Continuing problems led the Siamese to integrate the state formally into the nation in 1873. A governor was dispatched from Bangkok to oversee local administration, largely as a formal gesture aimed at proving to the Western colonial powers that the North was now an integral part of Siam. This step was recognized *de facto* with the establishment at Chiengmai of an international court composed of a British judge and Siamese colleagues, lasting from 1883 to 1925. National administrative reorganization in 1894 included the North, which was divided into two circles (*monthon*) comprising seven provinces (*changwat*); further re-

[18] Vella, 1957, pp. 92–93. The most readable political history of the region, though somewhat dated in the light of more recent studies, is LeMay, 1926, pp. 3–38.

gional decentralization occurred in 1932 with the abolition of circles.[19]

Despite these steps aimed at breaking down the regional political cohesiveness and social insularity of the North and shifting it into the national fold, the region long remained virtually autonomous; the gradual shift to national integration was scarcely perceived even at the highest administrative levels within the Northern provinces. It took the Shan rebellion of 1901–1902—bringing widespread dacoity—to publicize to the central government its weak control over the North.[20] This rude awakening intensified the Bangkok aristocracy's nation-building effort at the grass roots, the results of which have not been of a revolutionary order even to the present date. *De facto* national political integration has proved a slow process which still has far to go, and while this process has been working upon the lowland people for a century, it has scarcely touched the non-Tai tribal populations of the highlands.

Many Northern Thai still recall their independent political heritage with pride and continue to school themselves in the folk history and heroes of the former Northern kingdoms. Among townspeople and the educated, far greater emotion is attached to the heritage of independence and the rather recent realignment of the North to Bangkok than among the outlying peasantry, for whom statist political realities continue to have little meaning. Because of their closer dealings with the nation, its legal codes, its fiscal procedures, its in-

[19] The division of the nation into seventy-one provinces is part of a continuing campaign on the part of the central government to fragment power at the regional level in order to concentrate it at the center, a reflection of its unvoiced concern over the centrifugal forces at work. The trend to centralism as a continuing theme of Thai politics is documented in Siffin, 1966.

[20] Graham, 1924, II, 172; quoted in Moerman, 1967, p. 405.

ternal and international political problems, and its development schemes, and because of their daily contact with the representatives of Bangkok, Northern town dwellers show a greater awareness of the condescension accorded them and the double standards applied to them by outposted public bureaucrats, Central Thai business interests, and junketing officials and tourists. When such perceived behavior is compounded by the widespread local beliefs that taxation imposed at the center far exceeds services rendered to the region and that the regional terms of trade are kept purposely unfavorable, it is not surprising that an important segment of educated Northern opinion has it that the region continues to be discriminated against for the benefit of the Center.[21] In all fairness it can only be admitted that Central Thai attitudes and central government actions appear to be not entirely free of a colonialist view of the North, though these attitudes and actions, too, appear to be changing.[22]

[21] Keyes, 1967, provides the only authoritative examination of the political forces making for regionalism in Thailand, though the study is limited to the Northeast. A similar study for the North has yet to be undertaken.

[22] Reginald LeMay described the Central Thai attitude to the North during the 1920's as follows: "For many years past Siamese officials have considered it in the light of banishment and exile to be stationed in the northern provinces . . . , but it is hoped that, with the railway now through to Chiengmai and the gradual opening up of the countryside by road communication, the stigma attaching to provincial residence will soon become a thing of the past, and that the better class of Siamese officials will vie with one another in playing their part in the economic development of their country and in the decentralization which must from now onwards take place" (LeMay, 1926, p. 38). Despite LeMay's hopes, growing infrastructure has not eradicated the problem. Even today, bureaucrats do not cherish assignment to the North. For instance, staffing of the recently founded University of the North at Chiengmai has been its most severe problem, for professors refuse to transfer from Bangkok to the "boondocks" (*bannauk*).

Economy

North Thailand incorporates three major types of technology: the lowland wet-rice technology, the highland dry-rice and opium technology, and Western industrialism. Industrial technology has penetrated the North from the commercial-industrial enclave centered in Bangkok. Its introduction was long delayed due to the North's small resource base (small in terms of the demands expressed on the international market but not in terms of indigenous demands) and its concomitantly small consumer and capital-goods market. Only in the past generation has the central government's drive for national economic development introduced the economic infrastructure required to support industrial expansion within the region. Most important have been the introduction of modern transport facilities, communications networks, new power sources, and major irrigation projects. Anticipated repercussions have so far been disappointing, with few private industrial concerns accepting the challenges offered. The most important, though indirect, effects of these public investments have been felt among the lowland peasantry, a large section of which may be expected to undergo a profound though painfully slow economic and social metamorphosis under their continuing influence. Preliminary change is already apparent with the spreading use of the country bus and the motorcycle, the diesel-fuel tractor and power-driven rice mill, more exact control over water supplies and thus wider possibilities of double rice-cropping and crop diversification, and an ever expanding inflow of mechanical gadgets, scientific information, and provocative ideas.[23]

[23] Moerman, 1968, analyzes the influence of tractor plowing on the economy of a Tai Lue community of Chiengrai. Kingshill, 1960, reviews, in passing, various industrial incursions into a peasant com-

The lowland peasant technology of North Thailand centers on irrigated rice cultivation, with its dependence on flatland flooding during the monsoon months, use of the water buffalo, and secondary reliance on an assortment of complementary dry-season crops, fisheries, and peasant crafts. This technology is employed uniformly throughout the lowlands of the Tai culture area (except in the urban centers, where industrial technology holds sway). The relatively minor factors that distinguish the Northern technology from that employed on the Central Plain are attributable primarily to ecological variations.[24]

The highland peasant technology supports agricultural complexes centering on dry rice and the opium poppy. It exploits the natural fertility of freshly cleared jungle land and the regenerative powers of the forest through long-term fallowing. Rather than being bent on remaking the natural landscape, this technology, commonly known as slash-and-burn or swiddening, is adapted to it. Its success requires intimate knowledge of the highland ecology, skilled woodsmanship, and mastery of widespread territories. Though some few Northern Thai peasants have turned to the swidden technology as an occasional and relatively unrewarding diversion from their main pursuit as wet-rice cultivators, its principal

munity near Chiegmai Town. DeYoung, 1955, pp. 147–201, discusses the effects of such innovations as modern transportation, new consumer goods, animal health measures, modern fertilizers, mechanized farming and irrigation programs on the Thai peasantry at large, though his emphasis is on Northern Thai peasants in the vicinity of Chiengmai.

[24] Detailed descriptions of the lowland peasant technology in the North are provided by Moerman, 1968, and Kingshill, 1960. A more general description is found in DeYoung, 1955; he states, "The only appreciable difference in the rice farming of the various parts of Thailand is the type of rice grown" (p. 77). Also see Pendleton, 1962, pp. 134–215.

and most successful practitioners are the non-Tai tribal peoples populating the uplands.[25]

Each of these technologies is characteristic of a different population. And each of these populations—the hill tribes, the Northern Thai peasantry, and the Central Thai and Chinese-Thai town dwellers of the North—represents a different political and social alignment. Not unexpectedly, the economic institutions common to each of these groups are but another of their individuating characteristics. The larger towns of the North, those which are most intimately linked with Bangkok, are the most commercialized. It is here that the market system common to the West and the Bangkok enclave has staked its claim as an institutional frame for the industrial technology. Among the lowland peasantry an indigenous institutional structure prevails which may simplistically be referred to as a network of functionally diffuse patron-client relationships. And among the hill tribes the swidden technology is complemented by institutions of intravillage solidary cooperation, intervillage labor credit, and export-sector direct exchange. In each instance the economy cannot be comprehended without understanding its institutions as well as its technology; and in each case the institutional frame cannot be understood without an appreciation of the social and political systems within which it is enmeshed.

Furthermore, none of these economies exists in isolation. Though a simplified analysis may refer to them individually, their interrelationships are perhaps as important to understanding their internal structure and are surely as important to understanding their evolutionary dynamics as are their

[25] No single study treats upland peasant technologies of North Thailand in any great detail. Among the most informative, however, are Bennington-Cornell, 1964, and Thailand, 1962. Also see Judd, 1964; and Bernatzik, 1963.

individual characteristics. The upland peoples maintain long-established trade patterns linking them with their lowland neighbors and, through them, with the international commercial system emanating from the West. Similarly, the lowland peasantry has economic ties with the commercial centers of the North, a relationship which is becoming increasingly intimate as the industrial technology filters further and with rising intensity into the countryside. The incursion of the industrial technology, carrying in its train the institutions of the market system, is exerting corroding influences on the indigenous peasant economies and is straining their traditional interrelationships. A clarification of this evolving confrontation of economic systems constitutes a major object to which the following chapters will be directed. But such a goal must wait upon the presentation of an analysis of each system as a separate entity.

The Research Area

Chiengmai is tied to Bangkok by highway, rail, air, and telecommunications networks. By comparison, Chiengmai's intraprovincial transportation and communication links are primitive. Historically, the Ping River constituted the province's main trade route (with mountain trails a strong second), but with the construction of dams and other water-diversion devices for irrigation and power purposes, river transport has declined in importance. Today, the chief connective link is the all-weather road (euphemistically titled "Regional Highway 3") which follows the Ping River gorge north from Chiengmai Town through the wayside communities and districts of Mae Rim, Mae Thaeng, Chiengdao, and Fang to the Burma border. Each of these tiny towns (little more than villages themselves) serves as the administrative center for the peasant communities surrounding it while also marking the final commercial outpost of an industrial world searching for new supplies and markets.

Mae Thaeng straddles Highway 3 two country-bus hours north of the provincial capital. As the site for a district head-quarters, it gives its name to the political subdivision (Amphur Mae Thaeng) within which is located the miniature Ban Pong Valley, some five and a half miles long and three wide (see Map 2). A peculiar convolution of several miles of scrub land separates the Ban Pong Valley from the larger, southward-stretching Mae Thaeng Valley, the district administrative center, and the highway. A dirt road, deeply rutted in the dry months and a nearly impassable quagmire in the rainy season, connects the village of Ban Pong and its neighboring hamlets with the main road, Chiengmai, and the nation, but not without certain intervening obstacles, of which the most obvious are the thirty-two bumpy miles from Mae Thaeng to Chiengmai Town at the prohibitive passenger fare of six baht, the equivalent of a local day's wage.

The cluster of farm families which forms the community of Ban Pong is so closely integrated both socially and ecologically that in conjunction with its neighboring hamlets this valley village world could with little discomfort or reorganization maintain itself as a discrete social, political, and economic unit.[26] Despite Ban Pong's fundamental capacity for self-sufficiency, the community has been molded to the exigencies of the nation-state and the encroaching commercial-industrial economy by forces beyond its control.[27] The village headman finds himself subordinate and accountable to

[26] Ban Pong appears representative of contemporary Northern Thai peasant life, which is described in Kingshill, 1960; DeYoung, 1955; Moerman, 1968; and Wijeyewardene, 1967.

[27] This point has been developed in broader perspective in Van Roy and Cornehls, 1969.

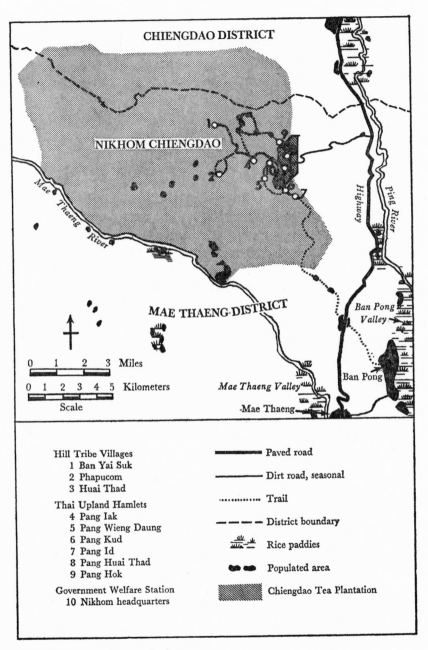

CHIENGDAO DISTRICT

NIKHOM CHIENGDAO

Mae Thaeng River

MAE THAENG DISTRICT

Highway

Ping River

Ban Pong Valley

Ban Pong

Mae Thaeng Valley

Mae Thaeng

0   1   2   3 Miles

0 1 2 3 4 5 Kilometers

Scale

Hill Tribe Villages
  1 Ban Yai Suk
  2 Phapucom
  3 Huai Thad

Thai Upland Hamlets
  4 Pang Iak
  5 Pang Wieng Daung
  6 Pang Kud
  7 Pang Id
  8 Pang Huai Thad
  9 Pang Hok

Government Welfare Station
  10 Nikhom headquarters

═══════ Paved road

──────── Dirt road, seasonal

············ Trail

── ── ── District boundary

Rice paddies

Populated area

Chiengdao Tea Plantation

Map 2. The Research Area

outposted representatives of the central government. The village schoolteacher is directed in his duties by superiors stationed in Chiengmai Town and Bangkok. The village temple and its monks are under the tutelage of the national ecclesiastical order. Village youths are called to fulfill military obligations imposed by the central authorities. Taxes are levied by the central government on landholdings, and, generally unknown to villagers, indirect taxes (in the form of a rice export tax, import taxes, and various business and sales taxes) play a part in determining many of the prices which villagers are charged in the market place.

Local merchants and itinerant peddlers introduce Ban Pong villagers to unfamiliar commodities. The radio and an occasional newspaper introduce new ideas. Christian missionaries visit to propound their revolutionary social philosophy. Nearby market towns and the provincial capital lure village families on educational holidays. Adventure and opportunity in the urban centers attract youths away from the valley, to which some return with changed ideas and attitudes. The incursion of new knowledge and tools tends to raise the local economic surplus, while the changing sense of social and economic priorities increases the inflow of commercial goods, thus tending to lower it.

The place of Ban Pong in the nation is thus inexorably changing—but at an excruciatingly slow pace. Ban Pong fits well the general remark made of Thai village life by De-Young:

[In] spite of the outward adaptation that peasant life had made to Western influences, the old basic patterns of life, in agriculture, in religion, and in social life, remain strong and secure. Thai peasant society shows none of the signs of disintegration that are so often evident when a peasant group is brought rapidly into contact with modernization and Westernization.[28]

[28] DeYoung, 1955, p. 201.

While such elements of economic change as those listed above may be glimpsed in Ban Pong's everyday operations, the traditional self-sufficiency provided by the irrigated-rice technology and its related institutions continue to play the underlying role in shaping village life. In this sense, Ban Pong stands as a typical example of Northern Thai peasant economy.

Similarly, the Ban Pong Valley is physically typical of the Northern Thai lowlands, a maze of paddi fields sharply outlined by a rim of steeply rising hills. The hill country surrounding the Ban Pong plain is populated at its higher reaches by various hill tribes—Meo and Lahu villages to the west, Lisu to the north, and Karen to the east. Directly northwest, about eight miles into the hills (and just south of the famous landmark mountain, Doi Chiengdao, 7,125 feet in altitude) are located the nearest tribal villages. In the same locale is situated a cluster of Northern Thai peasant hamlets, an exception to the rule that the Tai populate only the valleys. Here, too, is located a tea plantation, the only venture of its kind in North Thailand, and a hill tribe land settlement and welfare station, one of four which have been set up as Thai government attempts to deal with the hill tribe problem.

These communities are concentrated in a hill tract ranging in elevation from 2,200 to 3,900 feet and covering some fourteen square miles. The area is connected to the regional highway by a dirt road winding the four miles down from the government station and the plantation. Local tribal and upland Thai peasant communities are linked with one another and with Ban Pong by mountain trails. A one-hour journey by jeep or truck makes the ascent from the highway to the government welfare station; a half day's arduous journey on foot takes local people up the trails from Ban Pong to the upland peasant communities.

This cluster of communities, representing different cultures and economic structures, constitutes the Research Area in which was done the field work on which this study is in large part based. The upland Thai and tribal peasant villages of the Research Area are in no way unique to the Northern hills. They have been selected as case studies because, under the impact of both private enterprise and public planning, they represent in microcosm the diversity of problems and processes of economic change affecting North Thailand—and by extension much of the non-Western world—today.

Chapter 2

THE HILL TRIBE
PEASANT ECONOMY

Swidden Technology

Swiddening is commonly considered one of the most primitive of agrarian technologies. Characterizations which identify it as "rotation of fields rather than of crops; clearing by means of fire; absence of draft animals and of manuring; use of human labor only; employment of the dibble stick or hoe," and so forth certainly lend themselves to such a view.[1] The most widely accepted definition of swiddening, that it comprises "any agricultural system in which fields are cleared by firing and are cropped discontinuously," also fails to allude to any "progressive" attribute.[2] Nor can the primitive character of swiddening be gainsaid in terms of its capital component, the number of its stages of production, or its functional specialization and division of labor.

Nevertheless, in its capacity to extract a continuing dividend from the land without devastating the environment on which it depends, it has often proved exceptionally sophisticated. Unlike most technologies, swiddening seeks to preserve the very "balance of nature" which its continuing application requires.

---

[1] Pelzer, 1945, p. 17.   [2] Conklin, 1961, p. 27.

In ecological terms, the most distinctive positive characteristic of swidden agriculture . . . is that it is integrated into and, when genuinely adaptive, maintains the general structure of the pre-existing natural ecosystem into which it is projected, rather than creating and sustaining one organized along novel lines and displaying novel dynamics.[3]

The primitive position of swidden agriculture on the ladder of economic progress is also contradicted by its productivity.

It possibly is true that the economics of shifting cultivation . . . are fully as good as the economics of permanent-field cultivation carried on in many parts of southeastern Asia today. There is ground for believing that shifting cultivation . . . [can] yield a larger accumulation of wealth, acre for acre, than permanent-field farming of producing land in some parts of the rough country where it now operates.[4]

The qualifying clauses in this conservative statement are over-ridden by numerous examples of the remarkable productivity of swidden systems the world over.

Swidden technology does not follow a single pattern wherever it is employed, nor is it uniformly productive. It varies markedly with locale, crop complex, and societal infrastructure; cases range from the South American *milpa* to the African *chitemene*, the Indian *jhum*, and the Filipino *kaingin*.[5] In North Thailand it is known as *tham hai* (*tham rai* in the Central Thai dialect). Within this region it varies in its particulars and in its productivity among the peoples who practice it. Even within each culture it varies with ecology from village to village, from field to field, and from year to year.

---

[3] Geertz, 1963, p. 16.   [4] Spencer, 1966, p. 73.
[5] See Conklin, 1961; Spencer, 1966; and Watters, 1960.

Whatever generalizations can be drawn from North Thailand must therefore remain either extremely imprecise or, if more detailed, suspect in their application to individual cases.[6]

Swiddening in all its varieties relies for its success on three critical factors: land, labor, and climate.[7] The territorial expanse required for continuing swidden success is governed largely by the regenerative speed of the forest cover following field clearing, cultivation to the point of cropping infertility, and subsequent abandonment. Because the swidden technology is adapted to natural refertilization of abandoned field sites, it entails control of territories far larger than those in cultivation at any moment; invariably more land is left fallow than cropped. The effort of intermittent forest clearing and continual swidden management calls for a sizable labor input per unit of land under cultivation (though not per unit of total land possessed); swidden systems are thus frequently labor scarce in the same sense as the most industrialized economies, meaning that the volume of production is constrained by the labor rather than the land factor.[8] Thirdly, temperature and rainfall patterns limit cropping mixes and calendars, which relate back to questions of soil fertility, field-site rotation, forest regeneration, and labor requirements.

These factors combine among the Sino-Tibetan hill tribes of North Thailand to support a swidden technology bifurcated into two distinct agronomies, which in turn relate to an institutional configuration divisible into discrete "domestic" and "foreign" sectors. Each of these complementary agronomies centers on the cultivation of a single staple: the

[6] I prefer the latter option for it avoids the oversimplifications that inevitably result from broad generalization while also defining a *type*, or perhaps more accurately, a set of *norms*, from which individual departures stand out not as exceptions to the rule but as deviations from the average.

[7] See Spencer, 1966, pp. 26–52.   [8] See Myrdal, 1968, pp. 961–1092.

"domestic" crop is dry rice and the "foreign" crop is the opium poppy.[9]

The agricultural calendar is divided into two overlapping phases, each devoted to the production of one of these crops. The two phases coincide in the months devoted to the selection, clearing, and burning of field sites. These preparatory tasks occupy the tribal village from the end of February through April, months of respite from the intensive labor commitments required for cultivation and harvesting. Coming at the height of the dry season, these months are advantageous for "slash-and-burn" chores.

Village consensus determines the desirability of shifting the coming year's crop to fresh field sites or continuing on the old. The typical duration of rice-field occupancy is three years, though it has been noted that poppy fields may last as long as twenty years before serious declines in output appear.[10] Decision-making is complicated by the fact that opium and rice need different kinds of sites: opium requires cooler and "thinner" air (that is, higher elevations), drier terrain (that is, steeper inclines to ensure rapid moisture runoff), and "redder" soils (greater alkalinity). Furthermore, villagers must decide whether field-site relocation will also require village relocation; whereas fields are shifted every few years, village sites may remain the same for as long as two genera-

[9] The following description of the annual swiddening cycle relies heavily on Bennington-Cornell, 1964; Thailand, 1962; and Bernatzik, 1963; as well as on my own observations. Additional information, tribe by tribe, is provided in Young, 1962; and LeBar et al., eds., 1964.

[10] Bernatzik, 1963, makes this point, which differs from the findings presented in other studies. Obviously, however, the frequency of field-site shifts varies with local soil conditions and population densities, causing different studies of different village groups to arrive at apparently conflicting conclusions on this as on related matters. I have sought to avoid this type of problem by focusing on tribal norms.

tions.[11] To call the hill tribes nomadic, as is sometimes done, is thus somewhat misrepresentative.

Clearance of jungle growth for new field sites is ordinarily a cooperative project among the village men. Bush knives and axes are used to fell all but the largest trees, which are topped and girdled. After approximately a month of drying, the felled growth is set afire, great care being taken to contain the fires within the desired bounds. Only the clearing of residual debris, division of the fields into household plots to be separately worked, and construction of field huts and fences remain before the first rains signal that planting may begin in soils fertilized by the ashes of the fired growth.

Dry rice is sown in May with seed stored from the previous year's harvest or, occasionally, with seed borrowed or purchased from lowland traders or hill tribe neighbors. Several sorts of rice may be sown either broadcast or with the dibble: early- or late-maturing, ordinary or glutinous, and innumerable minor varieties differing in shape, color, texture, and taste. The numerous subsidiary crops planted among the rice include various sorts of beans, leafy vegetables, peppers, squash, sesame, sorghum, millet, maize, potatoes, yams, melons, onions, and tobacco, the proportions varying by tribe, village, and field.

June and July are occupied with weeding both the rice fields and the still unplanted opium fields and guarding the former from jungle depredators. These are also months for hunting and foraging in the surrounding jungles, a major supplementary means of supplying provisions and a much-cherished form of recreation. These pursuits are interrupted in August, when attention is turned to the harvest of maize,

[11] In North Thailand, then, "shifting cultivation" carries two meanings: field-site shifting and village shifting. See Spencer, 1966, pp. 64–65, 144–148.

vegetables, and early-maturing rice. After it has been threshed and winnowed, the rice is usually dried in roasting pans to insure against spoilage during the monsoon rains. Bundles of maize and millet are hung from rafters in the homes to dry gradually in the smoke of the roasting fires. Also in the later part of August comes the broadcast sowing of the opium fields; the heavy rains are relied on to drive the seed into the soil. Only further weeding and guarding against depredators is required to insure a healthy crop.

The main rice harvest comes during November and the first weeks of December. Households sometimes cooperate in reaping, assisting one another in sickling the standing grain and collecting rice sheaves at the center of each plot; but the yield of each plot belongs to the household that cultivated it. Carrying the sacks and baskets of winnowed rice by tumpline to the village ordinarily is women's and children's work, as are most chores requiring tedious but relatively unskilled labor. The harvest is stored in the homes or in special granaries conspicuously placed about the center of the village.

After this harvest, households turn increasing attention to the tending of their opium fields. Weeding is continued, the crop is thinned, and additional vegetable seed is planted in scattered patches to provide a subsidiary harvest. The poppies begin to bloom in January, and as they continue to mature into February the harvest is begun.[12] Each seed pod is incised with a special three-bladed knife, leaving a series of cuts from which the plant fluid oozes. After several days' wait the cultivator returns to the tapped pod and scrapes away the congealed exudent. Each pod may be tapped three times in this manner before the sap ceases to flow. Thousands of poppies must be individually dealt with, making the harvest a par-

[12] The technology of opium harvesting and processing among the hill tribes is detailed in Saihoo, 1963, pp. 39–41.

ticularly arduous chore. Following boiling and straining of the harvested lump of raw opium, it is wrapped in banana leaf or squeezed into bamboo joints for storage in secret spots. With this final harvest concluded, it must once again be decided whether to recrop the past year's swiddens or move to fresh sites, and so the cycle repeats itself.

The swiddening cycle is supplemented by other agrarian pursuits which fill the slack seasons. Foraging provides a number of edibles such as nuts, tubers, fruits, and herbs as well as fibers for cloth, grasses for thatch, and bamboo and wood for house walls and supports, for fodder, for fuel, and for a variety of utensils. Hunting is a source of meat and a pleasurable escape from the daily rounds for village males. Fishing is practiced where streams are sufficiently large. Animal husbandry is a relatively unimportant protein source, for livestock is held as a form of conspicuous wealth and is raised for intermittent consumption at feasts and for sacrificial offerings to the spirits on such occasions as sickness and funerals. Chickens, pigs, and dogs are most common, though goats, cattle, buffalo, and ponies are found in some villages. Gardens are maintained near the homes to provide medicinal herbs and to supplement the swidden harvests with such foods as papaya, pomelo, bananas, peppers, and gourds.

Tribal agriculture is supplemented by a variety of village handicrafts, some performed in all households (within which the labor forces is allocated along craft lines by sex and age group) and others requiring such skills as are only attained by occasional specialists. A diversity of tools and utensils, clothing, toys, ornaments, shelters and household furniture, and religious artifacts are domestically manufactured. Among the skills employed are weaving and plaiting, batik and other decorative work, architecture, metal-smithing, woodworking, papermaking, weaponry, and chemistry (for instance, the fermentation of alcohols, the refining of opium, the extraction of poisons).[13] These pursuits add complexity to the tribal technology and make the tribal economy far more self-sufficient than might otherwise be surmised, yet they remain subsidiary to the swidden technology, which is the economic mainstay and, as will be seen, the sole guarantee of economic independence.

Aspects of the hill tribe swidden technology most relevant to an understanding of the general structure of the tribal economy may be summarized as follows: first, tribesmen strive, in many cases successfully, to integrate the swidden technology into the jungle ecology on a continuing basis; second, the tribal economic product is ordinarily limited by labor scarcities rather than by land; third, the household forms the primary unit of production, though certain functions not directly involved in cropping are collective village undertakings; and last, the production system is bifurcated into dry-rice and opium agronomies, which occupy the households' productive efforts during different seasons of the agricultural year, are undertaken at different field sites, and entail somewhat different production techniques.

Institutional Bifurcation

Each of these basic features of the tribal technology carries institutional implications. The household as the unit of production is concomitant with a relatively small institutional role for the village and the tribal community at large in this regard. The scarcity of labor entails a complex web of institutions having to do with the interhousehold allocation of manpower, a matter which will be taken up later in this chap-

[13] A detailed account of village handicrafts among the Meo and Akha is provided in Bernatzik, 1963, *passim*.

ter. The tribal economy's ecological integration is a major factor in its continuing institutional differentiation from the adjoining lowlands. Most revealing of all these institutional realities, however, is the distinction between the "foreign" or "cash" sector, which runs in conjunction with the opium harvest, and the "domestic" or "subsistence" sector, which parallels the dry-rice harvest.[14]

The Domestic Sector

"The key to subsistence . . . lies in the size and constancy of the rice crop";[15] with a harvest sufficiently bountiful to feed each household and provide a residual seed stock for the coming year's needs, the tribal village can maintain itself with minimal resort to external economic relations. Even when this condition is met for the village as a whole, however, household harvests invariably fluctuate, with some exceeding, and others failing to meet, subsistence requirements.[16] Interhousehold economic dealings within the village thus inevitably emerge; rice transfers ordinarily are recompensed not with tangible payments or specific debts but with informal social "promotions" that carry with them subtle and often long-delayed economic advantages for the rice donors.[17] House

---

[14] Though the hill tribes do not employ the concept of the nation-state and therefore do not recognize the physical boundaries which in conventional economics distinguish the foreign sector from the domestic, transactions between the tribes and the lowlands have the typical "international" characteristics of labor immobility and problems of establishing workable media and rates of exchange. The terms "foreign" and "domestic" are thus used in the unorthodox sense of distinguishing between transactions among and within *cultures* rather than *political entities*, but not without reason. Cf. the use of this distinction in James Hamilton, 1963.

[15] Bennington-Cornell, 1964, p. 18.   [16] *Ibid.*, p. 19.

[17] The roles and functions of kinship in this and related aspects of the tribal economy is a topic which must be left to the attention of

holds consistently running surpluses which they provide to their less prosperous fellow villagers may in this manner gain improved marriage (that is, labor) options, richer swidden plots, control over village decision-making, and other advantages accompanying enhanced status and wealth. They also ensure such aid to themselves in return in the event that they fail to make ends meet at some future time. In the extreme case, when the gap between surplus and deficit households has grown so great that social dividends in return for rice "loans" have been played out, village solidarity breaks down, culminating in cleavage into separate villages.[18]

Village-wide surpluses or deficits ordinarily remain after interhousehold subsistence differentials have been netted out within the village to ensure that all meet minimal requirements so far as the aggregate harvest permits. In either case, households are drawn into intervillage economic dealings; either excess stocks are to be disposed of or deficiencies must be offset. Rice is ordinarily transacted among villages for specific compensation, usually on an annual credit basis.[19] Pros-

anthropologists. At any rate, the topic is of relatively minor interest in the present instance because economic structure varies little among the Sino-Tibetan hill tribes whereas the forms of kinship organization appear highly variable, leading to the conclusion that kinship is not a governing factor in the determination of tribal economics.

[18] See Jones, 1969, pp. 165–171. Bennington-Cornell, 1964, reports the following encounter: "A headman whose village had just lost two families stated that they had left in order to get enough to eat. We mentioned our understanding that a headman should provide for indigent people. He replied, 'I supported them for two years. That was enough.' There are the lazy ones who ride along without contributing" (p. 37).

[19] In the Mae Kok river basin of Chiengrai Province, tribal villages trade rice for cash at 0.30 baht per liter. Among these villages all such transactions are carried on at fixed rates. See Bennington-Cornell, 1964, pp. 31, 34. Furthermore, Bernatzik, 1963, p. 322, states that no "interest" is charged on loans returned within a year. On

perous rice producers thus gain economic ascendancy over their less productive neighbors in other villages and can through good fortune and astute dealings rise to positions of multivillage dominance. Entire villages which, because of some misfortune, suffer serious declines in their rice-producing abilities tend to fall into debt to wealthier households in neighboring villages, sometimes to such an extent that households are forced to transact long-standing labor obligations ("selling" their personnel) in ultimate compensation. An important factor mitigating against such indebtedness is village migration.

In speaking of "villages" this discussion does not mean to imply that the village acts as a unit in economic affairs. Rather, it is individual households *within* the village that rise to prominence or fall into destitution. Though households deal on an individual basis, however, the reciprocities which govern intravillage economic life (for instance, the sharing of rice harvests among households in case of unusual need) serve as an economic leveling factor. Thus, an individual household widely known for its wealth and power will invariably be located in a wealthy village. Though income and wealth differentials exist among households within each village, they tend not to vary as widely as intervillage differentials.

A village forced into debt by a continuing rice deficit will find its prospects for future prosperity diminished.[20] On the

---

multiyear loans, "interest" is paid only once and is always set at one-third of the agreed "price." These constraints on "price" manipulation indicate that a community of interest binds tribal life even at the extravillage level.

[20] Some villages encountering chronic rice-harvest deficits continue to function without suffering the physiological or social repercussions that might be expected. Their survival hinges on the opium harvest, which they use to buy rice from itinerant traders or other tribal

other hand, the opportunities opened to tribal ascendancy by a continuing surplus are cumulative, for expanded wealth and labor reservoirs deriving from astute management of the surplus permit increased social and economic leverage and the magnification of future surpluses. These mechanisms tend to produce intervillage economic differentials in wealth and power, just as they produce intervillage economic links between the wealthy and the poor. However, such tendencies to concentration of wealth and power are largely offset by tribal imponderables; an abundance of fortuitous circumstances (abnormal rains, plant diseases, epidemics among the labor force, jungle pest infestations, soil depletion, forced village relocation due to political pressures or bad omens, and so forth) help determine rice surplus and deficit situations, causing village harvests to gyrate unpredictably.[21] Therefore, intervillage patronage links of a relatively permanent nature do not emerge. The prosperity of any household or village, no matter how great for the moment, always remains a tenuous condition, dependent on the unpredictable bounty of coming harvests. As environmental controls increase with the incursion of Western technology, more lasting intervillage economic differentials may be expected to appear, leading to important changes in the structure of tribal economic life.

Beyond rice dealings and the network of intervillage obligations they entail, intervillage economic relations are minor within the tribal community. Some cotton, foodstuffs, and opium are transacted, and households in some villages are turned to locally for their superior artifacts, such as crossbows and pack-baskets, and their services, such as medicine,

villages, a departure from the tribal ideal of self-sufficiency in rice and use of opium to add to wealth.

[21] "Our impression is . . . that the rice [harvest] is only barely sufficient and the crop highly unpredictable for any one village from year to year" (Bennington-Cornell, 1964, p. 19).

shamanism, and sage advice. Within the village, too, inter-household economic relations tend to remain peripheral to the primary emphasis on household self-sufficiency. Beyond household production, tasks are intermittently undertaken on a village-wide cooperative basis, particularly field clearing, house construction, and hunting. Village specialists also are found, including the headman, spirit doctor, medical expert, midwife, barber, blacksmith, and silversmith, though not all villages contain every one of these experts. Specialists perform their services in return for the advantages accruing to status as well as for traditional rewards such as receipt of choice portions of the hunt and of sacrificial kills, use of particularly fertile swidden plots, and added voice in village decision-making.

In summation, rice identifies the domestic economy with the tribal community. Within this community, mechanisms operate at each level of aggregation and social distance (the household, the village, and the intervillage levels) to insure subsistence. Those households that provide more than their share in this endeavor are rewarded with enhanced social (and indirectly, economic) positions within the village; those that fall behind in the quest continue to be provided for in so far as the village is capable, but at a social (and indirectly, an economic) cost. Among villages, transactions are largely freed of the social constraint of reciprocal sharing, though they continue to adhere to the general institutional configuration of tribal culture.

The Foreign Sector

Despite the variety of goods and services produced by each household and by village specialists, the tribal economy is not totally isolated; it is not, as some economists would phrase it, entirely "subsistence oriented." First, physiological subsistence requirements are not always domestically met. Crop failures occasionally devastate large upland areas, and certain vitamin, protein, and mineral deficiencies are endemic. Thus, an intermittent trade is carried on with lowlanders for such consumption items as salt, rice, and dried fish. Second, the swidden technology requires certain capital imports from the lowlands, the most important of which is steel (usually scrap parts from junked vehicles to be worked in village foundries) for ax, bush-knife, and hoe blades, the tip of the dibble stick, the tridentated opium tapping knife and broad-bladed scraping knife, and the cutting edge of the rice sickle. Following crop failure, and in the absence of borrowable rice surpluses in neighboring villages, the lowlands are sometimes turned to as the only remaining source of seed. Among other capital imports, aspirin ranks high for the unusual reason that its salicylic acid acts as a preservative when mixed with processed opium. Third, the historic process of intercourse with the lowland civilizations, though based largely on traditions of conflict and coercion which have resulted in fear of personal contact with the valley peoples, has nevertheless generated a strong demand among tribesmen for various "luxury" articles obtainable only through trade with the lowlands. Included among the wide variety of such goods are matches, kerosene, enamel and ceramic pots and cups, blankets, cotton cloth and occasional items of clothing, rifles and ammunition, livestock, an occasional transistor radio, and silver ornaments. Such goods have become integral aspects of the tribal economy, setting standards of material well-being which all households strive to attain.[22] They rank as symbols of household wealth and provide an interesting clue to the evolving tribal conception of the good life.

[22] Ruth Sharp, 1965.

The problem is that imports must be paid for in cross-culturally negotiable items, or some commonly accepted moneystuff. Unlike the sense of brotherhood and social reciprocation which suffuses intravillage transactions and the community of interest which governs intervillage trade, the foreign sector—featuring a culture gap, labor immobility, and arm's-length negotiations in an atmosphere of uncertainty if not outright mistrust and latent hostility—requires that remuneration for imports be in cash or some other highly liquid asset demanded in the lowlands. In the hills, cash is limited to silver, either coins or ornaments. Paper currency, because it has no intrinsic value domestically, is rarely seen in the tribal world; silver, on the other hand, is highly esteemed. It plays a domestic role as a symbol of economic and social standing, being conspicuously displayed as necklaces, bracelets, earrings, anklets, and other personal adornments. It has also been found to play a complex religious role in at least one tribe.[23] But even silver must be initially purchased in the lowlands; its use as medium of exchange in foreign trade must depend in the first instance on some good of domestic origin.

Various products have been utilized for this purpose. Individual villages have attempted sporadically to sell in the lowlands such agricultural items as cotton, rice, tobacco, pigs, and chickens; jungle products such as foraged roots and herbs, animal skins and horns, and captured game; and tribal artifacts. None of these trade goods has provided an adequate or dependable cash income. Furthermore, the labor required for transport alone has proved sufficiently burdensome to limit such trade to villages located along the peripheries of the uplands. Only opium has proved effective as a basis on

[23] Kandre, 1967.

which the tribes can deal advantageously with the people of the lowlands.[24]

Various characteristics of opium's production and transactability lend themselves as do those of no other tribal product to the requirements of the foreign sector. First, opium is seasonably produced. Its cultivation and harvesting, during the dry, cool months, do not conflict with the rice crop. The labor force thus has its work distributed more evenly over the agricultural year than would be the case for almost any feasible alternative. A second advantage is opium's relatively low labor requirement (though even here the intensity of effort required in cultivation is still considerable). It has been estimated that the opium crop absorbs two-thirds as much labor time per household per year as does rice.[25] Opium's suitability to different field sites than rice, thirdly, permits more efficient land use by avoiding intensive employment (and thus rapid soil depletion) of the upland reaches most suitable for rice. In short, opium is an export good which minimizes conflict with production for domestic purposes.

The harvested product is of high unit value, forming a concentrated, fractionable, and not readily perishable putty-like substance. These qualities in conjunction facilitate its smuggling out of the hills and into the world narcotic whole-

[24] The importance of opium as a factor in the tribal standard of living is attested to by the strong correlation between estimated income through foreign trade and reliance on opium as the "engine of trade." See Young, 1962, p. 91, for a tabulation of tribal earnings through foreign trade (by tribe and trade goods).

[25] *Ibid.*, p. 90. This estimate accepts that the size of a swidden plot is a direct function of the household's labor force and need not be separately gauged—that is, it assumes labor supply rather than swidden fertility and capital stock to be the determinant of the level of output, a point of some significance which will be returned to in the following section.

sale trade.[26] Portability is a critical characteristic for any item entering into the tribes' foreign trade, for transport over the rugged terrain of the uplands is a time-consuming and arduous task. The advantage of opium in this respect is evident when compared with rice: the typical household may produce as little as 1,600 kilograms of milled rice (worth about 3,000 baht in the lowlands) to meet its bare subsistence requirement. The same household is capable of producing about 4 kilograms of processed opium (worth between 3,200 and 3,600 baht in the village—depending on its distance into the hills—and some 4,800 baht in the lowland market). To replace opium with rice as the foreign trade crop would therefore necessitate more than doubling the rice harvest, creating insurmountable problems of labor inadequacy and accelerated soil depletion, as well as of transporting thousands of kilograms of rice per household, not to speak of the final hurdle of locating buyers for the particular varieties of dry rice grown in the hills and of only peripheral interest to the Thai diet. Similar problems would be encountered in attempts to develop an export trade in livestock, potatoes, maize, and similar cash-earning products whose raising has occasionally but unsuccessfully been undertaken by individual households or proposed by "experts" on tribal affairs.

The overwhelming advantage of opium over all previously attempted alternatives is compounded by its drawing power. For no other tribal product but opium do lowland traders find it worthwhile to journey deep into the hills, searching out the farthest villages for their surplus, and for no other trade good would they be willing to risk carrying deep into the hills inventories of the very goods most sought by the

[26] "Definitely in the lowlands there exist secret trade organizations or syndicates, transforming, transporting and distributing the opium that is brought down from the hills" (Thailand, 1962, p. 38).

tribes: steel, seed, silver, and a variety of "luxury" consumables. This displacement of the conjunction of economic systems from the lowland market place to the tribal village carries a cost which the tribes must pay in lower opium prices (a difference of some 300–400 baht per kilogram) and higher import prices than prevail in the lowlands. But it is a cost they are willing to bear, for it permits them to avoid the lowlands, which means not only escaping the trouble of travel itself but of travel into an alien world feared as much for its unknowns as for its known hostility. Trade in the tribal village also eliminates for them the problem of smuggling the opium to market, a problem much greater for the tribesman than for the trader, who knows the ways of the police and blends into the lowland landscape.[27]

In its own way, then, opium is as critical an element of the tribal economy as rice. It serves as the primary tribal means of diversifying to offset the vagaries of the rice harvest. In years of rice crop failure, opium acts as the first asset liquidated to pay for substitute consumables outside the tribal community. In years of plenty, it can be hoarded in anticipation of future crop failures or traded for other forms of liquid wealth as well as for the usual subsistence, capital, and luxury import items. Those villages that do not produce opium are forced to reside on the periphery of the hills— that is, along the ragged fringes of the tribal world—in order to trade in a variety of goods of little value by trudging down to lowland market places to deal with Thai and Chinese merchants. If they live far into the hills they must inevitably suffer from the vagaries of the rice harvest.[28]

[27] Traders dealing with the tribes in their own habitat are usually Yunnanese Chinese (Haw), who are themselves a minority group in North Thailand and thus stand as cultural as well as economic intermediaries between hill and valley. Their role is discussed in Thailand, 1962, pp. 35–41, and their culture is described in Mote, 1967.

[28] "The absence of opium (or any other valuable product) as a

Though opium production and trade provide the tribes with a means of gaining access to a variety of goods considered essential to their well-being, it also forces them to deal with representatives of alien cultures. Dealings in the foreign sector for this reason remain devoid of the social implications which suffuse economic transactions within the village and which accompany those among villages. The foreign sector is thus distinguishable from the domestic sector not only in the tribal product transacted and the individuals engaging in the transaction but in the form taken by the negotiations themselves, with foreign dealings being carried on at arm's length, in economically disembedded terms, with money (i.e., silver) or its goods equivalents being the sole compensation for opium transfers.

Labor, the Key to Material Well-Being

It has been noted that the swidden system requires a far larger land-labor ratio than does the wet-rice technology of the Northern Thai valleys or the industrial technology of the nation's urban hubs. Yet even in terms of swiddening's extensive land requirements the tribal uplands have historically been underpopulated. The tribal concept of the uplands as a free good (or, more precisely, the lack of any economically significant property concept pertaining to uncultivated land) is a reflection of this fact.[29] Individual villages possess the sites they clear and cultivate on a usufructory basis, but long-fallowed sites return to the no-man's land of the jungle. To the individual village the uplands have always presented fresh cultivable sites; in this situation village rivalries over swidden

cash crop [among the Yao] has kept cash incomes at a low level as compared with the opium-growing tribes" (Kunstadter, 1967b, p. 655).

[29] Bernatzik, 1963, p. 321.

sites rarely occur and apparently never result in overt hostilities.[30]

Property concepts pertaining to capital are more specific, passing beyond mere right of usufruct. Capital is acquired by individual households, lent out to fellow villagers as a social obligation (invariably with the recognition that ownership remains with the initial holder), and lent to other villages for specific material compensation. Productive capital is generally of a rudimentary order, inexpensive, and durable; in an emergency, most forms can be improvised. Capital improvements to land (beyond clearing) are few and are ordinarily created as an integral part of the annual swidden preparation. Capital in the form of seed is critical but ordinarily available within the village as a residual from the preceding harvest; when not, it is acquired outside the village on the credit of the anticipated harvest or through the liquidation of a fraction of the household wealth. Capital in the form of livestock is not widely employed in the primary production process, though it is, of course, productive in being *repro-ductive*. "Nonproductive capital" (capital only in the sense that it is durable and a part of household assets) includes silver and opium hoards, dwellings, and household utensils and furnishings. Also, short-term nonproductive capital is

[30] At worst, swidden inadequacies in the immediate vicinity of large villages or nearby villages create internal pressures leading to village mitosis, a breakdown of internal solidarity resulting in separation into two new communities. Among the Lahu this condition frequently appears and has been carefully analyzed by Delmos Jones as an important aspect of tribal affairs, so important, in fact, that he asserts: "the most important social unit for the hill people of Northern Thailand is neither the separate village nor the total ethnic group. Rather, it is a group of closely related villages among which kinship connections exist and among which most marriages outside the village context take place" (Jones, 1969, p. 150). Such multivillage clusters can ordinarily be traced back to a single parent village.

held in the form of food stocks, apparel, and other semi-durables. To call such assets "capital," as is frequently done, is misleading since they are outputs but not inputs of the production process; the term "capital" will here be reversed for "productive capital."

In the swidden economy, with its limited labor force and its traditional capital complement, adding to traditional capital inputs does not raise output. This is because households typically clear all the land they are capable of working and store for this purpose the volume and variety of seed known from long experience to maximize output; they may from year to year be marginally off in their estimates of labor capabilities and capital requirements, but in general they operate efficiently, given their factor endowments as determined by their technology. In this case, investment above established rates is redundant. The incremental capital-output ratio, so widely employed as an analytic tool in development studies to indicate the role of capital formation as the engine of growth, misses the point when applied to this case.[31]

With land a free good and the capital component not independently capable of raising output under the given technological conditions, the critical factor in determining the volume of production is labor. The incremental labor-output ratio falls as household size increases, meaning that (with land and capital dependent variables) labor provides increasing returns to scale. The simple explanation lies in rationalization of labor effort as the fractional divisibility of the household labor input increases with household size.[32] The

[31] See the critique of capital-output ratios in Myrdal, 1968, pp. 1968–2004.

[32] The usual range of household size is from two or three up to fifteen or so. Among the Yao, at least, "The *desired* number of grown persons (over fifteen years of age) varied between five and twelve. The reasons given for limitation of household size were in-

larger household can, for instance, afford to weed its swiddens and guard them constantly against jungle depredators on a labor rotation basis while also performing other household chores; the smaller household must choose between one set of tasks and another at a time, thus intermittently neglecting its swiddens. The smaller household likewise runs risks which are limited in the larger; at any critical moment in the agricultural year a wrenched ankle, an attack of dysentery or fever, or a childbirth, for instance, can cut deeply into manpower.

Economies of scale at the household level are one of the obvious facts of tribal life.[33] The most superficial inspection of a village reveals that the largest households tend to be the wealthiest—indeed, the entire village congregates around them.[34] Theirs are the most sturdy dwellings and the best organized. Around them wander the greatest numbers of pigs and chickens, and inside are found the largest assortments of utensils and artifacts. Their numbers are the best clothed

---

variably that bad talk and quarrels would start if too many lived together, and that this made cooperation difficult" (Kandre, 1967, p. 601; my italics). Young, 1962, pp. 85 and 88–89, implies that average household size varies by tribe. These averages are positively correlated with the degree of reliance placed by various tribes on opium production. It appears, however, that variations in household size among villages *within* tribes tend to exceed differences in averages *among* tribes.

[33] "The larger the [household] community, the easier is the struggle for survival. The [Meo] is well aware of this fact and strives at all costs to enlarge the [household] community. Thus it is the self-evident aim of the [Meo] to have as many children as possible, and he demands ten children and more from each of his wives!" (Bernatzik, 1963, p. 62).

[34] This is not always the case, for a large household may be composed of a single married couple (the labor force) and a bevy of children large enough to destroy its wealth-accumulating opportunities until the dependents enter the labor force. By "large," therefore, we should mean "large and age-balanced."

and wear the greatest variety of silver ornaments, and they frequently appear the best fed. All this derives from the larger household's greater labor power. While labor productivity in the small household is barely sufficient in bountiful years to satisfy its subsistence requirements, the larger household harvests enough to accumulate an annual surplus, thereby achieving a measure of security in the event of crop failure and a degree of leverage in acquiring additional labor in future years.

The leading role of labor in the production process is well understood by tribesmen. An elaborate set of institutions governing its allocation has evolved, cutting across both the domestic and foreign sectors to give an inner unity and stability to the tribal economy by embedding it in the social process. These institutions have been alluded to in the preceding discussion, but their underlying function remains to be clarified.

The major means of expanding the household labor force are marriage and children. Neither labor source is costless, however, but both are sufficiently rewarding in improving the household's long-run economic position that they are consciously sought for their economic as well as their other contributions. This is most apparent among the Meo and Yao, who speak of marriage as a purchase of female labor.[35] In all tribes, wives must be paid for either through several years' uxorilocal residence, with the couple's contributions to household economic surplus accruing largely to the wife's parents (as among the Lahu), or through payment of a "bride price" of silver or livestock to the wife's parents (as among the Meo and Yao).[36] Polygyny is not uncommon, except

[35] "Marriage among the [Yao] is a business transaction involving the transfer of important amounts of wealth, and it is fundamental to the individual's success in life" (Kandre, 1967, p. 593).

[36] Thailand, 1962, pp. 48–50.

among the Lahu, whose relatively high regard for the female sex is reflected in matriarchal tendencies. Mates are selected (within the constraints imposed by kinship and clan incest rules and tribal endogamy) on the basis of skills, strength, health, and expected fecundity. Cases have been observed of the abandonment of infertile wives. Members of wealthy households have advantages in selecting marriage partners because of their own high reputation as producers, frequently better health, and ability to bear the initial costs of marriage. In impoverished households, in contrast, marriageable offspring frequently face a bleak future. Similarly, poor households face greater difficulties in expanding their labor forces through child raising due to their struggle at the margin of survival.

The other important source of labor arises from intervillage economic transactions. Households that encounter crop failure seek assistance first from their fellow villagers. When sufficient subsistence goods cannot be provided within the village (meaning that the village has either been deserted by relatively wealthy households or that the entire village has been dragged down into a state of impoverishment) whatever assets are available must be liquidated. It may be that the village stock of liquid assets such as opium, silver, and livestock is chronically small due to the village's small households, or it may be that previous crop disasters have depleted it. In either case the sole negotiable item remaining after the disposal of liquid assets is labor itself. In this situation, labor is not only the source of household wealth, it is also its residual form.

Impoverished households seek to maintain themselves until the next harvest, when with good fortune they may be able to rise at least to subsistence once again, by "selling" children and wives.[37] In the last resort, householders "sell" themselves. It should be noted that the transaction does not constitute an outright disposal of human bodies, as in the African slave trade of past centuries, but resembles more closely the adoption of the "sold" person into a new household as a socially inferior member. The sale, though unavoidable, places the impoverished household in an even more tragic position than before, for it deprives the household of a portion of the labor so desperately needed to pull it out of the vicious circle of an increasing productivity gap, which is reinforced not only by sales of the labor force but by declining labor effectiveness due to inadequate consumption levels. On the other hand, the "reason for buying children is almost always the desire to build quickly an efficient working household." [38]

Hugo Bernatzik has summarized the situation of labor transactions as follows:

Among the [Meo], in addition to the free there are also the unfree, who, however, are not to be confused with slaves. In the case of the unfree, it is rather a matter of [Meo] who are alone, whose relatives have died as a consequence of war, sickness, or old age, and who, having grown up within the unit of the large family, now have no possibility of enduring the struggle for existence as solitary individuals.[39]

That this is an overly idyllic picture is reflected in case studies of "bought children" and in the fact that a strong social stigma attaches to wage labor, an activity which tribesmen

[37] The practice of "selling" and "buying" children and wives varies among the tribes. "Akha do not buy, though others buy Akha. Neither Lisu nor Yao sell themselves, but both buy. Lahu both buy and sell" (Lucien Hanks, personal communication, October 1969). The problem is placed in historical and cultural perspective in Lasker, 1950, *passim.*

[38] Kandre, 1967, p. 594.   [39] Bernatzik, 1963, p. 62.

know can be easily confused with "bought labor" by the casual observer, including their own fellows.[40]

The "unfree" do not result solely from household disintegration under the pressures of rice-crop failures. Opium addiction is also a cause. One of the chief disadvantages of opium cultivation is that it provides the hill tribe peasant with an ever present inducement to turn to it for medicinal purposes as a pain killer, an antidote to diarrhea, and a source of consolation in times of emotional distress. The tribes are well aware of this danger and seek to avoid it, but not all are successful, as is apparent from the presence of addicts in many villages.[41] Addiction contributes to household poverty since it lowers export volume and labor productivity. In their search for the drug, addicts in the hills leave no stone unturned. Murder is not unknown. More frequently they resort to the sale of children and wives. When other avenues have been closed, addicts become attached on an occasional or permanent basis to wealthy households willing to use their labor in return for daily payment of a few pipefuls of the drug. In this manner, some wealthy households in remote districts gain command over a sizable "unfree" labor force.[42]

[40] Kandre, 1967, p. 604; Bennington-Cornell, 1964, p. 27.

[41] Young, 1962, p. 42. He estimates that some 15 per cent of aggregate opium production is domestically consumed (p. 90). Statistics on the numbers or percentage of tribesmen addicted are not available, partly because of the obvious political problems of conducting research into such matters and partly because of the medical problem of defining where casual consumption fades into habituation and finally into addiction.

[42] It is common gossip in North Thailand that some Karen tribesmen create their own captive labor forces of local Thai peasants by introducing them to opium and, after addiction has taken hold, providing it to them only in exchange for work in the swiddens or as porters in the overland trade with Burma. See Thailand, 1962, pp. 38–39.

The Dynamics of Tribal Economic Change
in Microcosm

Any summary of the hill tribe economy which describes only those characteristics that hold true without exception must inevitably degenerate into a list of platitudes, for technological and institutional variations are observable among tribal households right down to the intravillage level. I have adopted the alternative procedure of delineating norms, recognizing that though norms identify general regularities they do not reveal the range of variation from which they are abstracted. This procedure was chosen despite the fact that it invites criticism and controversy on marginal judgments, for what constitutes the norm in such a little known universe as the hill tribe economy depends entirely on the question of whether the data sample employed (in this case the footnoted references supplemented by personal observation) is representative of that universe. Only further field work can provide the answer.

It is to be expected that each tribal economic norm summarized in the preceding sections is not reflected in every individual case, for no "average" tribe, village, or household exists in the strict sense of the term. Though the inevitable deviations from the norm create methodological problems they also provide valuable clues to the process of economic change in individual cases and thus to the evolutionary dynamics of the tribal economy as a whole. The following analysis of three tribal villages reflects this advantage of "normal" summation.

Each of these villages (see map on p. 37) has been squeezed into the periphery of the hills by causal sequences revealed in their individual case histories, streams of events which appear to represent a widespread process of economic and political readjustment within the tribal world. In their new locations at the edge of the uplands they have been subjected to nearly daily contact with Thai people and the institutions and technologies of alien economic systems, generating a cumulative process of change which is gradually shifting their economies away from the tribal norm and is in turn dragging the tribal norm in its wake. The dynamics of economic change in these villages may be predicted to duplicate themselves as other villages are brought into closer contact with the Thai in the coming decades, either as a product of the pressures which are moving them toward the edges of the hills or as a result of Thai government involvement in tribal affairs as concern grows among the Thai elite over regionalism, meaning in this case the political security—or Thaiification—of the Northern border areas (see Chapter 5). Thus, the villages here analyzed serve as leading indicators of the trend of the tribal economic norm. Their deviations from that norm suggest the manner in which the hill tribe economy may be expected to change in the coming decades.

The Meo of Phapucom

Meo villagers within the Research Area recollect that their tribe first settled in the vicinity five generations ago. This memory jibes with anthropologists' estimates that the Meo have been filtering into Thailand since the middle of the nineteenth century. The age of the village of Phapucom is not recalled by its residents, however, because their ancestries, apparently following Chinese custom, are traced in terms of lineages (or "clans") which cross village lines with marriage and household realignments.[43]

[43] The details of Phapucom's history have been drawn largely from Lucien Hanks, 1964; and Jane Hanks, 1964.

Phapucom must have been in its present locale for decades, however, for by 1950 the village had swiddened all suitable sites in the immediate vicinity. Because of repeated cropping, none had refertilized itself sufficiently in the villagers' estimation to warrant a new cycle of clearing and cultivation. On both its eastern and western flanks the terrain slopes down to valleys too low for the application of the tribal swidden technology. Further west, fertile uplands have been occupied by other Meo, Lahu, and Lisu villages. Therefore, the decision was made in 1950 to relocate the village. In addition to its desire for fresh fields, the village decided to migrate in order to put distance between itself and encroaching Thai hill dwellers (discussed in Chapter 3), with whom the Meo had been involved in a series of unhappy incidents, centering primarily on foraging Thai-owned oxen which destroyed Meo crops by occasionally wandering into the swiddens.

The village moved some sixty miles south to a Meo village in Omkoi District, Chiengmai Province, populated with households of Phapucom's lineages and, more important, reputed to have fresh swidden tracts available. Anticipations were not realized. The soils of the Omkoi area had already been depleted. The terrain lacked an adequate timber cover and turned to mire in the rains, making it unsuitable for poppy growing. Poor swidden conditions did not permit the village to recover from the poverty into which it had sunk at Phapucom and which had been aggravated by the costs of village relocation (in lost time and energy as well as in the fees paid to make the trip south in the comfort of Thai country busses) and the costs of registering their new land with local Thai officials.[44] These blows to their livelihood and

[44] Upon moving to Omkoi, village households were approached by the local Thai district officer, who informed them that they would be permitted to cultivate the uplands only on payment of a special

their self-esteem may well have been decisive in turning a number of villagers to opium consumption.

Not knowing where else to turn, they petitioned a wealthy Thai owner of tea and orange groves at the foot of the hills near Phapucom, who had befriended them in the past. He willingly paid their fare back to Phapucom (for reasons identified in Chapter 4). They returned in 1960, literally without shirts on their backs. Not all the original villagers returned, however, and not all those who were in the returning party had been former residents of the village. The aged stayed on at Omkoi, probably favoring the security of familiar, even if impoverished, conditions over the risks of another relocation; several adventurous but poor Omkoi youths, related to and accepted into Phapucom households, took their places.

Further calamities plagued the village on its return. First, during their absence a Lahu village had migrated into the locale and occupied the finest swidden sites. Second, a tea plantation had infringed on their former territories. Third, a government hill tribe welfare station was constructed within a half mile of Phapucom shortly after their return, forcing them, from a sense of ethnic pride and for the sake of privacy, to move the village again, this time to a site several miles to the west. And lastly, their former problems with local Thai peasants were resumed. In 1963, for instance, four Phapucom households complained of losing large portions of their rice crops because of damage done by wandering Thai-owned cattle.

Three years after their return from Omkoi the village in-

---

land tax. The tax was paid but seems never to have reached the public coffers. Only later did the outraged Meo discover that no law exists on the Thai books which requires payment of taxes on upland use. See Kunstadter, 1967c, pp. 377–378.

cluded fifteen households with a population of 107, of which 50 could be said to form the labor force; 53 were below age ten, and 4 were aged.[45] The high dependency ratio added to the strain of poverty. The proportion of the labor force addicted to opium could not be accurately surveyed because of the secrecy which attaches to opium production and use and because of the difficulties in differentiating between casual and regular users. A speculative estimate places the number at about eight, which still leaves open to question the intensity of their addiction (that is, the quantity they consume and their degree of debilitation) as well as the frequency of use and the additional number of "casual" users.

Since the return from Omkoi, Phapucom's swidden harvests have consistently fallen below expectations. The typical household (three laborers and four children) considers subsistence output to be 1,600 kilograms of milled rice, a volume well below the standards of other hill tribe villages.[46] The typical householder's harvest in 1963 realized a volume of about half this bare minimum. Opium harvests have likewise been low. In contrast to the estimate that the average hill tribe household produces four kilograms of processed opium annually, the households of Phapucom harvest in the neighborhood of one kilogram each. Poverty has become chronic as a result of the unrelieved repetition of these crop shortfalls. Wealth, as measured in such tribal terms as silver

[45] For bench-mark purposes the labor force is defined as all those above age ten, excluding the aged (age fifty and over, though in other communities at higher living standards this may be set at age sixty). Population data for Phapucom have been derived from Lucien Hanks, 1963b.

[46] Using simplified consumption estimates of one-fifth kg. of milled rice per day per child below ten and four-fifths kg. per day for those ten or over, the village's annual requirement amounts to 19,368 kg. If output is 800 kg. per household annually, village output comes to 12,000 kg., some 7,000 kg. short of subsistence.

ornaments, livestock, multiple wives, and luxury imports such as flashlights, firearms, and radios, is conspicuously scarce.

Chronically low incomes and consequent wealth depletion have had disasterous consequences for Phapucom. Villagers have been pressed by poverty into accepting wage labor on the nearby tea plantation with increasing frequency; plantation records reveal that since 1960 the number of Meo seeking employment has risen yearly. Coincidentally, the Meo have become increasingly prone to seek and accept aid from outside the tribal community, creating reciprocative problems because of the conflicting cultural concepts of debit and credit involved. The origin of the Meo's dependence on charity seems to lie in the assistance received from their Thai benefactor, who supplied them with return transportation from Omkoi and has since continued to supplement their incomes with "loans" of rice and cloth. Reliance on "foreign aid" has been reinforced by the Thai government's provision of occasional material benefits (rice, blankets, salt, aspirin) through the local welfare station. The Meo have become so habituated to this practice that they often appear at the government welfare station in search of handouts, all thought of reciprocity apparently vanished.

Critical links in the chain of events contributing to Phapucom's depression and demoralization were the political and demographic pressures which squeezed the village onto marginal lands at the periphery of the hills. In tribal history virgin lands have always lain to the south; population pressures have always emanated from the north.[47] Phapucom was established as a southward extension of the Meo community seeping into Thailand from Laos and Yunnan. It was unfortunate enough to occupy a hill tract abutting on what appears to the Meo as a topographical and cultural precipice. Before

[47] Wiens, 1954.

it stood not further hills but the "uninhabitable" Ping river valley; behind it, and on both sides, lay fully occupied hill tribe tracts. The leap of sixty miles to Omkoi did not permit the village to escape its predicament, and so it returned to its old home to renew the struggle on inferior soils. Phapucom marks the end of a tribal era—the era of the open frontier. With land no longer abundantly available to this village, it replaces labor as the critical factor in the swidden technology. Yet the Phapucom economy remains institutionally and technologically geared to extensive land use and reuse. Its laborcentric institutions have not adapted to the changed ecology. Its labor-oriented technology only aggravates the problem. Declining crop yields in this self-perpetuating situation have affected standards of nutrition, health, and productivity, along with village self-reliance, in a cumulative process intensifying the village depression.

Through their effects on morale and nutrition, declining harvests have also stimulated opium consumption. As addiction and habituation have tightened their holds, opium users have devoted correspondingly less effort to the tasks of cultivation, hunting, foraging, and household maintenance. Consequently, standards of nutrition, health, and productivity have been further reduced, reinforcing the tendency to opium addiction.[48] Domestic consumption of opium has be-

---

[48] The habit of resmoking opium residues is both brought about by and reinforces declining productivity. The first smoking does not extract the product's full potency. Residues may be scraped from the pipe and reused four or more times, depending on the initial quality of the product. Though some narcotic effect remains to satisfy reuse, each smoking carries with it the hazard of increasingly harmful effects on the smoker's health. Though this danger is known to the tribal people, just as they know the harmful effects of addiction itself, villagers of Phapucom have gradually surrendered first to addiction and then, as insufficient opium has been harvested to satisfy their needs, to the consequences of resmoking.

come so great and output so low in some households that they have been forced to buy the drug from local Thai dealers at prices which are triple those at which the Meo ordinarily sell it.

Domestic deterioration has been paralleled in the foreign sector. As harvests have declined with soil depletion and lowered labor productivity, and as opium consumption has increased, cash income from opium sales has fallen. The consequent decline in imports has accelerated the trend in declining health and morale, in turn decreasing cash income as opium consumption has continued to gain ground. Though most households still manage to produce one kilogram of raw opium, only about one-third of the village total (worth about 5,000 baht) is sold. Some households are unwilling to sell more than four or five ounces. Several, it is said, consume all they produce.

The combination of inadequate rice harvests and declining cash returns from opium has forced the village to search for alternative income sources. One alternative is foreign aid. Lowlanders, traditionally wary of extending credit to tribesmen and knowing of the village's poverty, have been unwilling to go this route. Aid from the nearby plantation has been forthcoming on the face-saving understanding that eventual restitution will be made in labor services; in 1962 and 1963 such aid amounted to over 1,500 kilograms of milled rice as well as an unrecorded volume of cloth and other necessities. As for Phapucom's credit line with its hill tribe neighbors to the west, this has long since been played out (short of resorting to labor "sales").

Another alternative is wage labor, to which the Meo of Phapucom have turned despite its moral stigma. Revulsion at working under the supervision of Thai foremen and at being told when, where, and how to perform their chores has prevented Meo villagers from assimilating into the plantation economy. Their history of oppression at the hands of low-land peoples and the residual condescension and sometimes hostility of their Thai co-workers does not make plantation work pleasant for them. Consequently, wage labor is relegated predominantly to women and children, though they are paid lower wages than the men. During 1963, village income from this source amounted to not more than 4,500 baht.

A rough estimate of annual village income in 1963–1964 (February through January) may be hazarded by summarizing incomes in milled-rice equivalents, using a bench-mark conversion figure of 1.25 baht per kilogram of milled rice (the going price for the lowest quality sold in the locality in 1963). On this basis, milled-rice output amounted to some 12,000 kilograms; opium sales brought in 4,000 kilograms; plantation labor earned 3,600 kilograms; charity provided 750 kilograms. Total income equaled some 20,350 kilograms of milled-rice equivalents.[49] Since the village's annual subsistence requirement is about 20,000 kilograms *in milled rice alone*, it remains in a state of grinding poverty, foregoing many of the conveniences that are an ordinary part of tribal life.

As the village economy continues to falter, increased reliance must be placed on the foreign sector. The economy will in the process be restructured to fit its relations with its

[49] This estimate excludes a number of relatively minor sources of village income: foraging and hunting, services rendered by village specialists and household craftsmen, sale of vegetables and herbs to local Thai peasants, sale of artifacts in the lowlands (through the mediation of government officials), and charity from the government hill tribe welfare station. Income is so low that several adult men in the village remain unmarried due to their inability to pay "bride price"; it is not coincidental that several of the village's opium addicts are young unmarried males.

Thai neighbors. Economic transformation is being hampered, however, by the institutional fabric of village life. The hold of tradition remains strong: villagers continue to identify with the tribe, not with the Thai; they continue to cherish the dream of village independence centering on the swidden economy with its opium export surplus; they regard wage labor as a humiliating necessity rather than as an honorable trade. Hardships brought on by the deteriorating economy have not succeeded in quashing villagers' aspirations for a return to the more prosperous past. In stimulating opium addiction the current situation has actually reinforced their desire to return to swiddening rather than be assimilated into the lowland economy. In forcing the acceptance of charity and reliance on labor, their impoverished state has revitalized their traditional repugnance against lowland civilization.

Thus, the economic deterioration of Phapucom has raised new barriers to economic change in the process of tearing down the old, and it has strengthened some that have remained. Though structural change in the present situation seems the only alternative to increased poverty and ultimate village dissolution, such change can not come without severe dislocations, which may themselves destroy the village.

The Lahu of Huai Thad and Ban Yai Suk

General opinion has it that the Lahu are one of the more recent tribal immigrant groups to North Thailand. The earliest references place Lahu villages in Thailand no more than eighty years ago.[50] Much of the present population, in fact, has crossed into Thailand from northern Burma, their tra-

[50] Jones, 1969, p. 156. Later immigrants include Lisu, Yao, and Akha, who arrived in Thailand probably not more than sixty years ago.

ditional habitat, only since World War II. With the Chinese Nationalist debacle in 1949, elements of the defeated army, and with them a stream of Yunnanese refugees of all sorts, fled from China into the mountainous reaches of northern Burma, where their unwelcome arrival created a tense political situation. Political pressures in the area were only partly relieved with a massive airlift which evacuated many of the military forces from Burma to Taiwan in 1953. The unrest and hostilities of these years forced a number of tribal villages to migrate out of the affected area, some of them to Thailand.

Among the refugees were a group of Christianized (Baptist) Lahu, who arrived at Fang (northern Chiengmai Province) in 1954 in poverty, having left their wealth behind in their haste to escape.[51] Knowing nothing of their new "homeland," they petitioned a local Baptist missionary for aid, and he in turn introduced them to the very Thai businessman who would later come to the rescue of the Meo of Phapucom. He invited the Lahu to occupy the hill tract which had only a few years before been abandoned by Phapucom, and which now adjoined a newly formed tea plantation. As the Lahu understood it, the land was "donated" to them by its "owner." This take-over of Meo territories was to have important effects on Lahu-Meo-plantation relations after Phapucom's return (noted in Chapter 6). The Lahu founded the village of Huai Thad near the plantation factory, then at an experimental stage, and began cultivating the fallowed, and thus partly refertilized, Meo swiddens.

In 1962 a part of the village split off to form the new com-

[51] The histories of Huai Thad and Ben Yai Suk are dealt with in Jones, 1967, pp. 150–153; Devakul, 1965, p. 31; Lauriston Sharp, 1965, p. 89; and Jane Hanks, 1964.

munity of Ban Yai Suk, an hour's hike to the west. The reasons for the move are interesting, for they demonstrate the importance of documenting hill tribe economic affairs with an awareness of social institutions. One observer of this village split asserts that it was due to "insufficient land." [52] Another states in a similiar vein that "the more industrious, efficient, or energetic Lahu households, rather than renounce the norms of their ideal" of village brotherhood, split off in order to escape their communal responsibilities to the indigent.[53] Against these "economic" interpretations stand such findings as reflected in the following remark:

The . . . segmentation of the village of [Huai Thad] which resulted in the establishment of [Ban Yai Suk], was the result of a case of rape. . . . [In the controversy which followed the event,] kinship played such an important role that serious splits occurred [even] in households where husbands and wives were related to opposing sides.[54]

The first step in determining whether the village division actually occurred along income lines would entail a statistical survey of individual household incomes and subsistence requirements, and on this basis imputing the intravillage flow of rice among surplus and deficit households. Overriding the problems involved in this task would be the issue of whether the resulting correlation between income levels and village factions did not, after all, arise fortuitously or derivatively, while an exogenous determinant—in this case the controversy arising out of an alleged rape, or more broadly, the frequently remarked Lahu inclination to be "quarrelsome" and "factious" among themselves—was the primary cause.[55] The

[52] Devakul, 1965, p. 32.   [53] Lauriston Sharp, 1965, p. 89.
[54] Jones, 1967, p. 152.
[55] LeBar et al., eds., 1964, p. 30; Jones, 1969, passim; Devakul, 1965, p. 35.

question of which of these factors, economic imbalance or social instability, was the more influential not only appears unanswerable; it misses the point. The "two causes" must be analyzed as interacting elements in a single continuum of which village cleavage is one phase. Their analytical separation on the written page amounts to an obfuscation rather than a clarification of the stream of village economic history.

A year after the village split, Huai Thad had a population of 106, of which 61 constituted the labor force, 41 were below age ten, and 5 were aged.[56] Ban Yai Suk had a population of 107, composed of 63 laborers, 41 below age ten, and 3 aged.[57] Average household size in the former village was five, in the latter seven, a reflection, again, of varying levels of wealth. In both villages the dependency ratio, at 2:5, was more favorable than among the Mao of Phapucom.

The most important economic peculiarities of these two villages stem from their religion. Because of their abandonment of an important aspect of Lahu culture they have been isolated from their fellow tribesmen.[58] "In the minds of [other] Lahu, [these villagers] have been corrupted by Christian missionaries." They are no longer considered "pure Lahu." [59] Because of the barriers thus erected, communication with other tribal villages has been largely eliminated. Thus, information concerning available fresh swidden lands does not reach them, and village migration is constrained.

Christian doctrine as taught them also prohibits the cultivation and consumption of opium. Adherence to this stricture has left them economically stranded, with no export

[56] Derived from Sharp and Nakorntheb, 1963.
[57] Derived from Lucien Hanks, 1963a.
[58] The village of Huai Thad has, however, received Christian exiles from other Burmese hill tribes, including two Lisu, two Kachin, and one Wa.
[59] Jones, 1969, p. 169.

commodity available to satisfy their import requirements. Stopgap exports, including pigs, subsidiary crops, artifacts, and wage labor, must be resorted to. They are required, then, to live in close proximity to the lowlands. Even if they were to hear of superior swidden sites further into the hills they could not seek them out for this reason. Religion has immobilized them.

Though Christianity has in this sense locked them out of the tribal world, it has unlocked other doors. Missionaries (one of whom periodically lives in Huai Thad with his wife) have introduced the villagers to a host of new ideas, which have changed their daily dress, health habits, work regime, settlement pattern, and relations with the nontribal world. Missionaries have provided them with a romanized script and a literature and have offered their youth an education at seminaries in Chiengmai Town. The net effect has been to prepare them for assimilation into the lowland economy while permitting them to retain many indigenous Lahu social institutions, among them bilateral kinship, uxorilocal residence, and political leadership centering on the religious specialist.[60]

The level of welfare in these villages is above that of Phapucom. At Huai Thad, and even more so at Ban Yai Suk, plentiful and relatively robust livestock are apparent everywhere. Granaries remain well stocked throughout the year. Cash-on-hand is sufficient to make worthwhile an occasional trip by Thai peddlers up from the valley. Several adolescents have been spared from the production process to seek education at missionary schools. An air of community solidarity and pride suffuses each of these villages.

The chief source of income is the rice harvest and the various subsidiary crops which complement it. From a sample of Thai-speaking households it has been learned that the

[60] Jones, 1967, pp. 182–183.

typical household reaped 3,200 kilograms of paddi in 1963, about 800 kilograms less than had been harvested from the same plot the preceding year. Estimates for other crops are: sesame, 86 bushels per household (29 houeholds producing it); sorghum, 47 bushels per household (18 households producing); and maize, 7 bushels (31 households producing).[61] The representative household owns two breeding pigs and two dozen chickens, a banana grove (the stalks used as pig feed), and several papaya, breadfruit, orange, and/or pomelo trees. Several households at Huai Thad possess gardens of coffee trees provided by the Thai government.

The most common source of cash income is from labor at the tea plantation. In 1963 some households earned over 500 baht from this source. The two villages earned a total of more than 5,000 baht in plantation wages in that year. A second source of cash income is from sales of rice, bananas, pigs, and chickens to local Thai and Meo villagers. A third source is from sales of coffee beans, potatoes, and artifacts in lowland market places, with the nearby government welfare station acting as agent (see Chapter 5). Though a sample of Thai-speaking households provided an average annual cash income estimate of 1,000 baht, a more typical figure would lie at a lower level. In terms of milled-rice equivalents, household income in 1963 averaged some 3,500 kilograms, about double the Meo figure.[62]

With the village split of 1962, the wealthier faction moved to Ban Yai Suk. The new village cleared long-fallowed field sites to replace their former swiddens near Huai Thad, which were now too distant (and, it was said, too depleted) to warrant further cultivation. Not only is Ban Yai Suk wealthier,

[61] Derived from Thailand, 1963b.
[62] Computations follow the conversion rates mentioned above for Phapucom. This income datum includes neither income derived from subsidiary crops and livestock nor from hunting and foraging.

then, but with newly cleared swiddens it is assured of richer harvests. These factors, added to the distance of the new village from the plantation and the valley world, have given it a greater sense of self-sufficiency and insularity than is evident in Huai Thad. In terms of the trend to assimilation into the lowland economy the formation of Ban Yai Suk stands as a regressive step. Huai Thad, the poorer village, swiddening partially depleted soils and constantly tempted by the opportunities to earn income through commodities trade and wage labor, depends more heavily on its foreign sector and less on the domestic than Ban Yai Suk; some of its households have intermittently imported rice while those of Ban Yai Suk have not. This divergence in the composition of economic activity can be expected to grow so long as harvest at Ban Yai Suk remain bountiful.[63]

Prosperity and Depression

A comparison of these Lahu villages with the Meo of Phapucom is instructive. Both groups came to the same locale in dire economic straits. They have worked neighboring swidden sites and have even cultivated one another's fallowed rice fields. They have both supplemented the incomes earned from swiddening and related economic activities with wage labor at the nearby tea plantation. Despite adversities and foreign opportunities both have retained the swidden technology as the basic mode of production, at least in their domestic sectors. And, though moving in different directions, both have departed from the traditional economic equilibrium of the tribal community.

[63] While few households at Huai Thad had export earnings exceeding 1,000 baht in 1963–1964, Jones found six households in that village in 1965–1966 whose average cash income was about 1,900 baht; the trend is evident from these sample statistics (Jones, 1967, p. 156).

Despite these and other technological similarities, Phapucom has become increasingly impoverished while Huai Thad and Ban Yai Suk have raised their standards of living to a level approaching that of the lowland Thai peasantry. The simple conclusion that rising rates of soil depletion under population pressures on the extensive and intensive limits of fertile uplands are driving the hill tribes into economic depression is therefore inadequate. To this factor must be added a number of other variables, such as openness to foreign social contact (through cross-cultural religious ties, for instance), exploitation of economic opportunities in the foreign sector (such as acceptance of wage labor offers from commercial operations), the incidence and intensity of domestic opium consumption, and the burden of the dependency ratio.

These "causes" and others noted earlier may, however, themselves be traced back to their own "effects" that is, these tribal villages at the periphery of the uplands are caught up in a process of cumulative causation consisting of the interaction of past-binding institutions and traditionally slow-changing technologies forced to accommodate to, and themselves helping to shape the character of, various alien influences. Phapucom's increasing poverty can better be examined as a self-generating sequence of disasters appearing with the gradual degeneration of the economic and social fabric as the community attempts to adjust to the nearby presence of intruding economic systems. The relative prosperity of the neighboring Lahu villages can similarly be interpreted as the result of a series of successful adaptations to the changing economic environment. No "first cause" can be derived from either case; yet, having had its fundamental components uncovered, the causal sequence can be meaningfully extrapolated, a topic which will be returned to in Chapter 6.

Chapter 3

THE UPLAND THAI
PEASANT ECONOMY

Speculations on the Economic History of Miang

Early Western travelers through upper Burma, North Thailand, and Laos made occasional reference in their journals to a delicacy peculiar to the region, *let pet* (in Burmese) or *miang* (in Tai dialects). The first mention predates the nineteenth century: "We brought to, and spent the night near a small village. . . . Here the inhabitants get their livelihood by selling Laepac or pickled tea-leaf, of which the Birmans are extremely fond. . . . [It] is very inferior to the tea produced in China, and is seldom used but as a pickle." [1] A more extended discussion of miang production in Burma has been provided by Mary Lewis Milne, who discovered it to be the economic mainstay of the Palaung, a Burmese hill tribe.[2]

References to miang in North Thailand are found scattered through the early literature.[3] A British consular official came across miang groves in the hills northwest of Chiengmai Town about 1890.

[1] Symes, 1800, p. 273.

[2] Milne, 1924, pp. 222–238. Also see Shway Yoe, 1910, p. 298.

[3] An earlier statement, "No mention of *miang* is found in the writings of early missionaries to North Thailand nor in those of Reginald LeMay," thus stands corrected (Van Roy, 1967, p. 422).

Just at the bottom of the hill we passed a plantation of *mieng,* or Lao tea. The natives call these plantations *pa mieng,* or tea forest, if *pa* be rendered literally, this term causing it to be generally supposed that *mieng* grows wild. . . . The Laos do not drink the infusion, but prepare the leaf for chewing by burying it in pits, and it is one of their indispensable luxuries. You see a man put a lump of the fermented leaves in one cheek, which he leaves there while he proceeds to chew betel or smoke a cigarette, looking for all the world as if his face were distorted by the mumps.[4]

Another reference of about the same time and locale gives some details of miang's production and states further:

Salt is sprinkled over the leaves, and the whole rolled up into a hard ball about the size of a walnut. This is put into the mouth, and sucked all day. The people find it a great stimulant, and by its use are enabled to go without food for long periods. Large quantities of *mieng* are consumed, bullocks, and even elephants, being often laden with nothing else. It is regarded as a great luxury by the Lao princes, among whom it takes as important a place as the betel-leaf and areca palm nut.[5]

Passing reference to miang consumption is also made by Lillian Curtis, Reginald LeMay, and Erik Seidenfaden, who are other early Western visitors to the region.[6]

Such scattered remarks indicate that miang production, distribution, and consumption were well established in Burma and Thailand when first noticed by Western adventurers during the eighteenth and nineteenth centuries. Elsewhere, I have conjectured that its use by the Tai may date back to

[4] Satow, 1892, p. 194. This and several of the following citations on the traditional use of miang in North Thailand were furnished by S. H. Unemoto.

[5] McCarthy, 1900, p. 124.

[6] Curtis, 1903, p. 118; LeMay, 1926, p. 112; Seidenfaden, 1958, p. 112.

their earliest known kingdoms in present-day Szechwan and Yunnan, mainland China (c. A.D. 700).[7] It was in this region, it appears, that the Chinese first learned to consume tea as an infusion. The earliest mention of its use has been found in the *Yen tzu ch'un ch'ui*, written circa 500 B.C. In that book, an article of food called *ming ts'ai* has been translated as "tea vegetable." Its phonetic similarity to the term "miang" is evident.[8]

This line of reasoning, which links miang with the Tai through history, raises the question of how it came to be that the Tai, a valley-dwelling people, have continued to produce miang, derived from a shrub which thrives at elevations of 2,000 feet and up. Why, over the centuries, would Tai peasants have foresaken their lowland villages to traipse into the hills, abounding with such dangers as tigers, elephants, snakes, and evil spirits as well as isolated from the comforts and pleasures of valley life? Two reasons may be furnished. First, Tai peasants were frequently called on by their "Lords of Life" to participate in *corvée* labor; in fact, many spent a considerable portion of their lives serving under public indenture. Others were placed in bondage as a result of indebtedness or were enslaved during military campaigns. Though slavery in the Tai milieu was not inevitably unpalatable, it could be, depending on the whims of one's master. Those who did not enjoy their fate had the single option of escape into the lowland jungles or the hills. "If the demands of the government became too great, a farmer had only to escape to the forest and clear new land. . . . That the practice was common is indicated by the frequency

[7] Van Roy, 1967, p. 421. Experts on tea history tend to concur the the source of the shrub is the upper Irrawaddy watershed; see, for instance, Eden, 1958, p. 1.

[8] Sealy, 1958, p. 1-2.

with which the government issued decrees cajoling or threatening farmers who might be contemplating such moves." [9] In the hills, the traditional wet-rice agricultural techniques of the Tai proved unproductive. The sole alternative was frequently miang production.[10]

Second, the high esteem in which miang has traditionally been held by the Tai as a luxury consumable, along with the dangers and deprivations associated with its production, have assured it a high unit value. Those possessing the courage and determination to take up its production earn a high reward for their trouble. The move into the hills and to miang cultivation promises the adventurous peasant an income which, if he perseveres and avoids catastrophe, will raise his position in peasant society by a quantum jump. Miang production provides the industrious peasant with a shortcut to prosperity and status in the valley community, and this incentive, together with the prospect of escape from the *corvée* and slavery (conditions which today are replaced by population pressure on the margin of arable flood plains), has probably been sufficient inducement to ensure that miang production as a Tai industry will endure.

An alternative theory of the economic history of miang has been developed by Frank LeBar. Four Austroasiatic hill tribes—the Khmu and T'in of North Thailand and Laos, the Palaung of Burma, and the Lamet of Laos—produce and consume miang. Because various processes in miang production (steaming, storage, and fermentation) and consump-

[9] Vella, 1955, p. 330. Also see Wales, 1934, pp. 95–96, 123, 132, 161, 199–201; and Lasker, 1950, pp. 150–154, 189–193.

[10] There was also dry-rice swiddening and, in the nineteenth century (after its introduction through the British and Chinese), opium cultivation. But both these pursuits require the semimigratory habits of the hill tribes. Tai custom, which links the individual with his lowland community and a sedentary life, did not favor such adaptations.

tion (it is consumed as a masticatory) are similar to Austro-asiatic traditions, LeBar infers that miang production may well have originated among these tribes, that the lowlanders long acquired the finished product for their own consumption through a widespread "pattern of quasi politico-economic exploitation" of their tribal neighbors, and that the Tai have themselves only recently turned to its production as population pressures have mounted in the valleys.[11]

Several questions remain unresolved by this line of reasoning: Why do only a scattered few among the many Austro-asiatic hill tribes within the region cultivate miang? To whom did they export their surplus before the arrival of the Tai in the region? Why would dry-rice producers, semimigratory tribal people because of their swidden technology, tie their export sector to a perennial crop which takes five years to mature and may produce for some sixty years thereafter? Could these few tribes alone have satisfied what appears to have long been a widespread Tai (and Burmese) demand for miang as a luxury consumable? With population pressures only recently emerging as the reason for Tai migration into the hills, how could nineteenth-century reports state that "The Laos . . . prepare the leaf"?[12] On what other economic base could Tai villages generations ago have survived in the hills, as recent archaeological finds indicate?[13] How else can agricultural surveys dating from the 1920's have discovered large numbers of well- and long-established upland Thai miang-producing hamlets scattered over the Northern hills?[14] The patrimony of the miang industry is well worth further investigation, for a clarification of such questions as these will throw light on Tai-tribal relations in

[11] LeBar, 1967, pp. 115ff.   [12] Satow, 1892, p. 194.
[13] Ruth and Lauriston Sharp, 1964, pp. 237–239.
[14] The Record, 1922; Campbell, 1963; LeBar, 1967.

history as well as on the economic history of this and neighboring mainland Southeast Asian regions.

The most telling proof of the traditional importance of miang in the Northern Thai economy is the firsthand evidence gathered by a 1920–1922 botanical survey (sponsored by the Ministry of Commerce) of the dispersion of "miang villages" in the North. "The cultivation of miang in Siam . . . seems to be wholly confined to that portion of the country north of Latitude 18 [roughly, the North], but within that area the cultivation is widespread." [15] This statement is confirmed by a map published by the survey group showing clusters of miang villages scattered throughout the hills along the North's four major rivers.[16] On the basis of their three years of investigation the survey team concluded:

It is highly probable that the use of fermented tea leaves by the Siamese and Burmese dates back to very early times. Its use at ceremonial functions by both races suggest this, and it is not unlikely that these races were in turn indebted to some earlier inhabitants for their knowledge of the properties of tea.

And, "The internal trade in Northern Siam in miang is very large and comes next after rice and timber in value." [17]

The survey team calculated miang production in certain districts by tallying traffic passing key points along trade routes—"as there are usually several paths leading in different directions from each group of miang gardens, a good deal of the traffic was necessarily missed"—and their estimate of total annual miang production in Thailand (1920–1922)

[15] *The Record*, 1923, p. 17. Additional data on various aspects of miang production and trade in North Thailand are found in Siampakdi, 1943; Suwathapantha, 1947; Wicitrajantra, 1962; and Chotsukkharat, 1962.

[16] *The Record*, 1922, insert map.

[17] *The Record*, 1923, pp. 16, 20.

was thirty million bundles (*kam*).[18] A rough conversion, using figures of fifty bundles per man-day as the output norm and 100 days per year as the duration of the harvesting seasons, permits the imputation that the miang labor force about 1920 was certainly not less than 6,000, a sizable subsidiary industry for a region which in 1919 had a total labor force of roughly 860,000 and whose economic life centered almost wholly on wet-rice cultivation.

How do these survey data of more than fifty years ago compare with the current situation? Recent surveys of potential tea-growing areas in the North identify a number of locales in which miang cultivation continues.[19] A comparison of these sites with those discovered by the 1920–1922 survey indicates a high degree of consistency: that is, miang village clusters of the 1920's have continued apparently undisturbed into the present. Unfortunately, the later surveys contain no statistic which lends itself to an estimate of the present miang-growing labor force. I can only set down my impression that the upland Thai peasant population today amounts to about 75,000, of which (assuming the usual dependency ratios) some three-fifths make up the miang industry's labor force.[20]

[18] *Ibid.*, p. 20.   [19] Campbell, 1963; LeBar, 1967, p. 111.

[20] This datum is based on the roughest of approximations. The village researched intensively had a 1964 population of over 500. Local informants agreed with the estimate of government officials in Chiengmai Town that approximately 150 such villages are scattered through the Northern hills. This estimate indicates that the miang-cultivating population of North Thailand approximates 75,000 or about 3.6 per cent of the agricultural population of the six Northern provinces that are known to include miang villages.

LeBar questions this estimate as too conservative: "My impression is that the extent to which Northern Thai, in particular those in marginal areas, engage in supplementary swiddening and *miang* growing in the hills is vastly underestimated. As a possible indication of the extent to which *miang* is grown as a supplementary cash crop by

That the industry has grown in absolute terms is reflected in transport statistics. In 1958 (reckoned by the statistical personnel as a typical year) miang exports leaving Chiengmai Town by truck and rail were slightly in excess of two million kilograms (fourteen million bundles).[21] Such statistics vary widely from year to year and are severely limited in coverage as well as in the reliability of reporting parties; they are certainly underestimates of even the small corner of the industry they cover. Since most miang is consumed in the North, only a fraction is recorded in these regional export figures. Therefore, the industry today runs far in excess of its 1920 volume of 4,300 tons.

A comparison between present-day Thai upland peasant technology and institutions and those described by Western visitors generations ago leaves little doubt that the organization of the miang community remains esentially what it has traditionally been. Though hill dwellers today consume some Western imports in small quantities (transistor radios, patent medicines, permanent waves, formal schooling), such incursions have wrought little discernible change in the underlying pattern of life. The production process itself has been modified by Western improvements in only one important respect: miang is shipped to warehouses today by motorized transport, after being carried out of the hills on ox-back,

---

economically marginal lowlanders, I can cite the estimate by a group of villagers in Amphur Song, Changwat Phrae, that about 70 per cent of the 300 households in their village engaged in at least some *miang* growing in the hills, which were located a distance of about half a day by foot trail" (1967, p. 114).

Unpublished government records concerning miang cultivation show that some 5,400 acres are known to be gardened in Chiengmai Province alone (Economic Affairs Officer, Ministry of Economic Affairs, Chiengmai, personal communication, March 1964).

[21] Economic Affairs Officer, Ministry of Economic Affairs, Chiengmai, personal communication, March 1964.

rather than rafted to market places down the treacherous headwaters of the Chao Phraya River, as was once done. Though this modification has resulted in a closer articulation of the distribution network, it has had no appreciable effect on the basic organization of upland economic life. And though the impetus for migration to the hills has shifted from political to demographic pressure, the lure of fortune to be made in miang remains.

Miang Technology

Cultivation

One of the historical conundrums concerning miang is whether or not the shrub from which it is produced, *Camellia sinensis* var. *assamica* (the tea bush), is native to North Thailand. Today, miang (or tea) groves are found growing "wild" in the highland jungles. Whether these are natural biotic communities or the offspring of long-abandoned gardens cannot be answered. Whatever their origins, they often serve as the nuclei around which upland Thai villages are formed. Clearing the jungle growth from around such a grove is one way in which a peasant may enter the industry. The alternative is clearing suitable land and planting tea seed or seedlings, which take five years and more to mature to producing age. The investment of time and energy in such a venture is formidable for the ordinary Thai peasant, whose economic time horizon in his risk-laden environment and present-oriented society is ordinarily limited to weeks and months rather than years and decades.

Miang gardens appear as rather haphazard arrangements to the unpracticed eye. Shrubs are not set in neat formation, they are intermixed with clumps of weeds and occasional shade trees, and they fade into the jungle at their borders.

Adjacent gardens are not marked off except by fringes of weeds. Shrubs are left unpruned and from a distance do not differ much from ordinary jungle vegetation. To the peasant, however, each shrub is a unique, identifiable individual. Each has a known leaf-bearing capacity and distinct personality —a slow grower, a large-leafed plant, a difficult shrub to climb for harvesting, a young specimen with particularly tender leaf growth, and so forth. The peasant measures his garden property not by its acreage, nor even by the number of plants he possesses, but by the productivity of his individual shrubs.

Productivity depends on many variables. Soils are obviously important; they are fertilized by the mulch of cut weeds which if left unpruned would overwhelm the garden, and by the droppings of oxen which are left free to graze. Shrub spacing is also important, for close planting retards growth and leaf regeneration. The slope of the garden determines moisture retention; gardens in upland pockets do best for this reason. Gardens on slopes facing shaded sunlight do better than those located in dark hollows or open meadows. Bushes do best at high altitudes. Gardens in different areas of the North, because of unique combinations of these factors, have varying reputations. It is suspected, but not yet confirmed, that different varieties have evolved in different Northern districts, and this may also affect the volume and quality of output.

Garden management centers on harvesting, a year-round chore which follows a seasonally cyclical movement in its intensity and methods as a response to the miang shrub's regenerative capacity. The agricultural year is divided into four harvest seasons, which begin, according to the Northern Thai lunar calendar, during the cool months following the monsoon. During the first two months (approximately October and November), bushes are left to recuperate from the preceding harvest. This is a time for "rest and recreation" for hill villagers as well, a time for visiting friends and kin in the valley, for preparing materials to be used in miang production with the coming harvests, and for providing what little weeding and shrub care is required in the gardens. Enough leaves have matured by the third month (December) to warrant the first harvest, known as *mui*. This season's product is considered the finest of the year.

The *mui* season is short, generally lasting no longer than two weeks. It is followed by two more months of preparation for the more lucrative harvests to come. Wood must be cut for miang steaming, a step in processing. Villagers estimate that a minimum of three large trees must be felled and split to last a household one year; the ecological effects seem significant. A second task is the collection of bamboo, which is dragged to the dwelling and there split and woven into a variety of baskets used in production and sliced into string-like strips for packing the product.

By the sixth month (March) the shrubs have again regenerated enough leaf to permit the second harvest, *hua phi*. Picking lasts into the seventh month, and after another month's respite it recommences for the *klang* season. At the harvest's conclusion, bushes and gardeners are again given a chance to rest, but not for long, for with the *klang* season the rains have come, accelerating the rate of leaf growth. From the close of the tenth month to the end of the year the peasants are occupied with picking and processing the *soi* harvest.

The procedure during each of the four harvests is basically the same.[22] All members of the household except children be-

[22] On miang harvesting techniques see *The Record*, 1923, pp. 18–19; Chotsukkharat, 1962, pp. 259–264; and Milne, 1924, pp. 222–238.

low the age of nine or ten go to the gardens. Each laborer attacks a separate bush, tearing each mature leaf across [23] and retaining the tip ends of leaves in his free hand until grasping a bunch large enough to be tied into a bundle (*kam*) with a pliable bamboo sliver and dropped into a waiting basket. This picking procedure differs markedly from that required for high-quality tea, which consists of immature leaf and buds, called "flush." Miang consists of the most mature, roughest leaf, and of torn leaf at that. This difference helps explain why miang cultivators do not bother to prune, as tea growers do, and why miang technology provides a built-in resistance against alteration of the upland Thai peasant economy from a miang base to tea.

Picking is dangerous work, especially in the wet months. Each shrub must be climbed so that all available leaf can be stripped. Occasionally a slip results in a broken arm, leg, or neck. A backlashing branch may result in the loss of an eye. A wet day's work may aggravate a chronic cough, or it may trigger the return of a dormant case of malaria. It is not unusual to see a child as high as twenty feet above the ground crouching among tender limbs half stripped of foliage attempting to reach the highest leaves. In this manner a child can pick some thirty bundles per day; an adult, fifty.

At the close of each day the crop is brought to the family home. A fire is ignited in a pit in the dirt floor [24] over which,

[23] Leaf-tearing preserves the plant's health. Total defoliation would choke off respiration and result in death or stunting. Tea plucking involves taking only the "flush," leaving the old leaf to maintain bush health. Tea estate managers have scientifically determined optimal plucking ratios for different varieties, different locales, and different seasons, and I presume that experience has taught similar lessons to miang cultivators.

[24] One of the peculiarities of Thai hill villages is that most homes have earthen floors. Only the wealthiest residents can afford to build their homes in the typical lowland manner, on four- to six-foot

at ground level, is suspended a shallow cauldron of water. While the water comes to a boil, the bundles of miang are stuffed into a hollow log some three feet tall and two feet in diameter and having a bottom of woven bamboo slats. The log is placed over the cauldron, and the miang bundles inside are soaked with water while steam penetrates from below. Steaming takes between one and two hours. The bundles are then extracted from the log and given time to cool, after which their bamboo bonds are unfastened and retied. The bundles are then stacked in a plaited bamboo storage basket more than four feet in diameter and three feet tall. As the basket is filled, additional bamboo frames are added to raise its height, and stones are placed on top to provide enough pressure to eliminate air spaces and circulation which would cause spoilage. In Burmese hill villages, it seems, mortar-lined pits six or eight feet into the ground are generally used to store miang,[25] and I have seen one such pit in a Thai upland hamlet. In the lowlands, however, miang dealers are commonly equipped with thatch-roofed warehouses which enclose numbers of miang storage pits. Whichever storage method is used, "fermentation" naturally results. Tart (*fad*) miang is the partially unfermented product, particularly acrid and astringent in flavor. Sour (*saum*) miang, more mellow and juicy, results from three to four months of storage.

Of the harvests, *mui* produces the highest quality miang and brings the best price to the gardener. The second harvest, at the end of a long dry spell, produces inferior quality leaf and sells at the lowest price. The *klang* and *soi* harvests normally fall between these extremes. The approximate sea-

stilts. The absence of raised dwellings is also a reflection of household transiency.

[25] Milne, 1924, p. 234. Also see LeBar, 1967, pp. 109, 118.

sonal distribution of annual production is: *mui*, 10 per cent; *hua phi*, 25 per cent; *klang*, 35 per cent; and *soi*, 30 per cent.[26] Annual deviations from the normal year's output are said to vary by no more than 10 per cent. So far as output is concerned, once a garden has matured, miang cultivation is a relatively riskless agricultural pursuit in terms of productivity.

The Distribution Network

Oxen carry miang out of the hills and consumer goods in. Special bamboo baskets, tailored to fit leather or wooden saddles and closely woven to avoid scraping and tearing the miang as caravans wind their way through jungle cover, are tightly packed with miang bundles. Each basket contains about 200 medium bundles, about 30 kilograms; each ox carries two baskets. Caravans are frequently seen plying the trails, carrying miang down to the valleys or returning with milled rice (four *thang*, or 60 kilograms, per ox), salt and condiments, kerosene, and a variety of other consumer wares. Caravans vary from an ox or two to twenty and more. Frequently herders combine forces into large single caravans. One stout man can control no more than six oxen, so that those who possess larger herds ordinarily hire an extra drover or two, often a trustworthy neighbor and kinsman.

Ox care is one of the hill dweller's major preoccupations if he is so fortunate as to possess any of the animals. He constantly worries over their vigor and health, not only because various pests and diseases are constant threats to his herd but because his animals are one of his proudest possessions and speaking of them publicizes the fact of ownership and concomitant status. Attention is paid not only to the oxen

[26] These data are derived from the mean of reports furnished by eighteen miang gardeners in the Research Area in 1964.

but to their equipment, which includes saddles and baskets, and to their shelter, which consists of rough cattle sheds on the outskirts of the village. On long trails, wayside resting places are set up at which oxen are freed to graze and where shelters provide drovers with a place of rest and fresh water.

On its arrival in the lowland village the caravan unloads at its warehouse destination, a large shed within which deep mortor-lined pits are sunk for miang storage. According to informants, miang can remain in storage for as long as a year. I have been unable to discover, however, why further fermentation does not ruin the product during such extended storage. Sometimes miang is not transferred from ox packs to warehouse pits but is kept in the baskets and loaded on trucks for further shipment to Chiengmai Town or some other miang wholesaling center. Wholesale dealers maintain connections among themselves, so that miang gluts and shortages are minimized locally; and since miang harvests vary little and consumer demand is unusually stable for this traditional snack, price fluctuations do not plague the trade.

Dealers have local agents, who supply local retail vendors on a daily or weekly basis. The distribution network thus stretches from the hills to adjacent valley villages to larger market centers and back into the countryside in a wide circle. The entire distribution sequence culminates in the individual sale of a bundle or a quid by a peasant woman in the village market place.

Retailing and Consumption

Housewives purchase miang daily in village market places throughout the North, and casual passers-by purchase it from wayside shops. Most vendors are peasant women who come to the market with their wares at daybreak and leave before midday, returning to their homes or to their fields to labor with their families for the wet-rice or dry-season crop. Individual retail transactions feature the usual haggling which characterizes peasant market places. Haggled prices are not as fluid as they might appear, however, for they fluctuate about a standard established by traditions peculiar not only to this industry but to others of the North.[27] The standard price for a medium-size bundle never departs far from one baht. The haggling process characterizing this system has been ably documented elsewhere as "a highly structured economic behavior pattern with its own ethic, its own principles, and its own logic." [28] This transaction forms the final step in the distributive chain which carries the product to the consumer.

Two general varieties of the fermented tea leaves are sold, tart (*fad*) and sour (*saum*). The retail product is further differentiated by locales of origin and seasonal varieties, for variable soil and climate conditions cause perceptible variations in flavor. Certain districts (among them Chiengdao and Mae Thaeng) are widely renowned for their superior product. Sour miang is preferred by younger people, apparently because it does not have as harsh a taste; the small quantity which finds its way to Bangkok markets is entirely of this kind. Bundles of three sizes are sold—small (*kam noi*), medium (*kam kauk*), and large (*kam yai* or *kam luang*).[29]

[27] Socially regulated prices appear in Northern wage-labor rates, in pedicab fares between fixed points, and in market-place transactions. Similar findings are reflected in research on early twentieth-century Bangkok coolie wages in Ingram, 1964, p. 113.

[28] Uchendu, 1967, p. 47.

[29] Bundle sizes are actually measured by the hand of the picker. *Kam noi* is a handful of leaves with the index finger just reaching the thumb; *kam kauk* permits the width of one finger of the opposing hand to be placed between thumb and index finger; *kam yai* permits two fingers to be thus inserted. As hand sizes vary among pickers, and as the definition of bundle size varies among districts of the North (the definitions here used being common in the vicinity

Also, vendors sell the product by the quid as well as by bundle, laced with a flavoring agent or plain. The complexities of market-place transactions thus become apparent: prices are haggled but structured by tradition; the retailed product may be of various dimensions; it varies in flavor and quality in terms of the sections of the North from which it comes, in terms of its mode of preparation, and in terms of the season of its harvest.

A miang bundle no larger than a clenched fist is sufficient to serve a household as an evening snack and yet leave a wad or two to be carried by the householder to the fields the next day as refreshment during work. Much like chewing-tobacco, a quid may be sucked for hours. Everyone participates, even children. Usually, small lumps of rock salt are mixed into the quid, but on special occasions and among the wealthy, peanuts, sweet syrups, garlic, shredded coconut, or pork fat is mixed in to vary the flavor.

When asked why they consume miang, Northern Thai commonly reply that it provides them with energy after an enervating period of work. One close observer states that miang "is used for chewing by people carrying heavy burdens in the hills." [30] A pharmacological analysis of miang leaves at Bangkok concludes:

The various effects which Miang leaves produce on chewing are thus to be explained by the presence of caffeine. The question of habituation would be similar to that associated with the drinking of tea and coffee, which is not a true addiction, but is the result of becoming accustomed to the stimulating action of the active principle in the beverages.[31]

of the Research Area), sizes of individual bundles within each classification vary considerably. Product standardization has a long way to go in the miang industry.

[30] Seidenfaden, 1958.

[31] Ketu-Sinh, 1948, p. 170. This source was provided by Dr. Sombodhi Bukkavesa of Siriraj Hospital, Bangkok.

The importance of miang to the Northern diet is thus related to its stimulative effects, much desired by a hard working peasantry.[32]

Entourages, the Institutional Form

Village, Hamlet, and Household

The miang-cultivating community forms an integral part of Tai culture and the Thai nation, though, at a low position in the social pyramid, it is far more conscious of its cultural roots in the North than of its political ties with the Center. It is to be expected that the upland Thai community's social and economic institutions differ little from the norms of lowland peasant life, and that what marginal differences in life styles do appear are attributable primarily to ecological factors, to the requirement that the miang-cultivating household be so far removed from the lowlands as to make daily contact with the valley world impossible, and to the selective attraction to miang gardening and its attendant rigors of a particular personality type within the range of Thai peasant society.

The upland village, like its lowland counterpart, is a political rather that a social entity fitting into the nation-state as the lowest rung on the bureaucratic ladder. It has its own headman, who is directly subordinate to the commune chief and the local district officer. It is usually equipped with its own school and centrally-assigned teacher. It is occasionally visited by malaria control teams and local police officials and less often by forestry, census, and revenue officers. With these exceptions it is, even more than the low-

[32] LeBar, 1967, p. 106, states, furthermore, that miang induces salivation and thus "helps allay the hotness of the Northern Thai cuisine," an important consideration in a country where peppered and curried foods frequently induce ulcers and other digestive-tract disorders.

land village, left free of interference by the national political machinery.[33]

Internally, however, political arrangements differ more significantly between hill villages and those of the lowlands. The dispersal of miang groves that is made necessary by the rugged upland terrain scatters Thai peasant households over wide areas and divides them into tiny hamlets separated by miles of jungle trails. Each village is a rather arbitrarily created unit formed of a cluster of discrete hamlets. The village headman finds himself handicapped in his command over a scattered population, which is frequently factionalized among its component hamlets. To cope with the problem, some headmen appoint assistants (*hua na*) who act as *de facto* hamlet headmen though they are not officially recognized by the central government. The creation of this post, despite its informality, places an additional bureaucratic level between the individual household and the national political superstructure, thus serving further to insulate the peasant from recognition and performance of the rights and duties of Thai citizenship. The extra administrative level is a reflection of the weakness of the village as a political unit; it also weakens village unity further. In the hills the hamlet rather than the village must be recognized as the "village." [34]

Within the hamlet, community solidarity is recognizable in a general resort to kinship terminology as the form of reference and address. All within the hamlet are called "kinsmen" (*pi naung*) whether they are actually related by blood or marriage or not.

---

[33] It is a strange fact that among the many Thai hill dwellers I interviewed not one had served in the military. Since compulsory recruitment into the armed serves is general among the peasantry, hill dwellers present an anomaly. For unknown reasons, it appears that migration into the hills to avoid the *corvée* generations ago retains its usefulness as a means of avoiding the draft today.

[34] Wijeyewardene, 1967, pp. 69–74.

To call someone a *pinawng* means that our relationship, in the present situation, is somehow more intimate, more demanding of fellowship and special privilege, than we would accord to others. Close residence, shared experience, proximate age, and potential profit can all, like genealogical proximity, serve to admit some of one's many acquaintances as *pinawng*, "kinsmen." [35]

Within the hamlet, the solidarity suggested by "kinship" organization is accompanied by elements of stratification and factionalism. Social gaps appear between newly arrived households and the long-established. In part, this is a reflection of differing levels of material well-being and different occupations, for new households are invariably those that are poorest and that hire themselves out to their garden-owning or -renting neighbors as labor during miang harvests. Such stratification acts as both a divisive and a binding force. As in other communities, wealth and poverty influence the forming of friendships, factions, or camps. Yet, the wealthy and the poor also seek one another out for mutual benefits. Between the poor laborer and the relatively wealthy miang smallholder a symbiotic relationship emerges which ordinarily overrides divisive tendencies. In fact, hierarchical ties within the hamlet appear as minor examples of the "entourage" relationship to be analyzed below. Where factional interests overwhelm mutual benefit, hamlets tend to split into adjacent residence clusters separated by narrow belts of jungle vegetation; even in such cases, it appears, the factions continue to work together for economic gain, though they drop their common "kinship." This is an interesting variant of the process of village mitosis found among certain hill tribes.

Though households occasionally hire one another's labor, miang production is primarily household-centered. Upland Thai peasant households ordinarily consist of the nuclear

[35] Moerman, 1966, p. 360. Also see Wijeyewardene, 1967.

family. Married offspring take up residence on their own, with a tendency to establish themselves in uxorial proximity (perhaps within the wife's parents' compound, if such exists). The household typically does not extend beyond the married couple and their unmarried children. This pattern is maintained in the hills just as in the valleys. Man, wife, and adolescent children labor together in the garden. Except for relegation of the most strenuous tasks to men (usually) and those requiring greatest skill and detailed attention to elders, little rigidity is evident in the division of labor. However, during each phase of the agricultural cycle, individuals tend to specialize in favorite labor tasks, each taking informal responsibility for some particular chore, such as string making, basket weaving, weeding, ox care, and miang processing. Others join in whenever their chores are done. Invariably, chores are carried out in a jovial, nearly a holiday, mood—even in the hills, Thailand remains "the land of smiles."

The Household Life Cycle

As has been observed above, the contemporary Thai household migrates to the hills primarily for the purpose of improving its material well-being. Miang cultivation presents an economic and social opportunity. In generations past it was turned to as an escape from harsh treatment under uncompromising overloads. In the present generation it has become a means of moving up the economic and social ladder and thereby eventually obtaining coveted wet-rice fields, the ultimate symbol of success in the peasant context.

Population pressures have begun to appear in the Northern lowlands within the present generation. The consequent change in factor proportions is partly reflected in the increasing intensity with which wet-rice land is being cultivated. During the period 1950/51–1952/53 through 1961/62–1963/

64, for instance, rice yields per acre rose by 42 per cent in the North against an average of 18 per cent for Thailand as a whole.[36] Two demographic characteristics have been associated with rising population pressures in the lowlands. First, high fertility rates and declining infant mortality rates are together creating an aggregate national rate of population increase which is one of the highest in the world. Second, internal migration appears to be from the South and Northeast to the Center, and from the Center northward. Thus, not only is Thailand as a whole encountering strains from population growth, but the North is acting as a safety valve on pressures at the Center.[37] The effect has been the emergence of a substantial landless and land-poor peasantry in the North.[38]

The resultant economic and social problem for the landless minority is severe. To the Thai peasantry, life centers on the rice crop. The various annual tasks associated with rice cultivation take on a significance which far transcends the narrowly economic element. These tasks form the cultural core around which nearly all thought and action are developed. They are sanctified with religious significance.[39] And they are in turn based on exploitation of the household-owned irrigated acreage. Without wet-rice fields, the Thai peasant household is lost; it finds itself in a social limbo, cut off not only from economic security and opportunity but from normal social intercourse. At best, the landless household may succeed in associating itself as a "client" with some "patron" landowner, an extension of the wealthier household's labor force. More likely, however, it will remain in a state of perpetual drudgery at the base of the agrarian social hierarchy—survival at the margin of subsistence as

[36] Ruttan *et al.*, 1966.   [37] Caldwell, 1967.
[38] Wijeyewardene, 1967, p. 79.   [39] Jane Hanks, 1960.

itinerant wage labor. Among the few alternatives to this condition looms miang cultivation. For the more adventurous, the hardier, and the more far-sighted among the landless and land-poor, miang cultivation presents a magnificent opportunity to redeem a secure and respected place in lowland society.[40]

The typical Thai migrants to the hill community are recently married, landless couples in their early twenties. Their life outlook in the valley as wage laborers, and perhaps some experience along this line, has made them willing to accept the risks and deprivations associated with upland life. Their immediate hope is to find work with miang-garden owners as leaf pickers, woodcutters, and assistants in household chores and ox-caravan transport. Recognizing that employment is more readily available from past acquaintances, hill immigrants search out miang-cultivating households that maintain ties with the immigrants' lowland villages. Upland Thai hamlets reflect this tendency by frequently being composed of households with common lowland origins. If the immigrant couple is fortunate, they find a household which is willing to accept them as clients, providing them with year-round work in return for a kinship status carrying with it the obligation to share subsistence. Less fortunate immigrants are forced to hire out as piece-goods wage labor by the day, an economic position no less precarious than wage labor in the valleys.

[40] Besides the qualities listed above, an additional psychological orientation for movement into the hills appears to be a departure from the common Thai Buddhist belief in *karma*, which fixes one's place within the cosmos and which can be only marginally corrected as a result of one's lifetime's accumulated "merit." To move into the hills is to seek a major shift in one's cosmic position. The average Thai peasant would think such a step not only a hazardous tempting of fate but a preordained waste of time.

Such a marginal existence is often accepted because of the opportunity it provides to prepare a new miang garden by planting seed in a cleared area and maintaining it for five or more years in anticipation of entering the miang industry on a self-employed basis. Alternatively, it permits the couple to wait and search for some mature miang garden to become available on a rental basis. Until such a time, however, the couple depends on labor opportunities, which fluctuate with miang harvests. In all, about 100 days of harvesting are involved. At an average of fifty bundles of miang picked per man-day and a wage of one baht per ten bundles, the couple manages to earn approximately 1,000 baht per year as pickers. With luck they can augment this income by participation in other chores as adjunct members of a miang gardener's household. If labor opportunities appear in the valley, the couple often divide their attention between hill and lowland in accordance with the overlapping agricultural calendars of miang and lowland crops.

The couple's subsistence expenditures tend to outstrip their basic annual earnings of 1,000 baht.[41] At the lowest rung of the upland Thai economic ladder, they can hardly afford the "conveniences" of Thai rural life, such as shoes or sneakers, changes of clothing, meat and fish, mattresses and blankets, a radio, an occasional drinking or gambling binge. If they beget children their hardships are multiplied. Partly in order to offset the budgetary problem, children are often sent to stay with "kinsmen" in the lowlands.

When by one means of another the couple obtain a producing miang garden, their fortunes change. Miang gardens range in size from two-fifths of an acre (a *rai*) to over six

[41] The annual rice subsistence requirement in the upland Thai peasant community comes to roughly 290 kg. per year per adult, or an expense of 1,160 baht per couple.

acres each, but, as has been explained above, such data are not meaningful indexes of their value.[42] Garden owners state value in terms of annual yield per garden, and rent (when computed) is ordinarily calculated in proportion to average annual output, often as high as half the crop. Garden output of 10,000 bundles (equal to the annual picking capacity of the renting or owning couple) may be considered representative. At an index price of 4 baht per ten bundles sold, this yield represents a gross annual income of 4,000 baht. A rent of half the crop leaves the cultivator with a 2,000 baht net income, a situation twice as attractive as the one he faced as a miang laborer, not to mention the additional benefits accruing with his social elevation from laborer to gardener.[43]

As the miang cultivator's income rises with his move from wage labor to sharecropping garden tenancy or outright ownership, he realizes a "surplus" in excess of "subsistence" requirements and "enterprise" expenditures (the latter including wage payments, transport fees, garden rents, and

[42] LeBar, 1967, p. 114, mentions miang gardens as large as twelve acres (30 *rai*) in the hills east of the Ping River and north of Chiengmai Town.

[43] Institutionalized renting of gardens implies a strongly personalized and formalized land tenure arrangement. Occasional sales of gardens and the legitimization of ownership through their registration with the commune chief and payment of an annual land tax (ten baht per acre-equivalent) substantiate the thesis that Thai peasants have imported into the hills the land tenure institutions prevailing in the valleys.

This institution is not as formal as would appear at first sight, however, because the uplands, unlike the valleys, have never been legally opened to Thai peasant immigration. The hills remain, technically speaking, the public domain, the king's land. Clearing and planting for miang establishes the gardener as a poacher on lands which he has not been given the privilege of settling. Gross understatements of garden acreage would thus not appear uncommon. See Moerman, 1968, pp. 109–110; and Wijeyewardene, 1967, pp. 75–81, esp. n.4. Also see Chapter 5 below.

taxes), which is disposed of for "luxuries" ("nonsubsistence nondurables" such as patent medicines, liquor, sweets, lottery tickets, and "merit-making"), "prestige durables" (such as canned goods, amulets, sewing machines, wooden-walled houses, and corrugated iron roofs), and "remunerative durables" ("investments" such as oxen, additional miang gardens, and irrigated rice fields).[44]

These categories of acquisitions are not mutually exclusive. Remunerative durables serve prestige as well as investment functions, and they also provide the joy of ownership which places them in the luxuries category. Similarly, luxuries also raise status and some raise subsistence consumption, whereas prestige durables may improve levels of sanitation, health, and comfort sufficiently to raise labor productivity, thereby serving an investment function. Sufficient data have not been compiled to permit a specification of the marginal propensity to acquire each of these various types of items, but enough has been observed to speculate that the marginal propensity to subsist (expenditures net of enterprise, luxuries, prestige durables, and remunerative durables) is close to zero at incomes above the socially dictated subsistence base.

The major means by which miang gardeners can raise their economic (and with it their social) position is by turning

[44] Economists use as one of their favorite typologies the distinction between consumption and investment. The problem has always been that nearly all dispositions of income have a dual consumption-investment function; that is, the consumption-investment breakdown ignores one aspect of the general interdependence of the system. See Myrdal, 1968, pp. 994–1027.

The four categories of subsistence, luxuries, prestige durables, and remunerative durables, have been used here as the relevant breakdown of household expenditures because they closely approximate the indigenous view of the matter. These categories conceptualize the disposition of funds within the Thai peasant economy with minimal resort to an alien paradigm. See Neale, 1959; cf. Hill, 1966.

their surplus earnings into remunerative durables (though, as has been noted, dispositions of earnings among other expenditure categories also have effects on production). Oxen are the remunerative asset in which the gardener most often invests. They are readily available in valley market places as well as from neighbors in the upland community. Oxen are readily negotiable. A young ox may carry a price of 500 baht. It requires little care (though risks of injury or death are high) and forages for itself in the miang gardens and along the jungle periphery. Within five years it may be resold for double its purchase price. During the intervening period it can be used as a pack animal, transporting miang and consumer goods between hill and valley, thereby eliminating transport fees the gardener would otherwise have to pay caravan operators. In this manner a single ox may earn the gardener some 400 baht per year.[45] As additional oxen are acquired, the gardener can earn supplementary revenues in transporting for his neighbors.

As the gardener continues to accumulate surpluses and transfer them into oxen and other forms of remunerative and liquid assets (such as pigs and gold), he is enabled to expand his garden holdings. As his holdings grow, he becomes a landlord or a labor hirer, for his household can no longer harvest all its gardens.[46] The purchase price of a representative garden

[45] Since income accounts are not kept by the household and since peasants' vague memories of past incomes are not compartmentalized on an annual basis, rather heroic imputations are required to arrive at this figure. The most speculative estimate is that the typical ox caravan makes the hill-valley round trip twelve times per year. If an ox carries 400 miang bundles at a fee of 5 baht per hundred, annual miang transport income amounts to some 240 baht. If the ox carries 140 lb. of milled rice and the transport fee is 4 baht per *thang* (thirty-five lb. of milled rice), annual rice transport income is 192 baht.

[46] Besides using the labor of poorer neighbors, the gardener may avail himself of itinerant labor, offered by groups of adolescents who

may be hazarded as 8,000 baht, though (since gardens rarely come up for sale and cover a wide range of crop yields) significant deviations from this price may be expected to occur.[47]

As an owner-operator and rentier, the miang gardener has reached an enviable position within the upland community, a degree of physical well-being, security, and prestige not attained by many hill dwellers. If he has purchased the garden he formerly rented, he has as much as doubled his annual income. Garden owners who earn 10,000 baht or more per annum are not unknown. If the gardener's household increases to, say, four children, his annual subsistence expenditures reach an estimated 1,800 baht, leaving several thousand, at least, for supplementary expenditure. Clearly, the cultivator has freed himself from the vicious circle of self-perpetuating poverty in which landlessness had once trapped him. He has attained a position sufficiently elevated to permit the acceptance of other households as his clients.

Continued acquisition of remunerative assets from surplus earnings permits the gardener to further improve his position. To ease the managerial problem of supervising diversified

come to the hills during the wet-rice off-seasons, seeking fun as well as wages, earning five baht plus board for a good day's work.

[47] It would appear superficially absurd to attribute a price-earnings ratio of two to an investment as risk-free as a miang garden. Several factors may explain such a low figure. First, though risks in the output of a miang garden are small, risks to life and limb, and the risks general in a peasant civilization, are high. Second, and related, time horizons in the Thai peasant world are short—as is the usual case in peasant societies, the social rate of discount is unusually high. Third, the widespread poverty of this peasantry and the general illiquidity of most assets sharply limit purchasing power, thus limiting market demand. The rationale of such an unusual price-earnings ratio is, in fact, parallel to that behind high interest rates in agrarian Thailand (the prime rate is about 3 to 4 per cent per *month*). See Thisyamondol *et al.*, 1965; Usher, 1967a.

garden holdings, he may turn increasingly to renting them out, thereby increasing his position of patronage over a sizable number of tenants. As his holdings and annual income continue to grow, the dream of returning to the lowlands and the wet-rice economy as a landowner, esteemed among the households of his ancestral valley community, approaches realization. The successful miang gardener acquires in the course of a generation sufficient liquid wealth to purchase wet-rice fields, which sell for 7,500 baht and up per acre.[48] He purchases them gradually as liquidation of his accumulated wealth and availability of desirable plots permit. These fields he rents out to sharecroppers, as he does his excess miang gardens, in anticipation of the day when he will return to the valley.

The age of retirement from the upland life is reached, as the hill dweller himself is fond of saying, when he grows so old he can no longer climb the mountains. Some reach this age as early as their forties. Others remain in the hills into their sixties. On his return to the lowland community, he takes up life as a wet-rice cultivator. He may leave his miang gardens under the supervision of his children, or he may sell or rent them to former upland neighbors.

With his successful return to the valley world, the miang gardener's dream is realized. He has raised himself from land-lessness at the bottom of the peasant hierarchy to landowner-ship, a position of social as well as economic substance. This life cycle is not inevitable, however; successful return to the valley is not even the most common conclusion to a lifetime of effort at miang gardening. It is more likely that the household stumbles somewhere along the road to success—accident, disease, homesickness, miscalculation, or sheer indo-

[48] Four acres constitute an efficient size for a wet-rice landholding in the North.

lence determining that it never accumulates the remunerative assets required for success. But behind all miang gardeners' actions remains the dream of the glorious homecoming to the valley.

Entourages

Though the upland Thai peasant hamlet is unified on a "kinship" basis and through internal labor relations, each household remains an individual entity throughout its life cycle. Though it participates in the social life of the hamlet, its most enduring ties remain with the valley. It is in some ancestral village that the household is originally formed through courtship and marriage (though marriages occasionally take place among upland dwellers). It is in the valley that the household's true kinsmen reside and to which the household turns in time of distress. It is in the valley that the household usually maintains its religious affiliations and where it frequently sends its children to receive their education. And it is in the valley that it disposes of miang and acquires the goods to satisfy its material needs. The upland hamlet is little more than an *ad hoc* arrangement of dwellings clustered together to satisfy the individual households' desires for comradeship and mutual security as well as their needs for temporary labor alliances facilitating miang production. More lasting and deep-seated ties exist between each household and the lowland village of its origin or adoption.

The miang gardener finds himself in a peculiar situation. Unlike the Tai generally, he does not earn his livelihood in the production of a subsistence good; of the miang he processes he can consume no more than a tiny fraction, nor does even this amount serve him as a consumer staple. Beyond miang, his habitat is largely devoid of the consumer items he requires. He must therefore depend entirely on the disposition of this crop through trade channels in return for consumer goods as his guarantee of economic survival in the uplands.[49] These two interrelated peculiarities—that the miang cultivator is a specialist in a nonstaple and that he finds himself spatially isolated from the valley economy on which he depends—provide conditions which make the institutional underpinnings of Thai peasant economy stand out in stark reality.

The institutional regularity underlying Thai peasant economy is not readily apparent in the structure of the village, the hamlet, or the household. It is, however, clearly identifiable in the relationship between miang cultivators and their valley contacts. This institutional theme—here called the "entourage" [50]—is discernible in labor relations between upland Thai households (and even within households). The entourage has also been discovered to form the institutional base of Thai life in the lowlands.[51]

The institutional foundation of indigenous Thai (and, I suspect, Tai) economy, society, and polity is the entourage, "the Thai equivalent of our corporation, the building block of social activity." [52] The entourage is an informal organization in which each participant contributes and receives on a voluntary basis, sharing in the advantages of participating,

[49] One of the preliminary research attractions of the miang industry for me was the presumption that, in specializing in a nonsubsistence good, miang producers assign monetary values to all production and consumption items, permitting ready quantification of economic magnitudes. This preconception proved an illusion, however, when it was realized that the entourage, which institutionalizes the economy, embeds economic transactions in a broader social matrix, thus obscuring the monetary values which would otherwise have provided an attractive research aid.

[50] After Lucien Hanks, 1966.

[51] See Van Roy and Cornehls, 1969; and Van Roy, 1970.

[52] Lucien Hanks, 1966, p. 56.

yet occupying a unique position in a hierarchy of superior-inferior connections.[53] Two structural elements characterize the entourage: reciprocity and hierarchy. Reciprocity equates benefits contributed and rewards received in terms not only of economic but of social and political equivalencies, resulting in functional diffuseness and an "incalculable exchange" of values.[54] Hierarchy ranks participants in terms of a complex arrangement including the (Western) elements of class, status, and power on an undifferentiable basis, setting thereby the patron-client context within which reciprocative equivalencies are determined.

Clients are drawn to an entourage not only by the economic security offered by a wealthy patron but by the political and social advantages accruing from intimate connections with those superior in the hierarchy. Patrons are attracted to clients by the latters' usefulness as suppliers of goods and services as well as by their political and social contributions in improving the patron's community standing.

Entourages interlock to form a network of patron-client relationships running from the bottom of the Thai hierarchy to the top. Patrons are clients to their superiors. Clients ordinarily act as patrons to those below. Thus, the Thai social structure is a pyramid of linked entourages.

Each entourage is likewise a miniature replica of the aggregate system, having a cone-like structure with a patron superintendant over a coterie of clients at lower stations. Both the solidarity of the entourage (a function of the network of reciprocities generated between the patron and his clients) and its scope (dependent on its ability to attract clients of service to it) are ultimately manifestations of the patron's

[53] The structural regularities underlying the entourage are analyzed in greater detail in Van Roy and Cornehls, 1969.
[54] Lucien Hanks, 1966, p. 57. Also see Gouldner, 1960.

leadership abilities. Management of men rather than of resources is a major distinction between the Thai patron and
the Western entrepreneur. The voluntary nature of participation in the entourage requires that participants be expert dip-
lomats, that shrewdness rather than coercion be the mark of
the leader.

There is a wealth of observations pertaining to the perva-
siveness of entourage formations in Central Thailand, which
may be generalized to include the North; and several field
workers have discovered them in the North as well. Research
on land tenure and kinship in a village in southern Chiengmai
Province, for instance, is summarized as follows:

Thailand is well known for its absence of formal kin groups, or
traditional formal groups of any kind. Does this mean that organization is alien to Thai culture, and that therefore the Thais
start with a handicap in modern economic activity?
. . . Patron-client relationships . . . were part of the traditional Thai system, and there is evidence to show that these are
still widespread in a different form. In rural areas the clustering
of clients around a patron does not perhaps create a large or
formally organized association, but it has to be considered an
organization of a type, and is, moreover, essential to the social system as a whole. In [southern Chiengmai Province] important contacts with the administration appear to be largely chan-
nelled through "patrons" of one sort or another. These patrons
could be government servants, landowners, traders, or merely
wealthy kinsmen.[55]

Michael Moerman, in a study of the economy of a Tai-Lue
village in northern Chiengrai Province, notes the ubiquity of
entourages despite his primary thesis that "kinship" is the
binding force within the community whereas "commerce"
(by which he means the market system) links the village with

[55] Wijeyewardene, 1967, pp. 82–83.

the outside world.[56] This division between internal and external institutional forms in this instance misrepresents the situation as I see it. Moerman himself makes the point that a broad range of gradations appears between these extremes, that as the degree of social intimacy between acquaintances is gradually lessened, economic relationships tend to become functionally isolated from the social and political components, "market prices" tend to become more generally resorted to, and cash transactions tend increasingly to replace the more diffuse forms of reciprocity.[57] At all gradations of intimacy, however, Moerman cites cases of entourages, each with its own reciprocities, hierarchy, personality, and biography.

In the extravillage relationship between tractor renters from the neighboring town and local peasants, for instance, Moerman finds that, "Although they differ vastly in power, position, sophistication, and degree of solidarity, the farmer and the tractor owner still need each other."

In return for [the villagers'] business, [the tractor owner] does more than merely take their money and plow their fields. To a fortunate few, he is a patron willing to intercede with officials or to permit an occasional payment to go past its due date. He jokes and gossips with all the farmers, and instructs and advises them. Most tractor owners permit and encourage such broad-based social relationships. . . .

. . . Although [the tractor owner] behaves with a minimum of condescension, almost every interaction between him and the villagers indicates that he is thought to be superior. . . .

[56] The internal-external duality is most forcefully stressed in Moerman, 1966. The thesis is further elaborated in Moerman, 1968. The notion of a hierarchical continuum rather than a duality is a theme of Moerman, 1964.

[57] Moerman, 1968, p. 127, presents this concept in clear diagramatic fashion.

. . . Unlike the brash young men who drive and maintain the tractors, [the tractor owner] acts as a patron should act and therefore is not resented. He and the other tractor owners are able to assert their new dominance by means of old institutions: age-mate relationships and the bond between patron and client.[58]

In a footnote to this passage, Moerman reveals that "The majority of the tractor owners, in their wisdom and in their provincialism, participate in the . . . total relationships compatible to the villager," "Total relationship" should here be read as "entourages."

Within the Tai-Lue village, entourages structure economic and social life in such a pervasive fashion that kinship nomenclature is used to sort out the threads of the interlocking relationships. One of the major difficulties of Moerman's analysis of kinship organization results from the interplay of real and fictitious kinship relations in a setting where kinship terminology is used both to emphasize community endogamy and define entourage formations. His recognition of this problem is revealed in the following passage, among others:

The social resources [i.e., clients] of which a farmer [i.e., patron] avails himself in order to acquire land have further social consequences. The primacy of labor as a source for acquiring land, coupled with *a social system that makes cooperators of one's kinsmen and kinsmen of those with whom one regularly cooperates,* is certainly not irrelevant to the easy fellowship that seems to characterize village life.[59]

Moerman discovers a range of labor rewards, which he classifies as "fellowship" ("rewards that are neither reciprocated farm labor nor payments in valuables"), "exchange" ("the return of farm labor for farm labor given"), and

[58] *Ibid.*, pp. 70–72; also see pp. 108–109.
[59] *Ibid.*, p. 106, my italics.

☙ 118

"goods" (the return of rice or cash for farm labor provided, either as "gift" or "wage").[60] His detailed analysis of the reciprocities involved in each case is a valuable contribution to the theory of the entourage; but, in failing to deal at length with the hierarchical setting in which these reciprocities invariably occur, he again blurs the lines of entourage analysis.

One of Moerman's most important findings is that those Tai-Lue peasants who do not adhere to the institutional norm of the entourage are the despised members of the village community.

Generally, those who save, invest, expand their production, and use the market more efficiently [i.e., isolate the economic element from the social whole and therefore do not behave as entourage participants should] are the villagers who, for these and other reasons, are criticized as calculating, aggressive, and selfish. . . . [Successful] village entrepreneurs frequently fail to maintain the common peasant values of equanimity, generosity, loyalty to kinsmen, and conspicuous piety. They choose workers by effectiveness, not affection; save for investment instead of spending for prestige; devote their leisure to increasing private income and not to community activities. To put the matter baldly, it is not uncommon that villagers who are ambitious, enterprising, or successful are, in the eyes of their fellows, "sons of bitches." [61]

The workings of the entourage are most clearly exemplified in the relationship between upland Thai households and miang dealers in the neighboring lowlands. Typically (but not inevitably) the miang cultivator disposes of his entire

[60] *Ibid.*, pp. 116–117; more appropriate terms might have been "social reciprocity," "labor reciprocity," and "materials reciprocity," respectively.

[61] *Ibid.*, p. 144. The problem of individual nonconformity to the entourage form of economic, social, and political interaction and its development implications are investigated in Van Roy, 1970.

crop to a single wholesaler. The relationship between the cultivator and the dealer is not simply commercial, however. It is composed of a complex of economic, social, and political interactions overlapping on a continuing basis. The dealer is a patron to the cultivator. If his clientele of miang producers and others is large and his economic and social interests correspondingly widespread, he receives the honorific title *pau liang*, meaning "father protector," "father provider," or "father who feeds us." [62]

The *pau liang* stands near the apex of the peasant hierarchy. As an economic functionary he not only wholesales miang, he owns and rents out miang gardens, lends rice and other goods to his upland clients, transports wares between hill and valley on his oxen, ships miang to market places on his truck, owns and rents out wet-rice fields, and mills the rice of his fellow villagers. These various activities, and others, are dealt in by such men in confusing variety. But to isolate the economic functions performed by the *pau liang* is to abstract from the institutional frame within which he operates. The *pau liang* is not treated by his subordinates, nor does he behave toward them, as a wholesaler, moneylender, landlord, shipper, or merchant. He is not a demanding master but a benevolent patron. The relationship between him and his miang-cultivating clients does not respond in any immediate fashion to market forces but deals in terms of varying

[62] The title is a traditional one: "This term means literally, 'Father nourisher,' and is the name given all mission physicians by the natives" (Curtis, 1903, p. 123). It is similar to the Thai use of the term *ahsia*, an honorific title for Chinese merchants of outstanding fortune, and is more explicit than the generic Thai term *nai* (superior or patron). The similarity between the *pau liang* of North Thailand and the *lam* of Laos, "a person who acts as an intermediary between traders . . . and the tribal peoples . . . [,] a reciprocal relationship" (Halpern, 1961, p. 26), is worth further study along the lines of the entourage as the institutional form.

degrees of trust and affection, obligations to return benefits received and anticipations of benefits to be gained.

The two-way flow of benefits and rewards within the miang entourage transcends the economic dimension. Economic benefits do accrue to both parties—on the client's side through readily available credit, inside information on emerging opportunities, a guaranteed outlet for produce and a source of consumer staples, and a source of old-age and accident insurance; on the patron's side through an assured and foreseeable inventory flow, relatively efficient and honest operation of rented land and equipment, an ever ready reserve labor force, and a stable system of finance free of any need for detailed accounting. Yet rarely do economic benefits result as direct reimbursements for economic contributions. Integral contributions to the ongoing entourage relationship include on the client's part public demonstrations of respect, properly obsequious behavior in the patron's presence, a willingness to serve the patron in any manner called for. It is expected that the client be permitted to luxuriate in the shadow of the patron's higher status, that the patron offer him sound advice and protection in the face of life's vagaries, that he bestow on him the benevolence of his hospitality and friendship. The very obscurity which marks such functionally diffuse and time-extended reciprocative flows acts as a positive factor in maintaining the entourage, for participants are loath to dissociate themselves from situations in which they cannot be sure they have no vested interest.[63] The quantitative obscurity of this economic process thus helps explain the system's durability.

Let me turn briefly to a closer examination of the economic element in the entourage. From the tenants of his upland gardens or from independent owners who have turned

[63] Gouldner, 1960, p. 175.

to him as their patron, the *pau liang* receives miang shipments each season, part of which are his rental income. These loads may be transported down the hills to his warehouse on his oxen. They may be immediately disposed of to local merchants or may be stored by the *pau liang* in anticipation of merchandising the product himself directly to retailers in nearby village market places or to wholesalers in the larger market towns. His tenants and independent cultivators welcome the opportunity to dispose of their crops through him, for the establishment of a dependable sales channel and the strengthening of the link between them and their patron enhances their economic security.

The *pau liang*, in turn, finds the role of miang wholesaler a remunerative occupation. He has received a portion of his inventory as rental income. The remainder has been purchased by him at prices averaging .40 baht per bundle. The entire stock is sold by him at prices ranging between .50 and .70 baht per bundle. In addition, he earns standard transport fees for shipping the product down from the hills and on to the market centers. On his caravans' journey up to the miang gardens he may transport milled rice (perhaps grown in his fields by his tenants and ground in his mill) and other consumer goods requested by his clients.

This entourage is complicated in its economic aspect by an intricate network of credit arrangements. Rice is furnished clients in anticipation of coming miang harvests. Upland households leave earnings in the hands of the *pau liang* for safekeeping. The *pau liang* leaves oxen in the care of trusted clients, receiving a share of the transport earnings. Clients borrow funds with which to purchase oxen or gardens. Clients' adolescent children may reside at the home of the patron and labor for him in his rice fields or as his caravan assistants.

Unlike the merchant or moneylender, the *pau liang* maintains no detailed accounts of the myriad credit arrangements in which he is involved with his clients. He maintains no strict interest rate schedule, fails to specify due dates for the repayment of loans, and does not require collateral. A book-keeping system wherein economic obligations are entered in cash values and balanced against one another to derive net financial gains and losses is alien to the entourage. Rather, the network of credit transactions is systematized through a traditionally established order of equivalencies. The garden tenant, for instance, receives consumer goods from his patron in advance of the harvest; his obligation to reciprocate includes the understanding that he will sell his coming harvest to the patron at a specially low price, determined not only by the discount for goods earlier received but also by the degree of intimacy between the parties and correlatively by their relative social ranks.

The pattern of involvements existing at each moment between the *pau liang* and each of his clients is, in other words, complex, including accumulated economic credits, social obligations, and the requisites of political alliance. Strict account cannot be kept of financial transactions within this network of indebtedness, for individual contributions are inextricably bound up in the pattern of the larger whole and are often unquantifiable. The economic relationship is here indistinguishable as a discrete sphere of action. It can be properly viewed only as embedded in the broader socio-politico-economic bond maintained between patron and client through the ongoing interchange of goods and services, beneficence and homage, friendship and trust, a reciprocative system based on traditionally established equivalencies between unequals.

Though the *pau liang* epitomizes the institutional paradigm, patron-client relationships pervade upland Thai peasant life.

The association of a newly arrived couple with an established miang gardener, for example, is but a miniature entourage. The relationship between a miang gardener and his tenants, between a gardener and a local caravan operator, between a wealthy villager and his poorer neighbors—these and other points of interaction reflect incipient or ongoing entourages, each in constant flux as the perceived balance of accumulated debits and credits is continually being recomposed among hierarchically distinguishable participants.

The Upland Thai Peasant Economy in Microcosm

As discussed in the preceding chapter, any analysis of the regularities of a widely dispersed economic system must necessarily slough off the relatively minor variations which distinguish its component units. This procedural rule of thumb created particularly burdensome methodological problems in discussing the hill tribe economy because of intertribal variations on the underlying institutional theme. In the case of upland Thai peasants this problem is minimized; here, macrocosm and microcosm inhabit much the same frame of reference. Though upland Thai villages, hamlets, and households differ in their particulars, the underlying configuration of institutions characterizing their economy appears remarkably uniform throughout the Northern Thai uplands. It may be inferred, then, that upland Thai peasant communities tend to correspond closely to established economic norms, implying that economic deviation tends to be unimportant and that the pace of economic and social change tends to be slow.

A closer examination of a single cluster of miang-cultivating hamlets will serve to test these propositions. It will also serve as an illustration of certain structural features of the upland Thai peasant economy—for instance, the regularity of the miang cultivator's life cycle and the overriding significance of the entourage. The cluster of hamlets examined occupies a section of the Research Area described in Chapter 1. It lies adjacent to the hill tribe villages discussed in Chapter 2, the tea plantation to be discussed in Chapter 4, and the government land settlement and welfare station to be discussed in Chapter 5. Thus, it is being exposed to various alien economic influences. An analysis of the developmental implications of these influences will be reserved to Chapter 6. Here I will focus on a survey of the economic structures of these hamlets.

Village Twelve

As is typical of upland Thai communities, Village Twelve (*Muban Sib Saung*) is an arbitrary political synthesis of six otherwise autonomous hamlets separated by miles of mountain trails. Their sentiments and daily social contacts solidify them internally and link them with the lowlands rather than with one another.

The hollow political structure of Village Twelve is reflected in the lack of substantive duties and powers entrusted to its headman, whose primary purpose in taking the post appears not so much its prestige or authority as its salary, 105 baht per month. His duties consist of little more than attending occasional headmen's meetings in the valley; reporting local crimes, accidents, and outbreaks of disease; and keeping a population register.[64] Besides the headman, the sole village-wide functionary is the schoolmaster, an outposted employee of the nation's Ministry of Education. Though

[64] The village headman is informal leader only of his own hamlet. Problems in other hamlets are taken charge of by voluntary aides (*hua na*). Leadership as seen within the village thus differs radically from its perception by superior government officials, who view it from outside. This matter is reviewed in Chapter 5.

forty-one students are registered at the school, attendance is irregular, and it is frequently closed for lack of participation.

The village population varies between 500 and 600 with the miang seasons and is unevenly distributed among its component hamlets.[65] A household census conducted during February–March 1964 may be summarized as follows:

Hamlet	Population	Households
Pang Huai Thad	187	44
Pang Hok	105	26
Pank Iak	81	15
Pang Kud	79	19
Pang Wieng Daung	58	16
Pang Id	24	5
Total	534	125

Household size averages slightly over four, though this average varies significantly among hamlets; on the other hand, the overall dependency ratio, at 2.5, varies little among hamlets. The demographic pyramid reveals heavy concentrations in the below ten and thirty to thirty-nine age groups, with a sharp drop-off in population between fifteen and twenty-five and beyond forty. This unusual distribution is attributable to the high rates of in- and out-migration in keeping with the miang cultivator's life cycle, as earlier discussed.

[65] The implication that some 20 per cent of the Village Twelve population migrates between hill and valley each year is verified by the number of abandoned dwellings encountered during the miang harvesting off-season. In February–March 1964, eleven homes were found to be uninhabited, and at least five others were being used on a temporary basis by new arrivals.

The following statistics, derived from a census conducted by me during February–March 1964, are thus biased to non-annually-migrating households, which tend to be the relatively wealthy and long-established. Income and occupational data derived from this census are thus biased in favor of the prosperous end of the miang economy spectrum.

The hamlet-centered "kinship" system general among upland Thai as well as lowland peasants is also found among the hamlets of Village Twelve. Religion is similarly hamlet-centered. Among the six hamlets covered, two have Buddhist temples. The smaller one, at Pang Kud, is incomplete; construction was begun in 1959–1960, and by 1964 the hamlet had not gathered the financial resources and spare labor time for its completion. The temple's two novice monks are supported and its grounds are maintained by the hamlet. The larger temple, located at Pang Hok, is over twenty years old. Its aged monk and several novices are supported by the hamlet as well as by some households from upland communities outside Village Twelve, but the temple remains distinctly a Pang Hok landmark and asset.

Despite the presence of these two small temples, religious activity in local hamlets is kept at a low level compared with the valley. Little use is made of the temples. Furthermore, few homes have installed the Buddha altars common in the lowlands. There is little evidence of "merit making"—religious observances and philanthropic deeds to improve one's spiritual destiny. The sparseness of such typically Thai behavior may be explained by the close ties that local households retain with the valley world.[66] It is in their ancestral lowland villages that they participate in religious activity, and it is partly for this reason that they make frequent excursions to the lowlands. Such behavior demonstrates their attitude to life in the hills; it is temporary and disagreeable, but it is put up with in anticipation of the day when the Thai hill dweller finds himself sufficiently enriched to return to the lowlands on a favorable footing.

Hamlets differ in other respects. The origins of households in each hamlet vary. Households of Pang Wieng Daung,

[66] It may also be explained on the basis of the apparently eccentric psychological orientation of Thai hill dwellers; see note 40, above.

Pang Kud, and Pang Id come primarily from the neighboring valley village of Ban Pong and its surrounding hamlets. Some of those of Pang Iak come from Ban Pong while others are from Luang Prabang (Laos) and Doi Saket (east of Chiengmai Town). Pang Hok's households come primarily from Doi Saket.[67] Pang Huai Thad households are of more widely dispersed origins, coming not only from Ban Pong and Mae Thaeng but from Chiengdao, Fang, and southern Chiengmai Province.[68]

Hamlets also differ in the percentages of their households that have been attracted from miang production and its attendant occupations to tea production for sale to the nearby tea plantation and to wage labor in the plantation fields and factory (see Chapter 4). Since some households divide their attentions between miang and tea and since others vacillate seasonally between miang and tea production and labor, the task of differentiating between participants in the miang industry and participants in the tea industry becomes a rather arbitrary procedure in the marginal cases. Income sources, number of consecutive seasons of involvement, and social and political ties have been the variables employed here in determining household classification in the miang or tea industry. Households classified in the tea industry are examined in the following chapter. Of the sixty households classified as par-

[67] Pang Hok is a peculiarly insular hamlet. Unlike those of its neighbors, its households do not have patrons in the nearby valley villages. Unlike them it maintains a well-established temple with its own fully-ordained monk. The reason appears to be that its roots are in a village some thirty miles to the south, close enough to maintain old ties. Its households have not yet made the social adjustment to their new locale.

[68] Information on the histories of upland hamlets, which are constantly changing their populations as households move through their life cycles, is conspicuously absent. Only future archaeological work may provide clues to their biographies.

ticipants in the miang industry, twenty-two reside in Pang Hok, fourteen in Pang Wieng Daung, thirteen in Pang Iak, ten in Pang Kud, and one in Pang Id. All the households in Pang Huai Thad (the location of the tea factory and plantation headquarters) have been absorbed into the plantation economy. This situation explains why the dispersion of household origins is so great in Pang Huai Thad—the tea plantation has attracted wage laborers of diverse background from a wide area.

Income levels of those participating in the miang industry also differ markedly among the hamlets of Village Twelve. Per-household "surplus" income (net of "subsistence" and "enterprise" expenditures) ranges from a low of some 940 baht in Pang Kud through 1,800 baht in Pang Hok and 2,400 baht in Pang Wieng Daung to 3,600 baht in Pank Iak. (The one miang-cultivating household in Pang Id earns a net of —2,100 baht; it will surely not last long in the industry.) [69] As income levels vary, so do holdings of "prestige and remunerative durables." Oxen, for instance, are owned in the following numbers: Pang Id, none; Pang Kud, twenty-two; Pang Hok, thirty-six; Pang Wieng Daung, thirty-six; and Pang Iak, forty-five. Data pertaining to housing conditions, major household furnishings, and registered miang garden holdings follow similar patterns.

The Income Accounts

Information collected from individual households in the miang industry, supplemented by imputations based on labor

[69] Gross income per household for the village as a whole averages 6,592 baht. Though such an income (which may be translated into dollars at the rate of some twenty baht per U.S. dollar) suggests a standard of living far below physical subsistence, the miang cultivator actually lives comfortably according to his own standards at this income level.

productivity rates and household subsistence requirements, permits an estimate of incomes and expenditures for the sixty households comprising Village Twelve's miang economy.[70] An aggregative treatment would gloss over the occupational

Table 1. Occupational hierarchy, Village Twelve miang industry, 1963–1964

Occupational specialization	Gross income per household * (baht)	Index of specialization † (%)
Miang production and transport	10,800	72
Miang production	7,300	88
Miang and tea production	7,300	99
Miang sales and tea labor	5,100	92
Miang and tea labor	2,700	100
Miang labor	1,200	97

* Rounded to nearest hundred.

† Household income from the occupational specialization as a percentage of total household income.

income stratification which marks the miang economy and the individual household life cycle. The analysis is therefore broken down along occupational lines. Because single households frequently fall into several occupational categories, they will be classified by "occupational specialization," defined as that occupation or set of occupations which accounts for 70 per cent or more of total household income. Table 1 sum-

[70] The milled-rice subsistence requirement is set at 290 kg. per year per adult and 80 kg. per child. Supplementary subsistence requirements are estimated at 500 baht per year per adult and 250 per adolescent (ages eleven to fifteen) and child. Labor productivity rates are estimated at 50 bundles of miang per day per adult and 30 per adolescent over the hundred-day annual harvest period. In cases where the household's sole income is from miang labor, subsistence is presumed to equal productivity.

marizes the results of such a breakdown, ranking occupations, in terms of income levels attained, in accord with the household life cycle described earlier. It also indicates that, as households climb to superior occupations, they tend to diversify their economic interests—that is, the index of specialization tends to decline.

With the occupational shift up the income scale "subsistence" and "enterprise" expenditures rise as well, but not at so fast a rate; at the highest levels they tend to fall. First, subsistence spending rises as household size expands (chiefly a function of the age of the householding couple); since the household life cycle parallels the occupational hierarchy, subsistence spending may be expected to, and actually does, rise at a slow but steady rate, though it falls off among wealthy and old households as offspring depart to start their own households. Second, enterprise expenditures rise as households move to superior occupations, though they tend to fall off at the highest income levels; garden rental fees, transport fees, and labor costs rise as miang production is expanded, but, as the wealthy garden owner turns to renting out his miang property and accumulating oxen, such expenditures decline. The residual, "surplus" income, used to accumulate luxury consumables, prestige durables, and remunerative durables, thus rises rapidly with the shift to superior occupational specializations. The functional relationships are observable in Table 2.

The 400-baht deficit earned by the average household specializing in miang labor is not recognized as such by the household, which does not keep account of its economic situation on a fiscal basis. Though I have estimated incomes and expenditures for households in the miang industry, financial bookkeeping is unknown to them. It is, furthermore, alien to the realities of the entourage system and to the values of the

Table 2. Income uses per household, by occupational specialization, Village Twelve miang industry, 1963–1964 (in baht rounded to the nearest hundred)

Occupational specialization	Gross income	"Subsistence" and "enterprise" expenditures	"Surplus" income
Miang production and transport	10,800	3,200	7,600
Miang production	7,300	4,900	2,400
Miang and tea production	7,300	5,000	2,300
Miang production and tea labor	5,100	4,000	1,100
Miang and tea labor	2,700	2,000	700
Miang labor	1,200	1,600	−400

Northern Thai peasant. Thus, the deficit-earning household in the miang industry will only come to recognize its futility gradually as it becomes aware, through its empty stomachs, of its chronic inability to make ends meet in its chosen occupation. However, because such households normally migrate between hill and valley as seasonal labor opportunities in each locale warrant, it may continue to unknowingly subsidize its losing efforts in miang with its surpluses from rice. Even this case is not an example of peasant irrationality, however, because in the process of establishing itself in the hills it may well locate opportunities as clients to well-to-do households (working as permanent labor, ox drover, garden tenant) which would otherwise never have become available.

As expected, the rank correlation between occupational surplus incomes and asset holdings (prestige and remunerative durables) is high. Data for remunerative assets are presented in Table 3. Observations on prestige durables corroborate the hypothesis that the distribution of such asset holdings tends to parallel the occupational distribution of surplus income. This is particularly true of tile-roofed houses and of those having

Table 3. Asset holdings per household, by occupational specialization, Village Twelve miang industry, 1963–1964

Occupational specialization	"Surplus" income (baht)	Assets		
		Oxen	Miang gardens *	Rice fields
Miang production and transport	7,600	15.0	1.0	1.0
Miang production	2,400	2.6	.8	
Miang and tea production	2,300	2.5	.7	.1
Miang production and tea labor	1,100		.5	
Miang and tea labor	700			
Miang labor	−400			

* Nonownership of gardens among occupational categories that require garden use indicates the prevalence of renting. Thus, half the households which specialize in "miang production and tea labor" rent the gardens they work.

solid board walls and raised on stilts in keeping with lowland custom.

Entourages in Village Twelve

Richer households in the miang industry of Village Twelve tend to have clustered about them, in imitation of the compound style of architecture prevalent in lowland Thai peasant communities, the smaller and more ramshackle residences of poorer and generally younger kin, friends, and general hangers-on.[71] One such patron household in Pang Iak, for instance, has living in with it a bachelor from the householder's ancestral lowland village who performs a diversity of menial chores in return for an annual wage (kept for him by his patron) as well as his room and board and daily participation in family affairs. This same patron uses the labor services of several non-garden-owning neighbors on a regular basis dur-

[71] On the compound-architectural element in entourages see Lucien Hanks, 1966, pp. 58–61.

ing harvest seasons; his fidelity is returned in good measure by their praise of his stature in the hamlet, of his wealth, his generosity, and his wisdom. The pattern is repeated in other hamlets, though the scale of such entourages varies from case to case.

Entourages are not invariably formed by relatively wealthy potential patrons. In Pang Wieng Daung one of the wealthiest households, consisting of a particularly shrewd and hardworking widower and his two sons, is despised by his neighbors, who regard him as cunning and untrustworthy. His failure to inspire confidence by generating long-run relationships with those in search of work has resulted in virtual ostracism. Because of his difficulty in attracting labor on his terms he has turned his wealth to purposes other than expanding his miang output; he rents out gardens, seeks working relationships with the nearby tea plantation, and is rumored to have dabbled in opium smuggling.

The entourage formations that appear within upland hamlets are minor when compared with the ties between upland households and those in the valley. An exception to this rule is found in Pang Hok, which has strong roots in Doi Saket, some thirty miles to the southeast. Households in this hamlet have not formed the usual relationships with patrons in nearby valley communities. They dispose of their miang and purchase consumer goods with itinerant traders (representatives of *pau liang* from the valley), largely on a bargained, cash basis. Their arm's-length dealings provide price data which have proved useful in imputing the incomes and expenditures of households that deal more intimately with their valley patrons.[72]

[72] The price data derived from a survey of these households are presented below. The range of prices varies by season because of the differing qualities of the product, depending on the rains. The varia-

At the opposite extreme, a particularly intimate entourage relationship has been formed between a *pau liang* of Ban Pong and a miang cultivator of Pang Kud (himself a patron to neighboring households).[73] The two households are not related by blood or marriage, yet they behave and refer to one another as older and younger brothers. The *pau liang* has placed the cultivator in possession of a number of oxen, which the cultivator uses to transport miang and rice between Village Twelve and the *pau liang*'s compound in Ban Pong: he earns the transport fee; the *pau liang* earns the profits

tions by "year" may be interpreted as variations in the degree of intimacy developed between miang dealers and local gardeners. A "good" year is not necessarily one in which demand is high or supply low "in the market" but one in which the buyer is willing for one reason or another (and the reason may be any of a large number —not necessarily "market" conditions) to establish a more favorable relationship than usual. (Data are in baht per thousand bundles; n.a. = not available.)

Bundle size	Harvest season			
	Mui	Hua phi	Klang	Soi
Year of high prices				
Large	n.a.	500	600	n.a.
Medium	550	450	500	550
Small	n.a.	n.a.	150	n.a.
Year of normal prices				
Large	500	400	450	450
Medium	450	350	400	430
Small	n.a.	125	130	n.a.
Year of low prices				
Large	n.a.	350	400	n.a.
Medium	350	250	300	350
Small	n.a.	n.a.	125	n.a.

A weighted average of these prices is 400.10 baht. The bench-mark price used in all imputations has been 400.

[73] A similar example is provided in LeBar, 1967, pp. 112–113.

from miang and rice transactions. The *pau liang* permits the cultivator to oversee gardens which he rents out to other households of Village Twelve; whether the gardens worked by the cultivator have been given him by the *pau liang* has not been determined. The cultivator participates in the opium trade: he has received his cash fund for this purpose from the *pau liang;* whether the *pau liang* participates actively in the smuggling remains conjectural. The cultivator, in sum, serves as an extension of the *pau liang*'s economic interests into the hills; in contrast, the *pau liang* is the cultivator's economic life-line with the valley.[74] The well-being of each is furthered by the other. Mutual trust and respect permits each to improve his rank within peasant society. Though this entourage relationship is unusually strong, it represents an institutional regularity running through Village Twelve's miang industry.

In sum, Village Twelve's miang industry, organized along the traditional institutional lines of the entourage, is structurally stable, or functionally well integrated. Participants are furnished the means of realizing ther aspirations along established lines through participation in entourage relationships: opportunities for economic advancement are provided

[74] The commune within which Village Twelve is located contains nearly 200 *pau liang* by local count, of whom five, all in Ban Pong, are considered the foremost. One of these is the *pau liang* discussed here. He informed me that he possesses the following assets, some of which I had the opportunity to observe firsthand: more than forty acres of wet-rice fields rented out; two miang gardens rented out; a diesel-operated rice mill; a miang warehouse containing eight pits capable of storing approximately 80,000 bundles; a compound containing several dwellings of superior construction; a dry-goods store; a bus capable of carrying fifty passengers; and an undisclosed number of oxen and buffalo, some of them rented out to tenants of his fields and some distributed as pack animals among trusted miang-gardening clients.

through occupational mobility within the miang industry; economic security is available through the bounty of one's patron. Accordingly, economic deviation should be rare and strongly discouraged.

However, the presence of a tea plantation in the Research Area has generated acculturative pressures generally absent from the upland environment. The tea plantation actively induces local upland Thai peasants to shift from producing miang for their *pau liang* to supplying the plantation factory with raw tea leaf and working as wage labor in the plantation fields. Despite its continuing efforts in this direction, the plantation has failed to generate a lasting response, reflecting the basic functionalism of the indigenous institutional configuration. A closer examination of the corrosive impact of the plantation economy on the upland Thai peasant economy will be undertaken after the structure of the plantation economy itself has been analyzed.

Chapter 4

THE TEA
PLANTATION
ECONOMY

An Introductory Note on the Economic History of Tea

Until the middle of the nineteenth century the West's chief source of tea was China, where it had been produced on a smallholder basis since antiquity. Indigenous Chinese trade channels brought the domestic surplus to the ports (chiefly Canton and later Hong Kong), from where it was shipped by Western firms (primarily the British East India Company until 1834) to the London market. The failure of the Chinese to reciprocate the high British demand for tea and other oriental commodities produced a chronic bilateral trade deficit for the British as the eighteenth century wore into the nineteenth. Numerous efforts were made during the early decades of the nineteenth century to discover means of stopping the gold drain. Among the many exports tested on the Chinese market the most suitable to Chinese tastes proved to be opium; not only did it eliminate the gold drain, it poured profits into British traders' pockets. The world-wide repercussions of what evolved into a militarily enforced flow of opium from British India to China have to the present day not played themselves out.[1]

[1] A searching analysis of Britain's trade problem and of the various

Another exchange-conserving technique resorted to by the British, and the one of particular interest here, was the establishment of a tea industry within the confines of the British Empire. (One of the reasons why the commercial tea industry did not penetrate North Thailand until after World War II thus appears to have been Thailand's successful avoidance of British colonization.) The specific circumstance that sparked the idea of commercial tea production in British India as an alternative to the costly China trade was the discovery in 1823 of "wild tea jungles" in Assam, among the foothills of the Brahmaputra watershed. Adventurers in the employ of the East India Company discovered "hill people" (Kachin tribesmen) who consumed tea "as a vegetable pickled after the Burmese [and Northern Thai] fashion." [2] This discovery of tea in northeast India thus occurred in a cultural and geographical setting not dissimilar from that encountered in North Thailand; the parallels are important in understanding the tea-producing potential of North Thailand.

British experiments with tea cultivation in Assam quickly determined the profitability of its production on a commercial scale. Two requirements, however, led to the transformation of the industry from the smallholder system common in China to large-scale plantations vertically integrated into a corporate scheme within which the individual agricultural

---

efforts to solve it is presented in Greenberg, 1951; this history is carried forward by Fairbank, 1969. It was the quest to introduce opium to China that eventually resulted in its diffusion to the hill tribes populating the south China frontier, speeding the southward filtration of these peoples and culminating in the present cultural confrontations observed in the Northern Thai uplands.

[2] Courtenay, 1965, p. 37. On this point, as on many others concerning the historical development of the black-tea trade, see Griffiths, 1967, pp. 33–58.

unit operated as a component element in an international manufacturing, shipping, and wholesaling complex.

The first was *profitability*. To achieve this financial requirement a producing operation of over 500 acres, serviced by a mechanized processing plant and a resident labor force of more than three men for every two acres, was found optimal. This type of operation requires that the mechanical process be exploited to its fullest potential, that the labor force be integrated into the regimen of the processing plant, that a steady stream of raw leaf be fed through the system to minimize unit operating costs. It requires that labor-intensive tasks, particularly harvesting, be as mechanistically organized (that is, as standardized, regimented, and depersonalized) as possible.[3]

The second and related requirement was *effective competition* with the traditionally favored Chinese "green" tea. This was achieved by differentiating the product through an intensive European campaign to popularize "black" tea.[4] Since black tea lends itself to machine processing it fits the efficiency criteria of the profit-oriented plantation economy. Green tea, the traditional, hand-processed product, favors a labor-intensive technology of the cottage-industry type amenable to the institutional constraints of the Chinese agricultural smallholder system. By weaning Western tastes from green

[3] Problems of acquiring "efficient" (read docile) resident labor forces early led plantation owners to resort to labor importation. The resulting human migrations created problems of ethnic pluralism which continue to haunt the postcolonial world: for example, the Indians of Burma, the Chinese of Malaysia and Indonesia, the Tamils of Ceylon, not to mention numerous Western-hemisphere cases, the gravest one of which is the racial polarization presently confronting the United States.

[4] Courtenay, 1965, p. 48; Ukers, 1936, p. 42; Griffiths, 1967, pp. 579–591. The technological differences between black and green tea will be discussed in the following section.

to black tea the British ran the Chinese off the world market, for the Chinese were neither institutionally geared to adapt to large-scale, plantation-type operations nor sufficiently wealthy to acquire nor trained to operate the machinery required for black-tea production.

The plantation system of India, and later of Ceylon and the Dutch East Indies, thus defeated the Chinese in the international tea market not only because of the much-touted superior Western technology but equally because of the less publicized Western superiority in manipulating to their own advantage the market mechanism of their own invention.[5] Industrial technology meshed with market institutions to form an unbeatable combination.

Yet, the market system proved an unmanageable tool even in Western hands. The efficiency criteria that dictated large-scale tea estates and vertical integration also spurred the search for improved manufacturing techniques, the success of which resulted in market gluts in the face of an increasingly inelastic world demand. The rigors of competition among commercial-industrial giants produced their own antidote: in 1933 the tea industry cartelized itself on an international basis with the active consent of the major producing countries' colonial governments.[6] An international agreement was reached by producing countries controlling 97 per cent of the black-tea trade to limit output and exports in order to maintain prices. The companies survived, but only at the expense of higher prices paid by the Western consuming public and—more disastrous—at the expense of labor layoffs in the producing countries.[7]

[5] A subsidiary factor was the relatively low shipping cost to England from India, as against that from East Asia.

[6] Courtenay, 1965, pp. 184–185; Eden, 1958, pp. 178–179; Wickizer, 1944, pp. 72–96.

[7] See, however, Wickizer, 1944, p. 121.

The glut problem was further remedied by the devastation of World War II, which cut severely into producing acreage, labor, and capital stock, especially in the Dutch East Indies. Since then, a number of new producing areas (for example, East and Central Africa) and the entry of traditional green-tea producers into the competitive fold (for example, Taiwan and Japan) have made effective enforcement of the international tea agreement unworkable. Though the industry continues to be dominated by a few major exporting and importing countries and by giant wholesaling firms, it has been sufficiently opened up to competition to permit the entry of additional suppliers of high-quality leaf. One of these is Thailand.

Thailand has traditionally played a minuscule role in the international tea trade. In 1962, a representative year, tea imports totaled slightly over 1,609 metric tons, offsetting some 22 metric tons in exports (actually primarily re-exports) to leave a net import balance of less than 1,590 metric tons, representing a foreign exchange outflow of about thirty-three million baht. These figures are so tiny that they barely affect world trade statistics (total imports over the past decade have absorbed .002 per cent of the world supply) and are even so small that they do not appear in Thailand's summary trade accounts. The record of Thailand's experience, however, does not reveal its potential in the tea trade. Conditions in the North favor the introduction of this crop in a number of respects, and untapped markets, overseas as well as domestic, suggest that, with skilled merchandising, surplus problems need not emerge as production is expanded.

The potential benefits arising from the judicious introduction of the tea trade and its attendant industrial technology into North Thailand will be reviewed in the Afterword to this study. The remainder of the present chapter will be devoted to a structural analysis of the technology and institutions of the tea plantation as an economic system and to an examination of the economy of the Chiengdao Tea Plantation (see the map of the Research Area on page 37), the first tea plantation to appear on the Northern Thai scene.

Tea Technology

The economic institutions characteristic of the tea plantation hold significant implications for the peasant economies on which they ordinarily impinge, but these institutional implications derive from the technological particulars of the tea production process. Progressive modifications in tea technology have acted as a dominant causal factor in the industry's economic history. The defeat of Chinese producers by the British during the nineteenth century, the subsequent rise of giant tea producing and marketing corporations within the increasingly oligopolistic industry, the emergence of agricultural proletariats in tea producing districts with the "rationalization" of the production process, the decline of the industry under glut conditions on the world market, and the present opportunities afforded Thailand as an entrant into the international tea trade, among other evolving circumstances, all relate back to the technological specifics of green- and black-tea production. The distinctions between the green- and black-tea technologies will be briefly reviewed here; their institutional implications will be dealt with in the subsequent section.

Green Tea

The natural decomposition of harvested tea leaf involves the gradual freeing of enzymes from the leaf sap to act as a catalyst in the oxidation of polyphenols, a chemistry loosely referred to as "fermentation."[8] Green-tea manufacture relies on methods which kill the enzyme in order to delay or entirely stop further fermentation.[9] The immediate symptom of success is noticeable in the leaf's color after processing, for fermentation activates the leaf tannins, which discolor (or "tan") the leaf; early elimination of fermentation permits the leaf to retain its green hue. The technique of stopping enzyme action usually consists of roasting freshly picked leaf in large, shallow cauldrons over an intensely hot charcoal fire for no more than a few minutes while vigorously stirring the leaf to assure an even distribution of heat.[10]

Once fermentation has been forestalled by roasting, the leaf must be thoroughly dried to ensure retention of the product's flavor and retard its perishability. This is accomplished by first rolling the leaf between the palms of the hands (or in sacks) to cause abrasions, opening the cell walls to permit rapid evaporation of fluids, and by then drying the leaf over slow fires or in the sun. The finished product retains a greenish tint, though it is wrinkled, twisted, and brit-

[8] Eden, 1958, pp. 136–146.

[9] *Ibid.*, p. 169. Different varieties of green tea result from different exposures to fermentation prior to the elimination of further enzyme action. The product is also variegated by adding flavoring and aromatic ingredients, usually flower petals.

[10] The similarities between the early steps in green-tea processing and miang processing are striking. Steaming of miang bundles accomplishes much the same end as tea roasting, though it retards, rather than completely stops, the fermentation process. The equipment used is as similar as are the methods. The cauldron in which green tea is roasted is, for instance, identical to that over which miang is steamed. I have observed the adaptation of a miang workshop to a green-tea processing operation with scarcely any alteration in its layout.

An interesting case of a hybrid technology standing midway between miang and tea processing is described by Robinson, 1841, pp. 133–134; quoted in Elwin, ed., 1959, pp. 409–410.

tle from the roasting, rolling, and drying process. "There is no typical [black] tea aroma developed and when infused the liquors are pale primrose coloured. To the hardened drinker of black tea the brew is insipid and slightly bitter." [11]

Though attempts have been made to develop green-tea processing machinery, the highest quality product is hand worked. The entire manufacturing procedure lends itself to workshop rather than factory methods. To avoid unwanted fermentation, picking and transporting of raw leaf must be carefully and quickly done, for bruising will immediately generate enzyme action. To assure a high-quality finished product, picking must be discriminatory, with only the most tender buds selected; this is even more significant for green than for black tea, since delicacy of flavor, which depends on large part on the tenderness of the leaf, is a particularly prized characteristic of the "insipid" varieties. Roasting must be managed with a master's touch, for insufficient, excessive, or uneven exposure of the leaf to heat will produce an inferior product. Rolling and drying are also best accomplished on a personal basis, with individual lots of leaf receiving individual analysis and treatment. Superior green tea thus results from intimate attention to detail by the producer, who ideally follows the leaf personally from bush to roasting to rolling and drying operations. Green-tea production thus lends itself to smallholder operations, with individual producers caring for gardens in a manner not much different from that used for miang cultivation.

Black Tea

Whereas green tea is produced by eliminating fermentation through immediate destruction of the leaf's oxidase, black tea

[11] Eden, 1958, p. 169. This statement represents the biased opinion of a British black-tea enthusiast and industry spokesman.

is the result of a speed-up of fermentation under controlled conditions followed by a sudden cut-off at the desired stage. The manufacturing process is divided into four steps.[12] First, raw leaf is withered on trays in an airy loft or in revolving drums fed with a stream of hot air. The purpose is to reduce the leaf's moisture content to between 40 and 50 per cent of leaf weight. Then, the leaf is rolled by special machines which bruise and twist it, expelling its juices so that fermentation can take place rapidly. The resulting lumps of moist rolled leaf are broken and sifted by machine, and the leaf is then spread on tile or cement floors to permit unhampered fermentation. The total time from rolling to the desired state of fermentation is scientifically gauged, and at the proper moment the leaf is fed into drying machines, which blast it with hot air to stop enzyme action and to reduce the product to its final dryness of about 3 per cent moisture content and 20 per cent of its original weight. The finished product is graded and sifted mechanically before packing and shipping.

Every step in the manufacturing process involves industrial technology. It especially requires large capital outlays, industrial management abilities, and detailed knowledge of leaf chemistry. Because of the financial burden involved in running such an operation, factory facilities must necessarily be as fully and steadily utilized as possible to minimize costs per unit of output. This motivates the processor to pay as much attention to details of cultivation (the source of inventory) as to the operation of the factory itself.

The drive to maximum efficiency at the primary stage of production has led to the establishment of numerous tea research institutes in Asia and Africa.[13] So much research and development has been carried out that wherever tea is cultivated "the methods of planting, pruning, plucking, cultiva-

[12] *Ibid.*, pp. 149–160.   [13] *Ibid.*, pp. 181–184.

tion and manuring are closely correlated, and such differences as persist are mainly due to climate and *jat* [type] of tea." [14] In short, tea cultivation has, because of its intimate association with the efficiency criteria basic to black-tea processing, taken on many of the attributes of standardization and scientific control which characterize the industrial economy. It includes such scientific specialties as propagation, nursery management, pruning, soil management, and plucking, each with its own professional lore.[15] But outright mechanization of tea cultivation and harvesting has not yet been made feasible; these tasks remain labor intensive.

Because of its mechanical complexity and capital indivisibilities the technology of black-tea manufacture incorporates substantial economies of scale. However, the industry's inability to mechanize the primary stage remains its major technological bottleneck. "Even in the mid-twentieth century when the mechanization of the processing . . . of tea . . . has been carried as far as is technically possible, labour costs remain as much as 60 per cent of total production costs and about 90 per cent of the labour force is employed in field work." This means that "44 per cent of the total costs of a tea plantation can be attributed to harvesting." [16]

The Plantation as an Institutional Form

Economic development studies, even those concentrating on the agricultural sector, have rarely considered the plantation as a major institutional form and potential developmental force within the underdeveloped world. Though the plantation has occasionally been discussed by anthropologists, the scattered findings deriving from their work have yet to

[14] Harler, 1966, p. vii.   [15] *Ibid., passim;* see also Harler, 1964.
[16] Courtenay, 1965, pp. 45, 180.

be adequately synthesized. More systematic attention has been paid to the plantation by geographers, who have, however, tended to dwell almost exclusively on the system's physical and technological peculiarities.

Despite the widespread neglect of the plantation as an institutional form which frequently plays an important role in the economic development process, a large literature dealing with its everyday problems and specific ramifications has been accumulated within each of the industries lending itself to plantation organization.

The tea industry, for instance, inspires a steady flow of studies. The nature of these publications is of interest: they invariably speak lovingly and in detail of the natural characteristics and proper methods of cultivating the tea shrub; they dwell in rapturous tones on the intimate particulars of the manufacturing process and the functions and eccentricities of each piece of machinery; they analyze with an emotion bordering on chauvinism the imperialistic history of the industry and the international competition, vertical integration of firms, and complex distribution network in which it has culminated. Rarely, however, do they deal with the human dimension of the plantation. Conspicuous by their absence are discussions of the recruitment, compensation, and welfare of plantation labor forces and of the effects of the plantation on the non-Western cultures upon which it encroaches and which it seeks to bend to its own ends.

The economic and social dualism so often remarked of the developing countries has historically been crystallized on the plantation. It is on the plantation that the Western and non-Western worlds meet head on. The Westerner sees the plantation as *a firm*, a business venture no different in its basic rationale from Adam Smith's pin factory or Henry Ford's assembly plant. Indigenous peoples see the plantation not as a firm but as a unique social organism, or *cultural enclave*, a way of life into which they are drawn despite themselves and which differs in nearly all its essentials from that to which they have been conditioned by many lifetimes of accumulated experience.

As a Firm

Financial gain has been the ultimate goal of the plantation throughout its history; "the purpose of a plantation, under normal circumstances, is to produce a crop that is demanded by the world market in an efficient enough way to make a profit." [17] I emphasize this obvious point because the profit motive has played an important part in shaping the plantation into what it is today and because this motive and the institutional edifice upon which it builds and which it helps to solidify clashes so sharply with the pre-existing social, political, and economic institutions of the peasantry it employs.

The rules of the game of profit-seeking in a commercial setting are essentially simple. They consist of minimizing unit costs while maximizing revenues. The key to success resides in manipulation of the component elements of costs and revenues. Profits grow under competitive conditions as (1) the quantity of inputs per unit of output is reduced, or (2) the quantity of outputs per unit of input is increased, or (3) input costs are lowered, or (4) output prices are raised, or from various combinations of these factors. The success of

[17] *Ibid.*, p. 53. Courtenay's statement that "under normal circumstances" the plantation is profit-motivated is important, for it implies that a non-profit-oriented plantation can exist. Though the plantation has evolved into what it is owing, in large measure, to profit orientation, profit orientation is neither a necessary nor a sufficient condition. It may well be that, given different constraints, the plantation may serve socially as well as privately beneficial ends. That is, there exist in this world measures of success other than profits.

tea plantations as firms has devolved from their capacity to pursue all four of these courses simultaneously. The plantation as a firm has historically played strictly by the rules—so strictly, in fact, that it presents one of the most conspicuous examples of the rapacity of the commercial institutional configuration freed of social and political constraints.

Of major importance to the success of the tea plantation has been its attempt to diminish average costs by employing industrial production processes. The tea plantation represents, for the agricultural sector, a capital-intensive industry; it is in a sense a factory in the fields. This characteristic has permitted it to achieve significant economies of scale. For instance: "In the early days in Assam the [tea] leaf was hand rolled, as in China, and a man could manipulate 30–40 lb. (14–18 kg) withered leaf a day. A modern tea roller [operated by a single man] can accomodate 800–1000 lb. (364–455 kg) of withered leaf and roll it in 1–1½ hours."[18] The economies of scale implicit in mechanization have been extended to all plantation operations by scientific management, standardization of operations, and careful training and supervision of labor. They have resulted in the transformation of an industry from one composed of household-scale operations to one divided among giant estates serviced by veritable armies of laborers working in close synchronization with the machine process.

Exploitation of industrial economies of scale is associated with another important attribute of the plantation: it is almost invariably foreign-owned. The heavy investment required of an industrial plant is rarely available locally, and even if funds were available at the source of production it would be even rarer to find locally the required competent

[18] Harler, 1966, pp. 153–154.

technical personnel to manage and operate the plant.[19] Thus, its very industrial character has determined that the plantation be a foreign intruder into the indigenous environment of the producing area, not only in its commercial spirit but in the fact of its ownership and control.

The economies of scale which mechanization and scientific management have permitted on the input side have transmitted themselves to output. In a competitive world market with secularly rising demand, increased volume of a standardized product results in increased revenues for the industry but not necessarily for the firm. However, the world tea market for a long period (from about 1870 to World War II) faced a situation of declining competition as it grew. The quest for market domination led to consolidations among those most successful in reaping scale economies and thus to control of the international trade by a relatively few international giants. In an oligopolistic industry, tea wholesalers

[19] The reason why funds and skills are not locally available are themselves largely the outgrowth of the plantation's operating procedure. Because its heavy capital investment requires that the plantation be foreign-financed, it is also therefore foreign-controlled, resulting in the export of its profits to its overseas owners. Funds which would otherwise be locally accumulated from the profitable operations of the plantation are thus siphoned off to the "mother country," which only re-exports them to enter into further lucrative enterprises whose net receipts will in turn flow back to their foreign owners. Similarly, managerial and engineering skills are not locally available because they have been given no opportunity to develop. The search for profits does not permit funds to be "wasted" on training of local personnel when trained manpower is already available in the "mother country." The absence of local scientific expertise thus perpetuates itself, a phenomenon traditionally reinforced by the belief among those already trained that local manpower is intellectually inferior, as proved by its lack of skills. These vicious circles are discussed by Myint, 1964, pp. 54–68; and are implicit in the discussion of underemployment in Myrdal, 1968, pp. 2041–2061.

turned to "market management" (i.e., output- and price-fixing) and tea estates to "resource management" (wage squeezes) as means of assuring continued profitability of operations. Since the Depression years, however, such international cartelization of the industry has declined as first demand and later supply conditions have fluctuated uncontrollably, but the pursuit of profits irrespective of indigenous social considerations has not lost its grip.

The effort to reduce per-unit operating costs by seeking economies of scale through mechanization has been paralleled by the effort to secure cheap labor. Where mechanization cannot be utilized in all operations for technical reasons, as for instance in the harvesting of tea, the plantation must resort to manual labor, which it regiments to mesh with the mechanical processes in use. Labor is seen as a supplement to the machine and is subordinated to the demands of the industrial discipline. It is regarded "merely as an undifferentiated mass of 'cheap' or 'expendible' brawnpower." [20] This attitude is frequently demonstrated in scientific discussions of tea production. Even in this relatively enlightened generation it remains common to speak of measures beneficial to the material well-being of the plantation labor force not in terms of their intrinsic merits but solely in terms of their output- (and thus profit-) promoting qualities. For instance:

Several factors are involved in *the rise of outturn of tea per worker* . . . [;] one factor of the greatest importance is the improved health of the labour force. In 1944, mepacrin was issued as a febrifuge to all the labour, in place of quinine. As a result, it is recorded that on one estate the average number of fever cases treated monthly fell immediately, in that year, from 150 to 8. . . .

In addition to the above, the houses of the labour force are

[20] Myint, 1964, pp. 56–57.

now periodically treated with DDT, and a further improvement in general health has resulted. At one time the labour needed persuasion to work but now it wants to work! Other factors involved in *the increased outturn per worker* are the greater incentive of improved pay and conditions.[21]

This essentially commercial view of labor is similarly reflected in the following statement, among many others:

A Ceylon planter notes that "tea estates are highly organized pieces of machinery which cannot function without efficient management and a permanent labour force." On his own estate of 1,400 acres, a permanent "army" of 1,500 men, women and children are employed. He adds that "the estates are so organized that crop is taken six days out of every seven all through the year." [22]

In short, the plantation management's attitude to labor typically parallels its attitude to other factor inputs. Labor is treated as a commodity, and in keeping with the rules of the game its cost is minimized. In the opinion of one leading development economist, "the falure of the . . . plantation to become the 'leading sector' in the underdeveloped countries was due, not to their producing primarily exports as such, but to their cheap labor policy which has perpetuated the pattern of low wages and low productivity." [23] This interpretation implies that the developmental dynamics of the plantation as an institutional subspecies of the firm have acted as a barrier to development itself.

[21] Harler, 1966, p. 150, my italics. Though I use this quotation to exemplify the plantation operator's short-sighted view of labor, it is actually an unusually liberal one, for it at least recognizes the existence and means of breaking the vicious circle of poverty brought on by the cheap labor policy. In short, it recognizes that plantation labor may actually respond positively to commercial institutions.

[22] Myrdal, 1968, p. 445; quoting Williams, 1956, pp. 191, 206.

[23] Myint, 1964, p. 64.

As a Cultural Enclave

The most distinctive mark of the plantation, perhaps, is its equipoise between labor-intensive cultivation and mechanical processing.[24] One particularly searching analysis refers to plantations as

large-scale, capital-intensive, highly specialized commercial enterprises employing wage labor. Although a plantation uses land and is concerned with products grown on the land, in its scale and methods of operation it is more analogous to a modern factory than to an owned or rented family farm worked by unpaid family labor or occasional hired help. The spread of plantation culture must be viewed as a spread of industrialized agriculture.[25]

The plantation thus breaches the oft-observed gap between the industrial and agrarian ways of life. In the context of the tropical countries in which it has been developed to exploit the commercial potential of such crops as sugar, rubber, palm oil, coffee, and tea, it places a "modern" technology in the midst of a "primitive" one. It also places in an alien context important institutions of the commercial-industrial world.

In broader perspective the evolution of the plantation under the pressure of profit-seeking suggests a somewhat different interpretation of its place than that which emerges from its analysis as a firm. "It has been suggested that the characteristic feature of the plantation is the industrial treatment to which its crop is submitted. . . . It is simpler and more useful to characterize the plantation as something foreign introduced into the geographical [and cultural] environment." [26] In its physical aspects the plantation is obviously an innovation. Its industrial machinery, its occidental architecture, and its managerial personnel are imported. Its revolutionary agri-

[24] Courtenay, 1965, pp. 50–57.   [25] Myrdal, 1968, p. 445.
[26] Gourou, 1966, p. 147.

cultural technologies reform local landscapes and its introduction of new plants alters the ecology, bringing an unending series of further changes, many of them so subtle as to go unnoticed but nevertheless carrying far-reaching economic and social consequences.

Of greater immediate significance are the intangible innovations brought in with the plantation. The profit motive as an institutional characteristic is foreign to the non-Western economy. In North Thailand, for instance, we need only remind ourselves of Moerman's finding that "villagers who are ambitious, enterprising, or successful are, in the eyes of their fellows, 'sons of bitches.'"[27] Such a situation, in which unfettered pursuit of self-interest, and, we may add, of financial gain for its own sake, is disparaged by the community, is the usual case among people outside the Western, commercial milieu. Thus arises the much-debated topic of low (or even negative) responsiveness among non-Western populations to wage incentives.

Not only is the profit motive foreign, but so is the rationale of industrial efficiency. The scientific mentality, geared to nineteenth- and twentieth-century Western concepts of cause and effect, of the machine process, and of technological progress, is beyond the indigenous world view. The firm employs foreign financing and exports its profits to its foreign owners. Even its product is foreign, usually being introduced as a new crop and being exported to meet foreign demand. "The impulse toward establishment of plantations . . . emanated from the West, in response to Western demands."[28] The plantation is an alien intruder, a cultural enclave.

Despite its Western origins and orientation the plantation has traditionally been located in the underdeveloped world

[27] Moerman, 1968, p. 144.   [28] Myrdal, 1968, p. 443.

for the simple reason that its inability to mechanize many agricultural chores directs it to areas of labor "surplus." [29] It was early found, however, that plantation labor was not readily forthcoming in the underdeveloped world even where a potential labor force was available. For reasons generally misunderstood by colonial governments and business interests, peasant populations were not attracted to the plantation. Various expedients were turned to as alternatives to outright slavery, which did not long retain the acceptance it had received on the earliest, Western hemisphere plantations. [30] Colonial governments restricted peasant land tenure, interfered with indigenous crop distribution channels, raised taxes, discouraged labor movements out of plantation districts, imported labor forces from other areas, and employed other means of forcing local people to shift from peasant agriculture to wage labor. The effects included severe economic and social dislocation, resulting in massive labor flows as indigenous institutions were disrupted without workable alternatives being introduced. The more humanistic approach of postcolonial governments has not eliminated all these destructive processes. Furthermore, despite the diversity of efforts to secure plantation labor forces, one method has rarely been considered, even in the postcolonial era. There has been little enthusiasm in the plantation districts for experimenting with the wage scale to test labor responses. [31]

[29] *Ibid.*, p. 444. The fact that labor more than geography has determined the distribution of the tea plantation is illustrated by the United States experience. At the turn of the century tea was introduced to South Carolina, where it did well. The experiment was abandoned, however, when the cost of labor was found to be excessive. The failure of Argentine tea on the world market is attributable to the same reason.

[30] *Ibid.*, pp. 1103–1106, esp. p. 1104, n.1; Myint, 1964, pp. 60–62; Gourou, 1966, pp. 148–153.

[31] This "mental block" is being overcome in the postwar genera-

Why have high wages (and superior living conditions) not been one of the major incentives offered by plantations?

The owners of the . . . plantations usually explained this situation in terms of the very poor quality of labour they could recruit from the subsistence economies. . . . According to them, the uniformly low level of wages which prevailed in all types of underdeveloped countries merely reflected the uniformly low level of labour productivity in all these countries. . . .

[Furthermore, the employers held the general belief] that, in general, indigenous labour not only had low productivity but had limited capacity for improvement; and that it was used to the customarily low material standard of living and would not respond positively to the incentives of higher wages.[32]

This psychology lingers on. The industrialist's belief that low productivity (the presumed concomitant of inherent mental inferiority) deserves low wages has produced among the landless agricultural proletariat of the underdeveloped countries the very inferior quality of humanity (due to undernourishment, poor housing, lack of medical care, minimal education, low morale, and deculturization) originally envisioned. The cheap-labor policy of the plantations has developed into one of the most repressive of the vicious circles that characterize underdevelopment.

The disregard for the human dimension of the plantation is attributable to the alienation of its management from the indigenous culture on which it imposes. Not only have plantation operators traditionally either felt contempt for or pa-

---

tion as higher wages are coming to be resorted to for political reasons and are being found to entail frequently significant incentive effects. See Harler, 1966, p. 150. Econometricians' efforts to determine the degree of supply responsiveness to price changes in peasant agriculture are also generating a new climate of opinion. See, for instance, Behrman, 1968.

[32] Myint, 1964, p. 54.

tronized "natives" as their inferiors, but their ethnocentricity has shielded them from investigating, and thereby understanding, the impact of the Western firm on non-Western cultures. The result, which serves to perpetuate the very conditions which have led Westerners to consider non-Western cultures "backward," is cultural dualism: "The characteristic element in the system is the clash of civilizations. The plantation is an enclave in another form of civilization. There is no need to talk of 'plantations' when the clash of cultures does not occur." [33]

The Tea Plantation Economy in Microcosm

Khun Luang, the Entrepreneur

Khun Luang (a pseudonym translated literally as "Mr. Big," an honorific title by which local people refer to him) was born in 1907 in Central Thailand of Thai parents with mixed Sino-Thai ancestry. While still a young man he received a position with the British-American Tobacco Company (a concessionaire of the Thai government) and was assigned to promote Virginia tobacco as a dry-season crop among North Thailand's lowland peasantry. In this capacity he was exposed to the practically untapped economic potential of the region and became well acquainted with its people and folkways.

In the early 1930's he was shifted by the Company to a post in the Netherlands Indies, where he was introduced to the tea trade. He became interested in the possibilities of tea as a Thai product. Following his hunch, he sought and finally gained admission to the Tocklai Institute, a foremost experimental station and training facility operated by the Indian

[33] Gourou, 1966, p. 148. Also see Boeke, 1948.

Tea Association in Assam.[34] Gaining entry was no easy matter, for the British tea industry was at that time, and continues to be, governed by a close-knit, discriminatory elite. His interest in introducing tea production to Thailand, and even his nationality, had to be kept secret. At any rate, he emerged from the Institute after two years with a professional knowledge of the tea bush and its cultivation as well as of mechanical tea processing and plantation management.

Returning to North Thailand, he resumed his promotional work for the British-American Tobacco Company on a larger scale and branched out into other activities, including fruit orchard management and experimentation with tea cultivation at various sites. Early successes in tobacco curing, however, led him to concentrate his efforts in that direction, and by 1940 he had established himself as one of the nation's leading independent cured-leaf producers, though he remained tied to his patrons in the British-American Tobacco Company as his sole outlet.

The nationalist movement that overwhelmed Thailand during the late 1930's, coupled with the Japanese occupation starting in 1941, spelled the death of Western holdings— among them the British-American Tobacco Company. To fill the gap left by its departure and to channel revenues into government coffers the Thai Tobacco Monopoly was formed under official auspices. Khun Luang was cut off from former associates; in terms of indigenous institutions, he was divested of the entourage within which he had been an important client. Management of the tobacco trade was placed in the hands of an autonomous government agency which immediately set about the task of forming a new network of entourages, carefully eliminating elements of the former structure in order to consolidate its power. Though Khun Luang

---

[34] Eden, 1958, p. 182; Griffiths, 1967, pp. 437–448.

was permitted to continue as a private producer, all cured leaf was henceforth to be sold to the Tobacco Monopoly at monopsony prices. Because he had been cut off from a position of influence within the network of tobacco industry entourages, he was stripped of his power to determine the market for his product. Further expansion of his tobacco venture had become politically and socially, as well as economically, unfeasible, so he turned his energies in new directions.

As the War subsided, Khun Luang directed his attentions increasingly to tea experimentation. His theory that the North is well suited to tea and that, in fact, miang shrubs are themselves identical with the Assamese varieties of tea in their wild, unpruned form was ridiculed by the Bangkok tea merchants whom he tried to interest in his envisioned venture. His principal experimental station was located at his orange orchards near Ban Pong, adjoining the Research Area.[35] Higher in the hills, to the west of this site, (at the upland Thai hamlet of Pang Huai Thad), he had set up a pilot hand-operated green-tea factory supplied with raw leaf brought in by local miang producers. The high-quality product which it was capable of turning out reinforced his suspicions. Its success proved not only that tea could be produced in the Northern hills but that large tracts of mature bushes were immediately available if their owners could be persuaded to turn from their traditions of relying solely on miang sales and intimate entourage relations with their *pau liang* to cultivation of tea for sale to large-scale processing plants.

Construction of a mechanized factory was begun at the

[35] More recently, a government-run agricultural experiment station at Fang (northern Chiengmai Province) has attempted to work with tea and popularize its local production. See Campbell, 1963, pp. 20–22.

site of the former hand-operated facility in 1949. It entailed a heroic effort. For instance, the factory's tea drier, a particularly cumbersome piece of equipment, required a month's labor of thirty men to be dragged the six kilometers up the mountain from the nearest road; a path had to be hacked through the jungle for it, streams had to be forded, steep slopes had to be graded, quagmires had to be contended with. Other machinery required corresponding efforts. Though the factory was completed in 1951 it was not until two years later that a dirt road could be completed to link it with the lowlands and the regional highway during the dry season.

Khun Luang's original intent was to rely on independent miang smallholders to supply the factory's raw leaf inventory, a scheme of enterprise patterned after the traditional Chinese system. It was thought that in this way the difficulties of recruiting, training, supervising, and caring for a resident labor force—a seemingly endemic problem of plantation operations—could be avoided. For reasons to be considered below, this procedure proved costly, and Khun Luang was forced to alter his plans.

At an early date he decided to integrate smallholders into his operations by purchasing miang gardens and then redistributing them to peasant households rent-free, the only requirement being that tenants sell all their crops to the tea factory (at bargain rates). This variant proved as unmanageable as the original procedure, for among other problems, tenants frequently chose not to abide by the agreement, disposing of their crops as miang to local *pau liang*. Also, the absence of clear laws on upland land tenure (see Chapter 5) made him fear that investment in scattered miang garden holdings would not be secure.

By 1960, Khun Luang had decided to develop a fully integrated plantation (the Chiengdao Tea Plantation) which would be free to rely on its own resources for its raw leaf inventory. Extensive land clearing and terracing was begun on hillsides neighboring Pang Huai Thad and sloping toward Pang Kud and the Lahu village of Huai Thad, a project which continued well into 1964. As plantation fields approached maturity, scattered miang garden holdings were resold to local peasant households. The long-term trend of operations has thus been toward consolidation and vertical integration. This trend has extended, as we shall see, to Khun Luang's marketing operations as well.

About 200 acres of the plantation's land had been planted in tea by 1963, but only 16 acres or so were considered to have reached maturity. It thus still remained necessary to purchase the bulk of raw leaf inventory from local miang smallholders. At the close of that year the Land Department of the Ministry of Interior granted the plantation a concession for 800 acres (including previously planted land) for the purpose of fashioning a model modern enterprise. Only at this late date, therefore, did Khun Luang receive a right to his tenure; the concession sharply curtailed his risk, thereby giving him freer rein to play out his hand. The concession is to run fifty years, a unique departure from the standard twenty-year term formerly granted without exception to land-development schemes in Thailand. Khun Luang requested the thirty-year extension by arguing that a shorter grant would not warrant the anticipated investment. That he overcame political precedent stands as a tribute to his ability to gain admission to entourages in politically advantageous circles after his previous fall from grace upon the establishment of the Thai Tobacco Monopoly.

The vitality of the concession has been enhanced by a public loan of five million baht, which will finance the construction of a larger and more modern factory near the present location, its size adequate to absorb the expected yield of all plantation fields at maturity. Because of the limited supply of tea seedlings (for which a special nursery had been established), only 50 acres were planted in the year following recepit of the loan. These gardens are expected to reach picking maturity by 1970. Ultimately, it is hoped, all 800 acres will be planted with a total of six million shrubs and worked by a resident labor force of over a thousand families.

Difficulties in marketing processed tea from the local facilities were for some years as great as those associated with the acquisition of adequate raw-leaf inventory to keep the factory running. Khun Luang's attempts to interest Bangkok's Chinese tea wholesalers in his product consistently met with failure.[36] His search for buyers led him at an early date to fabricate his own wholesaling outlet, a "Chinese" firm complete with Chinese personnel and façade. The purpose of this stratagem was to persuade retailers that the product was but another imported brand. When the ruse was discovered by rival wholesalers, the firm's bankruptcy followed, bringing an estimated loss of over two million baht.

A more fruitful tactic following the failure of this scheme was Khun Luang's organization of the Thai Tea Association, a group of fourteen small processors and merchants with himself as president. With this pressure group as his justification (or, in indigenous logic, with this entourage providing him the requisite stature and contacts), he could legitimately approach the government with a plan to develop

[36] The wholesale tea trade in Thailand has long been controlled by Chinese merchants and Western trading concerns. The refusal of the former group to accept domestically produced tea is due primarily to family ties with overseas producers and traders. The latter group find Thai tea unacceptable because they have obligations to parent companies which own their own tea estates in other Asian countries.

the tea industry. He apparently found a receptive audience (or amenable patrons), for in 1957 the Public Warehouse Organization, an agency of the Ministry of Economic Affairs, began forcibly wholesaling domestic tea to importers. The agency's operations are financed by a 5 per cent commission on domestic tea sales, a small price for Khun Luang to pay when the alternative is no sales at all. The marketing problem has thus been absorbed by the public sector with the virtual guarantee that all Thai tea will find buyers (the role of the Public Warehouse Organization in the tea trade is statistically reviewed in Table 8). As sponsor (i.e. patron) of the domestic tea trade and as willing participant (i.e. client) in Public Warehouse Organization dealings, Khun Luang has in effect built himself a vertically integrated operation from raw leaf to retail good. By skillfully manipulating his fellow producers and government connections he has re-entered the network of elite entourage formations in a superior position.

Inventory and Factory Operations

Khun Luang's tea-producing operations consist of three sectors: factory, fields, and smallholdings. The original cost of the entire venture has been largely concentrated in the factory; it is estimated to total 1.3 million baht. For accounting purposes, however, the current market value of plant and machinery may be considered nil; the original investment has been fully amortized. This estimate excludes improvements to land, which have gained a sizable *real* value with clearing, terracing, and planting in tea shrubs and shade trees. But because this property falls in the public domain (Khun Luang being merely its concessionaire) it, too, has no *market* value.

Operating expenses for the factory, which is equipped to manufacture black tea dust, a commercial variety sold mostly to restaurants, may be summarized as follows for 1963: fuel, 6,870 baht; maintenance, 5,031 baht; operations, 11,000 baht; total, 22,901 baht.[37] Of the total, 16,333 baht went for wages; even in the factory, then, labor costs predominate. Ancillary expenses, not included in this total, were maintenance of the dirt road (3,869 baht) and maintenance of a truck used to haul plantation supplies and processed tea between the factory and Chiengmai Town (expense undetermined).

In 1963 the 90,706 kilograms of raw leaf which arrived at the factory permitted it to operate 151 days on a single-shift basis. Twenty-four hour capacity, which would require nearly two metric tons of input, has never been reached, though the plant is outfitted to permit night work. On a 270-day single-shift annual schedule (leaving three months of shutdown during the tea-bush dormancy season) the factory could process over 160 metric tons of raw leaf. It thus falls short by nearly half of exploiting its current potential on a single-shift basis alone.

A typical day's factory operations require approximately fifteen workers, the number fluctuating with the intensity of work. Included are machine operators, wood stokers, leaf conveyors, and a supervisory technician. All plantation wage earners take shifts in the factory at their standard pay. However, they prefer field work to the factory, primarily because supervision is relatively lax in the field, but also because most laborers are unfamiliar with and awed by mechanized operations.

The plantation's tea fields had only partially reached picking maturity by the end of 1963. Aggregate output of the sixteen acres that had come of age had reached a magnitude

[37] Data on factory, personnel, and inventory costs are derived from Khun Luang's ledgers, which he permitted me to review and transcribe in summary form.

far short of that sufficient to supply the factory with adequate raw leaf inventory; plantation output had, in fact, not improved significantly since 1958 (see Table 4). As newly planted fields mature, however, this volume is expected to increase above its current eleven metric tons per annum.

Table 4. Tea picking, purchasing, and processing, Chiengdao Tea Plantation, 1958–1963 (kg.)

Year	Pickings from plantation fields	Purchases from tenants	Purchases from independent producers	Total inventory *	Factory output †	
					Green tea	Black tea
1958	10,220	2,652	160,103	172,975		33,863
1959	9,907	2,124	238,572	256,628		60,283
1960	10,413	2,663	74,658	87,734	83	20,345
1961	11,463	4,741	102,762	118,966		28,599
1962	11,230	5,215	32,721	49,266	2,207	9,038
1963	10,941	5,841	73,924	90,706	2,730	15,149

Source: Derived from Chiengdao Tea Plantation ledgers.

* Total inventory for 1959 included 6,025 kg. of processed green tea purchased from local independent producers to raise the quality of black tea dust to minimal wholesale requirements.

† The manufacturing process reduces the weight of the product to about one-fifth its raw state.

The picking season lasts from April through November, though it can be extended through December in years of unusually low inventory. Unlike plucking for miang, tea harvesting is a continual chore, for severe pruning of the bushes forces constant regeneration of fresh leaf; harvesting does not interrupt leaf regrowth because only the freshest flush is plucked, leaving the mature leaf to provide the plant with respiratory vigor. A labor force which in 1963 totaled 439 performs field chores, though less than 20 per cent of these laborers remain resident throughout the year. Between twenty and forty employees tend the ten-acre tea nursery, which takes on particular importance because it nurtures the plants which form the source of tea shrubs for the plantation's expansion program.

To supplement plantation pickings, raw leaf is purchased from tenants of Khun Luang's miang gardens. Of the many scattered smallholdings he once possessed, he retained only five in 1963, totaling ten acres and furnishing the factory with less than six metric tons of raw leaf. Tenants are charged no rent on the condition that they sell only to the factory. Rent is implicit, however, in price terms, which tend to fluctuate about half a baht per kilogram below the plantation's buying price from independents. Tenants have furnished raw leaf in steadily increasing amounts; between 1958 and 1963 the quantity rose by more than 200 per cent (see Table 4), primarily because of improved bush yields as tea pruning and related techniques have been learned.

Since its first year of operations, the plantation has relied primarily on independent smallholders for its inventory. By 1959 it was purchasing raw leaf from 237 peasant households (see Table 5), some situated as far as eight miles from the factory site. Following this peak year a program to reduce the number of independent suppliers was activated in keeping with Khun Luang's policy of consolidation. Table 5 shows that by 1963 this program had resulted in a decrease to 69 independent suppliers. Of this total, 24 sold their entire output to the factory and may be considered to have been drawn entirely into the vortex of the plantation economy. In 1963 these 24 households earned 81,835 baht (3,410 baht per household) from tea sales. Total plantation purchases from independent suppliers in that year amounted to 142,186 baht. Though the annual number of suppliers has declined to one-third its peak figure, annual sales per household have continued to fluctuate around a bench-mark value of 2,000 baht (Table 5).

The entrepreneur's decision to diminish his reliance on independent suppliers resulted in a decline of approximately 65 per cent in the volume of raw leaf purchases between 1959 and 1960 (see Table 4). This policy was in part necessitated by the fact that the chemistry of tea manufacture requires

Table 5. Raw leaf purchases from independent smallholders, Chiengdao Tea Plantation, 1958–1963

Year	Households	Total purchases (baht)	Purchases per household * (baht)	Price per kg. (baht)
1958	187	357,485	1,912	2.23
1959	237	521,963	2,202	2.19
1960	92	169,218	1,839	2.27
1961	102	158,676	1,556	1.54
1962	28	80,868	2,888	2.47
1963	69	142,186	2,007	1.92

Source: Derived from Chiengdao Tea Plantation ledgers.

* Purchases per household for 1963 are based on a total volume of 138,469 baht, which excludes purchases from an undisclosed number of Meo hill tribesmen from distant villages.

a rapid, uninterrupted, and coordinated flow of high-grade leaf from bush to processing operation so as to insure acceptable wholesale quality. Reliance on the bought-leaf scheme works against those requirements: miang gardeners have generally failed to employ proper methods of tea plucking and bush pruning, and the result is low-grade raw leaf; tea transport on shoulder poles and ox-back from distant gardens to the factory causes premature fermentation, which also lowers leaf quality; miang gardeners harvest at fixed intervals rather than continuously throughout the year, resulting in intermittent periods of idleness and overload on the factory's storage capacity and manufacturing operations. Owing to these factors the quality of much of the finished produce was actually lowered below minimum local consumption standards in 1959.

More important than these essentially technological problems have been difficulties deriving from the cultural schism between the plantation and the Thai peasantry. Whereas the above-mentioned technical difficulties result in a finished product of inferior quality, institutional disharmonies result in a wildly fluctuating inventory, an unpredictable production schedule, and a volatile sales record. The details of this conflict will be summarized in Chapter 6. Let it suffice here to state that the plantation's problem in controlling miang smallholders stems from upland Thai peasants' continuing reliance on their traditional entourage relations, which frequently take precedence over their dealings with the plantation. The effect is that smallholders dispose of only residual raw leaf supplies to the plantation; in years of high demand for miang this causes inventory deficiencies on the plantation, in years of low demand it results in inventory gluts.

In 1962, for instance, an unusually large decline below ideal conditions appeared in the number of smallholders supplying the factory and in the volume of raw leaf forthcoming. That year saw the demand for miang rise to unusual heights, drawing all but twenty-eight smallholders away from contact with the plantation. Smaller producers, who tend to maintain the most volatile (because least intimate) relations with their *pau liang*, were the first to be attracted away. Table 5 shows that raw leaf purchases from the small group of relatively large suppliers who remained faithful to Khun Luang consequently reached a high of 2,888 baht per household while total purchases dropped below 81,000 baht. That this aberration was only temporary is indicated by the following year's return to more typical data. The erratic fluctutuations in the value of raw leaf inventory during the period 1958–1963—more than 600 per cent when 1962 is used as the base year (see Table 4)—indicates the instability, and thus the costliness, of factory operations under this supply system.

To compete with smallholders' traditional entourage ties, Khun Luang offers milled rice on credit to all raw leaf suppliers desiring it. In 1963, 9,344 kilograms were distributed in return for 7,958 kilograms of raw leaf (the implicit discount on the rice was about 15 per cent below its retail value, assuming that the rice and the leaf were both of ordinary quality). Another attempt has been the guarantee of a standard minimum buying price of 2.00 baht per kilogram for "acceptable" leaf.[38] Higher rates are granted those who promise in advance to sell their entire annual output to the plantation. These inducements have not appeared effective in drawing smallholders into the plantation economy.

The Labor Force

The plantation is managed on a day-to-day basis by a salaried staff of eight: an inventory purchasing agent, a bookkeeper, and six field, nursery, and factory foremen. Most

[38] Khun Luang's policy of reducing sources of supply was instrumented through the use of "acceptable" as an ambiguous purchasing standard. Since 1960, raw leaf arriving from distant hamlets has not received the guaranteed minimum price on the grounds that long-distance transport deteriorates the product below "acceptable" quality. The desired commercial effect has followed: these hamlets have curtailed economic relations with the plantation. An undesirable social side effect, however, has also developed. Upland Thai peasants have learned of what they consider arbitrary treatment of some of their fellows by the plantation; the policy has intensified the schism which separates the plantation from the local Thai peasant economy.

of these personnel are Chinese-Thai and have the managerial skill, unremitting attention to detail, and trustworthiness so widely acclaimed of this Southeast Asian minority. Total annual salaries amount to 39,000 baht, paid monthly. The staff's diligent supervision of plantation chores leaves Khun Luang free to devote the bulk of his energies to executive responsibilities in his various other interests, particularly his cultivation of influential contacts among the nation's elite.

Wage labor, whch totaled 431 men, women, and children in 1963, is drawn from two distinct sources: Thai peasants from the valley and from upland hamlets, and hill tribesmen from villages hear the plantation. Both Thai and tribal peasants consider employment on the plantation less attractive than participation in their own economic systems as they are ideally conceived. Wage labor on the plantation is accepted as a last resort only because circumstances occasionally do not permit each individual to reap the rewards of the system in which he has been educated to participate. Plantation wage labor permits peasants to subsist; it does not permit them to pursue the goals and aspirations indigenous to their own cultures.

Virtual anomie prevails among the plantation's Thai labor force. Thai laborers invariably apply for work only after all opportunities in the valley and in miang have been exhausted, and they tend to depart at their first chance. Labor turnover is consequently high. A sense of community has not been given a chance to develop. Most Thai employees reside at Pang Huai Thad, which adjoins the factory. The hamlet is marked by an absence of residential stability and concomitant social conditions. Many of its households are only casually acquainted with each other and often do not know neighbors' names, nor do most show other evidences of familiarity; interhousehold kinship within this hamlet is far less common than in neighboring upland Thai hamlets; homes are not kept as sanitary and orderly as is commonly observed elsewhere; and no system of intracommunity leadership has been developed. In sum, the impression is that of a number of strangers temporarily thrown together in a disagreeable endeavor from which each seeks to extricate himself. The only major semblences of order are the uniform employment of all households on the plantation and the barrackslike arrangement of the central group of wooden dwellings (imitating the construction but not the style of superior peasant housing), which have been built by the plantation as an inducement to a resident labor force.

Sixty Thai peasant households could be considered, on the basis of their occupational specializations, to reside within the plantation economy during the census period, February-March 1964.[39] Following the rationale worked out in the preceding chapter to analyze the upland Thai peasant economy's income accounts, the average plantation household had a gross income of about 4,300 baht in 1963, met "subsistence" expenditures of about 3,000 baht, and retained a "surplus" of nearly 1,300 baht (disposed of largely for "luxury consumables" and "prestige durables"). Table 6 shows that sources of earnings lay almost exclusively in tea labor and tea sales to the plantation, with households specializing in tea sales finding themselves in superior economic positions, a pattern paralleling the economics of miang production.

Khun Luang took the occasion of the construction of the tea factory in 1949–1950 to befriend the nearby Meo hill

[39] These households are not the sole source of Thai labor, however. Some wage earners arrive intermittently at the plantation from miang-cultivating households in neighboring upland Thai hamlets, particularly during the slack months between miang harvests.

tribesmen of Phapucom and use their services as porters and construction workers. He has more recently aided this particularly impoverished village with gifts of rice and sundry other goods; in his effort to attract labor he willingly paid the village's way back from southern Chiengmai in 1960. Concurrently, some Meo have begun to resort to wage labor on the plantation. In 1963 Meo wage labor was provided primarily by women and children during the slack seasons of

Table 6. Occupational hierarchy and income uses per household, by occupational specialization, Village Twelve tea industry, 1963–1964

Occupational specialization	Gross income (baht)	"Subsistence" expenditures (baht)	"Surplus" income (baht)	Index of specialization * (%)
Tea sales	5,640	3,737	1,903	86
Tea labor and sales	4,706	3,387	1,319	100
Tea labor	3,565	2,643	922	99
Miscellaneous †	7,650	3,995	3,655	100

* Household income from the occupational specialization as a percentage of total household income.

† Schoolteacher, seamstress, and shopkeeper.

the hill tribe agricultural year. These villagers were joined by an unkown number of casual laborers wandering in from more remote Meo villages to provide the plantation with a total of 150 Meo workers.

A more carefully planned scheme for attracting a resident hill tribe labor force was implemented in 1954 with the grant of a parcel of fertile land to the community of refugees from Burma who founded the Lahu settlement of Huai Thad. In return for the land (which was not really Khun Luang's to give) the Lahu promised to provide wage labor on a prearranged annual schedule. However, the schedule interfered with their own agricultural labor needs. In addition, recurrent incidents growing out of their Thai peasant neighbors' and Khun Luang's attitudes to them strained relations. Of a total local Lahu population of 213, only 80 provided any part-time labor to the plantation in 1963. The original labor agreement had fallen into disuse.

Total regular wage labor in 1963 was thus divided among 161 Thai, 150 Meo, and 80 Lahu. To get a more accurate representation of the significance of each group in plantation operations, however, the gross data must be altered to man-days, of which the Thai furnished nearly 13,000, the Meo 1,500, and the Lahu slightly over 1,200.[40] As Table 7 shows, the average Thai worker thus furnished about 81 man-days of labor, the Meo 10, and the Lahu 15. Since the plantation could have been operated with 88 full-time wage earners at its 1963 volume, the labor turnover rate approached 4.44.[41]

Total wage payments in 1963 amounted to 77,608 baht (discounting 3,205 baht for "special" labor employed in June to transplant tea seedlings), 86 per cent going to the Thai, and 7 per cent each to the Lahu and the Meo. The average Thai laborer received a daily wage of 5.15 baht, the Lahu 4.20 baht, and the Meo 3.80 baht.

A daily wage rate, rather than a piece-goods rate, has been

[40] No man-day adjustments have been made for women and children because of the inadequacy of pertinent statistics.

[41] The maximum number of days worked by full-time resident wage earners on the plantation is 180. On a 180-day schedule the 15,704 man-days of regular labor paid for in 1963 could have been performed by 88 full-time employees. Since the actual number hired was 391, annual turnover was 4.44. (The implicit assumption that the work load is evenly divided over the agricultural year is not unreasonable for a tea plantation, which strives for this very goal as a cost-saving device.)

Table 7. Labor force, Chiengdao Tea Plantation, 1963

Labor category	Labor-ers	Man-days of labor	Man-days per laborer	Total wages and salaries (baht)	Wages and salaries per laborer (baht)	
					Yearly	Daily *
Salaried staff	8			39,300	4,913	
Wage labor:						
Thai	161	12,986	80.7	66,892	415	5.15
Lahu	80	1,218	15.2	5,083	64	4.20
Meo	150	1,500	10.0	5,633	38	3.80
Special labor †	40	800	20.0	3,205		4.01
Total	439			120,113		

Source: Derived from Chiengdao Tea Plantation ledgers.

* Wage rates differ by sex, age, and seniority but not by ethnic group. Men receive between 5 and 6.50 baht depending on their seniority on the payroll. Women receive between 3 and 4 baht. Children receive smaller wages, depending on their productivity records. Thus, average daily wage statistics by ethnic group reflect different age, sex, and seniority characteristics, with Thai laborers being relatively more heavily represented by adult males of high seniority and Meo laborers being weighted by higher proportions of women and children intermittently employed.

† Special labor was hired during the month of June to transplant tea seedlings to newly terraced gardens. Because this was a nonrecurring expenditure and because these laborers were hired for that one month only, the relevant data are segregated and average wages on a yearly basis have not been computed.

adopted because the latter system has resulted in low-quality pickings, though it has also provided appreciably larger harvests during periods when it has been in force. Conversely, the system in use in 1963–1964 proved difficult to manage because pickers tended to slow down their rate of work unless closely attended. Though the foreman system which has been instituted to cope with this difficulty does not result in as rigid a work situation and as controlled an inventory as it suggests, it has gone far toward destroying the atmosphere of mutual trust requisite for development of the traditional patron-client relationship within which Thai peasants have been conditioned to act.

The Plantation Income Accounts

Plantation expenses in 1963 were estimated at 349,000 baht. Of this amount, 44 per cent was paid out for raw leaf inventory, 34 per cent for labor, 9 per cent for field management (net of labor), 8 per cent for marketing, 3 per cent for various incidentals (including road maintenance and employee benefits), and only 2 per cent for factory operations (net of labor). Labor costs fell well below the 60 per cent typical of tea plantations because the preponderance of raw leaf was purchased directly from smallholders, making labor costs an implicit element in inventory value.

The plantation's revenues are more difficult to estimate than its costs, for no written accounts are kept (at least none known to me), nor are Public Warehouse Organization records open to public review. Factory output by volume is known for the years 1958–1963, however. By imputing the average wholesale price for the product at 22 baht per kilogram (the average price at which the domestic product is sold by the Public Warehouse Organization), 1963 gross sales can be estimated at 393,338 baht, 10.5 per cent of the Public Warehouse Organization's gross revenues for that year (see Table 8).

Since estimated gross sales were some 393,000 baht and estimated total costs were 349,000 baht in 1963, net profits for that year may be imputed at 44,000 baht, an 11 per cent rate of return on gross sales and a 3 per cent return on the estimated original investment of 1.3 million baht. Compared with interest rates ranging from 5 to 7 per cent on time deposits

Table 8. Tea marketing: Public Warehouse Organization and Chiengdao Tea Plantation, 1958–1963 (in thousands of baht and
percentages)

Year	(1) Tea imports *	(2) Public Ware- house sales	(3) Aggregate effective demand for tea *	(4) Domestic produc- tion as % of demand *	(5) Chiengdao plantation sales †	(6) Plan- tation as % of domestic produc- tion †
1958	30,086	2,213	32,299	6.9	(745)	(33.7)
1959	32,836	3,218	36,054	8.9	(1,326)	(41.2)
1960	32,428	3,480	35,908	9.7	449	12.9
1961	32,512	3,488	36,000	9.7	629	18.0
1962	33,127	3,629	36,756	9.9	25	0.7
1963	20,921	3,747	24,668	15.2	393	10.5

Source: (1): Thailand, Ministry of Economic Affairs, Department
of Customs, *Annual Statement of Foreign Trade of Thailand* (annual
issues, 1959–1964). (2): Thailand, Ministry of Economic Affairs, Public Warehouse Organization, personal communication concerning tea
sales receipts, 1964. (3): (1) + (2). (4): (2) ÷ (3). (5): Table 4,
"Factory output," × 22 baht per kg. (6): (5) ÷ (2).

* The appreciable decline in tea imports and effective demand in
1963, and consequently the rise in the percentage of domestic demand
satisfied by domestically produced tea, was due to a sudden change
in Public Warehouse tea import restrictions in that year.

† Aggregate wholesale value of plantation tea sales is estimated on
the basis of an imputed price of 22 baht per kg. The relatively low
quality of output in 1958 and 1959 caused the price to drop below
this imputed value; the inaccurate resultant sales values have been
placed in parentheses.

and with interest rates in the unorganized money market as
high as 5 per cent per month, Khun Luang's investment cannot be considered to have borne out expectations if it is
assumed that the venture was fundamentally profit motivated and that it had passed through its gestation period by
1963.

Neither of these assumptions holds true in the present instance. First, Khun Luang declares, and his actions corroborate, that he does not expect his tea venture to come of age for at least another decade. His recently inaugurated expansion program certainly will not contribute to revenues for several years. It was only in 1959–1960 that he altered his plans from expansion on the bought-leaf factory model to one of full-scale plantation organization. Thus, current profit rates cannot be accepted as final evidence of the firm's financial success.

Second, profits have not been Khun Luang's sole motive in developing the plantation. His actions and statements are marked by his ambivalence toward the commercial orientation in which he was schooled by Western business and colonial contacts during his youth and toward the entourage orientation indigenous to Thailand. The latter of these seemingly irreconcilable world views carries overtones of benevolent patronage of the peasant people who labor for him, if civic duty toward his plantation population. This approach is reflected in the Theravada Buddhist philosophy which Khun Luang is fond of reciting: physical comfort lies at the periphery, not the center, of the life process; psychic tranquility and satisfaction (*sabai*) come as rewards for sharing wordly possessions and privileges with one's fellows at the expense of physical convenience (*saduak*). Actions springing from this world view raise the individual not only within the cosmic hierarchy, assuring reincarnation in superior form, but also in public esteem during the present lifetime; for only through renunciation of hedonistic tendencies and their replacement with a spirit of compassion, charity, and consideration can the individual's position on the scale of accumulated merit be recognized by his fellows.[42]

Khun Luang's entrepreneurial training conflicts with his Thai heritage.[43] He has accepted the commercial philosophy that wealth accumulation through scientific management of innovative schemes is a primary life goal. Yet, he retains his regard for the cultivation of mutually satisfying and beneficial interpersonal ties through his largess, always accompanied by the promise of more to come. This ambivalence in world views stands as a microcosmic expression of the conflict between the entourage and the market as alternative institutional paradigms, a conflict between the indigenous and the alien which troubles the elite of Thailand as of other underdeveloped nations.[44] In visualizing, planning, and introducing a new crop and mode of production into North Thailand, Khun Luang has attempted to rationalize his behavior in terms of both systems, thereby resolving the conflict by seeking both private and social gain in a single

[42] Lucien Hanks, 1962, 1247–1261.

[43] It has been pointed out that the conflict between social duty and self-gratification is characteristic of Western entrepreneurs as well as of Thai (note, for instance, the many references to the civic responsibility of the business executive in such works as Mason, 1959), and that it is therefore specious to point to the Thai heritage as its source in the present instance. This argument misses the mark: the dimensions of the conflict between commerce and the entourage are so overwhelming as to be patently different from the superficial, Madison Avenue–inspired community involvement campaign of the American industrialist, not only in magnitude but also in kind. In the commercial setting, the social repercussions of enterprise must be constantly brought to the entrepreneur's attention (by, for instance, several years of exposure in the graduate business school classroom), and it is rare to find a businessman losing any sleep over the matter. In Thailand the problem is uppermost in the "entrepreneur's" mind without anyone bringing it to his notice, for it is self-evident in the confrontation of cultures with which he must cope.

[44] This conflict is treated further in Van Roy and Cornehls, 1969; and Van Roy, 1970.

venture. Unlike the classical entrepreneur, who in the competitive setting unknowingly or disinterestedly works for the betterment of the community at large in his effort to maximize his own returns, Khun Luang strives for both ends in single actions only through a constant and vigorous conscious effort.

In conclusion, though technological matters present the Chiengdao Tea Plantation with no insurmountable problem, particularly as its major financial worries have been lessened by generous public assistance, its operations insofar as they relate to labor relations and supply contacts portend less favorably for the future. A decade of educating and enticing landless lowland Thai, miang smallholders, and tribesmen to the opportunities of tea has come to an unresolved and therefore unsatisfactory conclusion. The plantation has failed to attain its objective of freedom from unpredictable inventory supply through the expedient of strengthening ties between the entrepreneur and his staff on the one hand and raw leaf suppliers and wage earners on the other. Only those in dire straits have turned to the plantation; it has failed to make itself an attractive alternative to livelihood in upland peasant economies.

The continuing existence of these difficulties is traceable directly to the cultural climate in which they have been generated. The specific points of friction between the plantation and local people (to be returned to in Chapter 6) are superficial symptoms of a clash of economic systems. Though the Chiengdao Tea Plantation is Thai operated, it is a Western product. It has not avoided the institutional clash with indigenous economies which have traditionally been ridden over rough-shod by foreign-owned tea estates; it has only dampened the blow by recognizing the cultural gap and by seeking to deal with it. It has not solved the problem because the entrepreneur has not been willing to foresake the profit motive, the major institutional constraint on the plantation both as an efficient unit of economic activity and as a cultural enclave.

Chapter 5

THE PUBLIC SECTOR

Indigenous Political Systems

Each of the economic systems analyzed in the preceding chapters is supported by political structures that distribute power in such a way as to activate individual motivations to the maintenance of the system's stability and continuity. Political institutions, insofar as they serve important functions in ordering economic life in the Northern Thai uplands, have been alluded to in passing in the preceding discussions. Here these threads will be drawn together in an attempt to specify how political institutions in each upland culture preserve economic stability. An analysis of the linkage between polity and economy contributes to an explanation of the dynamics of economic interaction and change among the upland cultures, which will be considered in the following chapter.

The Hill Tribes

The tribal institutions that are most critical in determining the politics of contact with neighboring peoples relate to territoriality. The concept of the nation-state is unknown in the tribal world, as is the related but less formal concept of ancestral homelands. Only at the village level are institutions employed to deal with the distribution and use of land and its fruits among the tribal population. Here, tenure rules pertain only to swiddens and household sites, the lands cleared by the village but divided among households to be individually cultivated and inhabited. Unused sites (excluding swidden plots on short-term fallow) fall outside the tribal institutional rubric; they are free to all. Similarly, there is no division of hunting territories among villages or tribes.

Land is claimed solely in crop usufruct. Property rights pertain to crops under cultivation rather than to the land itself. Thus, the concept of inheritance in land (though not in crops) is absent. Limited institutionalization in regard to land use appears to stem from the land surplus which tribal villages have traditionally faced. In a situation where land can be treated as a free resource—a situation which is beginning to fade away in fact but not in tribal conception —it has not been necessary to develop institutions to cope with the problems associated with limited territories.

Continuing political integration does not ordinarily pass beyond the village level among the hill tribes, although, as has been observed earlier, multivillage communities have been thought to exist among the Lahu, and among wealthy villages of all these tribes extravillage political dominance may be achieved through the provision of credit in return for extended labor obligations, which sometimes fade into slavery. Occasionally, too, villages that possess headmen of outstanding sagacity, or shamans of widespread reputation, or practitioners of other highly respected skills, may attain dominance over their neighbors.

Within the village, formal political authority is vested in the headman, ordinarily a wealthy village elder of an important lineage selected by adult village males for an unspecified term. One of the most divisive problems facing the Lahu village of Huai Thad is its ambiguous authority structure, for both the headman and the Christian "teacher" have been invested with much the same powers; the problem is one of fitting Christian political doctrine to tribal traditions and has been instrumental in fragmenting the village. Similarly, the failure of the headman of the Meo village of Phapucom to pull his community out of its protracted economic depression (through no fault of his own) has lowered his prestige and turned villagers to their spirit doctor, producing a subtle rivalry for power and fragmenting political organization.[1]

Tribal polity at the village level remains largely "informal," or embedded in institutional arrangements which require conformity to traditions of social responsibility that carry generally accepted rewards and penalties. I suspect, for instance, that kin and wealth relationships within the village, rather than the headman's decisions as autocratic leader, govern field-site distribution, the when and where of village migration, and household arrangement, despite the headman's (or the "elders' ") purported absolutism in such matters.

The institution of wealth- and income-sharing among prosperous and impoverished village households ordinarily acts as political stabilizer as well as economic leveler. It actually operates in the agriculturally unpredictable upland environment as a form of diffused reciprocity, a kin-group, and on a more generalized basis a village-wide, insurance scheme to guard against household crop crises. Goods are transferred among households not in anticipation of known returns from

[1] Lucien Hanks notes that "in former times the tribal elder was probably the same person as the religious leader. The headman with secular functions seems to have risen late in response to colonial demands. . . . Thus modern pressures on secular leaders, if unwithstood, may push the tribe toward a former state of affairs without particular damage to tribal organization" (personal communication, October 1969).

the receiving household at a known future date but in the expectation that reciprocity will be forthcoming when the mix of harvest surpluses and deficits among village households is altered. Intravillage prestations are thus actually the tribal version of a progressive income tax and transfer (or income maintenance) system, with levies being imposed by convention on the wealthy to assure the subsistence of the village poor. The collapse of this arrangement—as for instance, in the case of factionalization between incessantly hardworking (and surplus-reaping) households and incorrigibly indolent (and deficit-earning) households—leads to a continuing one-way redistribution of income and wealth, and results in the destruction of the village as a political entity.

The hill tribes, in sum, lack much of a "formal," or functionally discrete, public sector. Political structure remains largely implicit within "informal" arrangements; in other words, polity is embedded in the general matrix of economic and social institutions. However, in the institutional realm of greatest concern, the territorial interaction of the tribal economy with its neighbors, the tribes lack even an *in*formal political structure; the tradition of treating unswiddened land as a free good, for instance, leaves the tribes at the mercy of alien land tenure institutions which may be introduced to fill the vacuum.

The Upland Thai

Only the most superficial analysis would consider Thai political institutions to be composed solely of the bureaucratic superstructure which is imposed by the nation-state. The Thai peasantry generally deals with the bureaucracy and its formal rules and regulations as alien intrusions into the indigenous polity. What this indigenous polity consists of is clearly visible among upland Northern Thai peasants, whose physical, social, and economic distance from the center of bureaucratic power is so great that they operate largely autonomously of official interference. The bureaucratic intrusions into the upland Thai community have been specified in Chapter 3; they include the requirement that certain clerical functions be performed by local headmen, that villagers pay land taxes, that children attend school, that local people submit to occasional harassment by visiting functionaries from various government departments. These various articulations with the nation-state are weak, as is seen in the frequency with which the rules and regulations are circumvented, ignored, or misapplied locally.

Indigenous political life among the upland Thai is similar to that of the hill tribes in that it is embedded in the broader institutional configuration. As among the tribes, power in the Thai peasant community is fundamentally a function of the household's labor resources. Beyond its internal labor capabilities, the household improves its political position by entering into reciprocative arrangements with its neighbors (that is, by forming or joining an entourage), thereby indirectly extending its labor resource base. The entourage is as much a political as an economic vehicle. It differentiates power positions just as it does economic positions by arranging patrons and clients in a closely knit hierarchical network. The superior household gains a larger voice in the affairs of the community as it gains control over a greater number of clients. In this perspective, it is not the corporate community or the supervening bureaucracy but the entourage which is the unit of political life.

Though Thai peasants pay taxes to the central government (both explicitly and, through government-controlled price adjustments, implicitly), they fail to see any benefits accruing from them. To the peasant, the socially desirable tax system is implicit in the entourage. Patrons receive material benefits ("income taxes") from their clients relative to their clients' "abilities to pay," and they return goods and services ("transfers") to them on appeal or as a matter of course to meet subsistence and other needs.

In the Thai system the guarantee of household security differs from that prevalent within the tribal system in being fragmented among specific reciprocating dyads (patrons and clients) rather than being diffused on a kin-group and village-wide reciprocative basis. This difference permits greater political and economic differentials to emerge within the upland Thai peasant community than in the neighboring tribal village; it also permits greater social mobility in the Thai than in the tribal world while simultaneously introducing a greater element of personal insecurity.

Unlike the hill tribes, the upland Thai possess an established set of institutions defining land tenure. These institutions have been adapted from lowland traditions developed in a setting wherein superior wet-rice land is not regarded as a free resource, although unimproved arable land has historically been plentiful. The concept of national territoriality is vague in the peasant mind, though the peasantry does recognize that all land from Burma to Laos "belongs to the King" and that unclaimed land within this realm may be occupied under conditions of squatter's rights. Thus, miang gardens cleared out of the jungle and nurtured to maturity become household property, to be worked and disposed of as the household pleases; this understanding is reinforced by the act of registering gardens with the commune headman and paying annual taxes on them. (That the peasants' understanding of land tenure arrangements does not coincide with the state's legal interpretations is a problem discussed in a later section.)

In sum, the indigenous polity of the upland Thai is an extension of the institutional configuration prevalent among the Thai peasantry (and elite) of the lowlands. Power is expressed in terms of entourage relationships. Politics are thus highly personalized, with political leverage fragmented among innumerable dyadic contacts. Land tenure is also highly individualized; procedures have been developed whereby holdings may be secured as private property. The relative scarcity of superior garden plots and the many years of care involved in reaping a return, in combination with the history of institutional adaptation from the neighboring lowlands, account for the emergence of a highly developed land tenure arrangement in an upland environment that at first glance appears to provide land in superabundance. Among the upland Thai as among the hill tribes, however, political arrangements remain largely informal.

The Plantation

The political structure of the plantation is polarized between the entrepreneur and his salaried staff on the one hand and the wage-earning labor force, including independent suppliers, on the other. Plantation life centers on the two-way flow between the labor force and the entrepreneur of raw leaf in return for a money wage. An antipodal reciprocitive relationship between a controlling center and a subordinate periphery here replaces the diffused form prevalent among the hill tribes and the fragmented form found among the upland Thai; I will refer to this exchange nexus as redistribution.[2]

The depersonalization, or desocialization, of the plantation economy in the presence of a vast, undefined agrarian proletariat (composed in large part of the landless Northern Thai

[2] See Polanyi et al., eds., 1957, passim, esp. pp. vii–ix, 250–256.

188

peasantry within shouting distance of the plantation) that competes with the resident labor force for plantation jobs, leaves bargaining power overwhelmingly at the center. Any laborer withdrawing his services partly or wholly from the plantation in an effort to sway conditions in his favor (in imitation of his options within the typical entourage) knows he will find himself separated from his job; he is readily replaced by substitutes.[3] Though Khun Luang does not pursue his politically advantageous position with the rapacity which untrammeled profit-seeking might warrant, he nevertheless uses his position in ways which appear to the labor force capricious and exploitative and against which they know of no recourse except dissociation.

To the Thai labor force, the plantation appears a caricature of the entourage because it breaks with all reciprocative conventions. The entrepreneur appears as a *pau liang* of such inordinate power that they as clients possess no political leverage worthy of contributing to the entourage. He also appears to the labor force to be so far removed socially that he is unresponsive to his clients' felt needs; he could do much for them, they think, but he fails to meet his responsibilities. For these reasons and because of the insecurity fostered by life in the shadow of seemingly arbitrary power, laborers seek escape from the plantation whenever alternative labor opportunities arise. This explains Khun Luang's difficulties in attracting a resident labor force and the concomitant high rate of labor turnover on the plantation.

Khun Luang, as might be expected, does not see his position in quite the same perspective. As has been pointed out in

[3] Through collective action the labor force could gain bargaining strength, but the tradition of the entourage, which proscribes cooperative activity among equals in favor of hierarchical ties between unequals, rules against the formation of labor unions, mass movements, or similar peer groupings in the indigenous Thai setting.

the preceding chapter, he visualizes his "enterprise" not only as a profit-seeking venture but as an entourage whereby he raises his rank within the Thai social order. He sees himself as benefactor as well as manager of his labor force and states that he considers his provision of a steady wage and various fringe benefits (housing, wages in milled rice as well as cash, minor medical treatment) to steady employees as indicators of his benevolence. The plantation is to him but one strand of a wider-ranging network of relationships, however. He is, for instance, much more concerned on a day-to-day basis with his place as patron of the entourage formalized as the Thai Tea Association and as client in the entourage of elite participants from which he has reaped such benefits as the tea plantation land concession, a government loan, and a guaranteed sales outlet. Though he is aware that the plantation strengthens his hand in dealing with the Thai elite, it is the labor force en masse and not wage earners as individuals who are of political value here. He agrees with his employees that they are of little political relevance on the plantation.

The institutional character of the plantation polity, then, depends in part on the perspective from which it is analyzed. Local people see it as an unappealing, redistributive departure from the entourage; because of its disproportionate or non-reciprocative political structure, they avoid the plantation whenever economically feasible. The entrepreneur sees it as a commercially-oriented entourage, a system in which he benevolently provides for his clients in return for their support as laborers and raw leaf suppliers. From both perspectives, however, the politics of plantation life remain informal and subordinate to the ongoing economic relationship between center and periphery, with power concentrated at the center.

The Local Bureaucratic Superstructure

The form of each of these indigenous political systems is a reflection of the dominant economic pattern. Power is diffused among the hill tribes through village-wide reciprocative patterns and frequent, unpredictable crop fluctuations; among the upland Thai it is fragmented among entourage participants through similar reciprocative conventions which, however, cross hamlet lines; on the plantation it is concentrated at the center of a redistributive arrangement of participants. In all three systems polity is embedded in the wider network of ongoing economic and social relationships; in none is power, as opposed to wealth and status, considered a discrete object of action by the people involved, nor is the "public sector" separate in terms of personnel vested specifically with the authority to regulate power relations.

Each of these systems is self-sustaining in the absence of a formalized public sector; yet each falls within the sphere of a superior political entity, the Thai nation-state, and each is therefore brought into contact with a dominant, formal public sector, the intruding central government bureaucracy. In each case the imposition and enforcement of national policy primarily for the benefit of classes of the citizenry far removed from the Northern hills creates difficulties which interfere with and complicate but do not destroy indigenous social, political, and economic systems. Some of these impositions do benefit local people, but even where they are perceived, the benefits ordinarily are considered to be far outweighed by the burdens which appear to be their inevitable accompaniment.[4]

[4] A summary of the various external political agencies which reach into the Northern hills is provided in Kunstadter, 1967c, pp. 379–394.

The chasm between the Thai bureaucracy, even at the local level, and the hill tribes is of cultural dimensions. Representatives of the two systems deal with one another on separate planes of reasoning. The concept of nation-building, on which government dealings with the tribes are largely founded, is foreign to the tribal mind. Restrictions on crossing national borders, for instance, appear arbitrarily repressive. Similarly, the tribal peoples do not comprehend the rationale behind the government's efforts to suppress opium production, to limit swiddened areas, to relocate tribal villages nearer to the lowlands, and to Thai-ify the tribes through increased exposure to the lowland culture. Historically, political relations between the lowland peoples and the tribes have been strained; this tradition has not been forgotten in the hills, nor is it absent among the lower-level civil servants who most frequently come into contact with tribesmen. Governmental rules and regulations enforced at the local level merely reinforce the traditional hostilities, for to tribesmen they appear to be aimed primarily at eliminating the very freedoms on which their livelihood depends, and local bureaucrats do little to discourage this attitude. The minor successes achieved by the government in its management of tribal affairs have been outweighed by the political strains that interference has perpetuated.

From the point of view of the upland Thai peasantry, government officials from the district officer on up are of such high rank in the Thai social order that they exist in a limbo outside the local network of entourages.[5] Like Khun

[5] The gap between upland Thai peasants and the Thai bureaucracy is, of course, not as great as that between the bureaucracy and tribal people. Thai village and commune headmen serve as bridges across the gap, for they are not only members of the peasant community but, technically, of the bureaucratic hierarchy as well. Tribal village headmen, with a few remarkable exceptions, have no official sanction

Luang, they exercise power which Thai hill dwellers have no means of countering; they are therefore feared and generally avoided, though they are accorded the demonstrations of respect which their high positions in life have earned them. In small part, this situation is an outgrowth of regional resentment against Central Thai supremacy; in part, it is a reflection of the social discontinuity between the peasantry ("those who work for a living") and the civil service ("those who receive a salary"); in larger measure, it is a result of the villagers' lack of knowledge concerning the goverment's contributions to the maintenance and improvement of local life.[6] However, it remains primarily the effect of the widespread inability of the peasant and the local civil servant to participate in common entourages.

This social gap does not exist on the plantation. The entrepreneur's high-reaching connections—known to local officials because of his ability "to get things done" and implicit in his luxurious style of living, his "Bangkok" dress and speech, and his occasional Thai elite and Western guests—places him in a position far more powerful than their own. Even district officers are delighted to receive from him any sign of favoritism and bend over backward to offer him any assistance, for his patronage is considered to carry great weight at higher levels; it therefore raises their status in the eyes of their local acquaintances. Because of Khun Luang's high rank, the plantation may be said to stand politically above the local bureaucracy. The labor force thus finds itself wholly within the power of its employer, without recourse even to the nominal protection of commune and district administrators.

---

from the Thai government and thus have no voice in the bureaucracy.

[6] Moerman, 1961, pp. 4–8.

The local bureaucracy's differential political impact on indigenous systems is clearly demonstrated in its formulation and administration of land tenure regulations. The laws governing land use are enacted at the highest level of the government—since the 1957 *coup d'état*, in fact, by proclamation of of the prime minister. The basic law is broad and ambiguous, requiring that its details be worked out on a pragmatic basis by local enforcing agencies. Land law as it pertains to the uplands falls under the jurisdiction of two agencies, the powerful Land Department (Ministry of Interior) and the relatively weak Forest Department (Ministry of Agriculture).[7] Within these agencies interpretations of the technical details of the law and of the necessity for enforcing particular provisions change as they filter downward to the local administrative level. By the time they reach the local level the intent of the law, itself unclear even at the ministerial level, has become roughly fitted to the *de facto* indigenous situation.[8]

Revolutionary Proclamation Number 41 (1960) states that forests are public domain and that such land may not be turned to private use.[9] Similarly, the Land Code (1954) deals specifically with a class called "state land," which presumably is synonymous with the public domain.[10] These laws do not spell out what land constitutes forest or public domain nor what is to be done with different classes of squatters.[11]

[7] The differing degrees of political leverage of these two agencies are themselves effects of the interplay of entourages within the government. Entourage relationships at the ministerial level are analyzed in Riggs, 1966, pp. 211–310.

[8] Yano, 1968; Seth, 1968.   [9] Premarasami, 1963, esp. pp. 404–406.

[10] Srirachaburutra, 1963.

[11] The vagueness of the Thai law on such matters has been noted by others; for instance: "I have not been able to find a written reference to the law which is supposed to claim for the Thai government all land over 2,500 feet (800 meters) elevation. Presumably house

Such matters are implicitly left to the discretion of local representatives of the Land and Forest departments. The realms of authority of these two agencies have not been carefully defined and differentiated; enforcement of the law becomes at the local level more a contest for power and status between forestry officers and district officers (themselves outposted representatives of competing entourages within the bureaucracy) than an effort to clarify and pursue the intent of the written word.[12] In this contest district officers clearly have the advantage. Forestry officials, intent more on resource conservation than on the immediate effects of such a policy on the upland peasantry, are generally impotent in their efforts to clear the public domain of poachers; not only are they backed by a relatively weak ministry, but their efforts clash with the immediate interests of their local clientele.

District officers, on the other hand, are lax in their enforcement of tenure laws. They generally ignore the presence of hill tribes; when questioned on the matter, they appear uninformed on even the most basic information regarding the tribes—the locations and histories of villages, the magnitudes of populations, the names and linguistic skills of tribal leaders, the trade links between tribal households and the lowlands.[13] By ignoring the tribes, they avoid the tricky problem of dealing with minority groups which they have inadequate power to remove from the "government lands." District officers seem better informed on the essentials of upland Thai hamlets. They appear oblivious, however, of the fact that these hamlets, like the tribal villages, occupy and cultivate the

---

sites, gardens and irrigated fields could be excepted from this if title were registered" (Kunstadter, 1967c, p. 377).

[12] Riggs, 1966, pp. 211–310, 197–199.
[13] Manndorff, 1967, pp. 529–530.

public lands. They treat these hamlets just as they treat those of the lowlands, and the atmosphere of normalcy is reinforced by upland Thai peasants' efforts to appear respectable by registering and paying taxes on their gardens just as they would with wet-rice fields and by following standard procedure in appointing headmen and complying with ordinary bureaucratic directives.[14] The only local resident who appears fully conversant with the technical insecurity of his tenure position is Khun Luang, who has coped with the problem by selling off his scattered holdings and replacing them with a fifty-year concession for 800 acres of plantation land, received directly from the Land Department in Bangkok.

Though the laws remain imprecise and the jurisdictions of administrative agencies continue to overlap, government regulations appear to be consistent in incriminating both upland Thai and tribal peasants as trespassers on the public domain. This implication is confirmed by the plantation's acquisition of a special concession to operate in the same area. The only mitigating element is the vague Thai legal tradition that peasants have some traditional right to take out squatters' rights on the "Kings land."[15] The lack of clarity of the law at the local level, however, permits officials of different departments and ministries to define and discharge their duties pragmatically and in accord with their vested interests. Thus, local forestry officials complain of infringements on the wild tracts and harass upland dwellers, while district officers tend to accommodate or ignore them. Inconsistent bureaucratic administration at the local level only adds to the complexity of relations within and among indigenous economies and be-

[14] As is common in the remote lowlands, many miang gardens are not registered or are only partly registered for tax-evasion purposes, despite the fact that this increases insecurity of tenure. See Yano, 1968, and Moerman, 1968, p. 99.

[15] Yano, 1968, pp. 856–858.

tween them and the bureaucratic superstructure; it has not altered the structures of the indigenous upland systems.

Central Bureaucratic Intervention

The Recent Surge of National Interest

The princely states which for centuries controlled present-day North Thailand did not consider the uplands part of their domains; they left them untouched except for minor trade relations and occasional forays to maintain ascendancy over the tribes and to protect routes of trade and conquest from falling into the hands of neighboring states. This situation was not altered with the establishment of suzerainty over the North by the Central Thai kingdom and by the North's later absorption into the Siamese nation-state. The unified kingdom remained valley-centered; though the uplands fell within its "boundaries" (a concept introduced from the West during the nineteenth century), they and their populations were left largely to themselves.

The historical disinterest of the Central Thai in the uplands and their tribal inhabitants accounts in part for the ambiguity of the law and for the overlapping of local bureaucratic jurisdictions in the hills. During the past decade, however, a series of circumstances has focused international interest in this very area, forcing the Central Thai bureaucracy for the first time to turn its attention to the formulation of clear policies and operational administrative devices concerning the economic development, political security, and social stability of the Northern hill tracts.

In the mid-1950's the United Nations and several major Western powers moved into high gear in their drive to combat the international traffic in narcotics. Thailand was one of the producing countries pressured to diminish the illicit production and export of opium and its derivatives. These efforts culminated in the enactment by the Thai government of Revolutionary Proclamation Number 37 (1958), which prohibited the drug's sale and consumption (though not, explicitly, its production).[16] Despite this pronouncement there is little reason to believe that opium output, estimated in 1962 at more than 75 metric tons (with some venturing to guess it approached volumes as high as 500 metric tons), has been reduced in subsequent years.[17] The root of the opium problem in Thailand lies at the source of production, the Sino-Tibetan hill tribes. The search for a means of halting production has newly involved the Department of Police and several other public agencies in Northern upland affairs.

As interest in the opium problem increased there arose a cry within the Ministry of Agriculture, particularly among forestry officials, that the hill tribes were deforesting the Northern uplands and thus endangering agricultural prospects in the lowlands. The belief gathered force that the form of swiddening practiced by the hill tribes is destructive of watersheds, that it causes flash flooding as well as altered climatic and rainfall conditions. Whether these widespread suppositions have any empirical content remains conjectural. Nevertheless, severe floods accompanying several monsoons during the 1950's left the hill tribes the scapegoats of Northern Thai public opinion. Conservationists estimate that two million acres have been denuded by the tribes at a current rate of 160,000 acres per year. The Department of Forests, having estimated that 40 per cent of deforested land in Thai-

[16] This was not the first act to outlaw opium. The first use of the printing press by the Thai government, in 1839, was to produce 9,000 handbills banning opium smoking and trade by royal proclamation; Thailand, 1965, p. 409. The long series of narcotics-control measures in Thai history traces back at least to 1811; see *Ibid.*, p. 219.

[17] Thailand, 1962, p. 63.

land is the result of swiddening, has demanded the immediate cessation of such practices and has imposed a rarely enforced penalty of five years' imprisonment and a fine of 20,000 baht on illicit forest clearing.[18] Typically, these strictures are raised against the hill tribes; nowhere have I found Thai swiddening, miang gardening, and other Thai peasant uses of the uplands proscribed.

The most pressing problem has arisen more recently, though ripples broke the surface of apathy as early as the early 1950's, when the aftereffects of the Communist revolution in mainland China, ethnic disturbances in Burma, and the political fragmentation of French Indochina stirred population movements whose repercussions were felt in North Thailand. Fears of Communist subversion and insurgency in border areas have more recently arisen at the center of power, resulting in a great intensification of interest in the Northern uplands and a sweeping reappraisal of the impact of pre-existing policies (or more correctly, the lack of them).[19] By and large, restrictive policing measures that have been developed to halt the opium traffic, to preserve the natural upland ecology, and to seal the borders have had a destructive effect on political relations between lowlanders and hill tribes. Tentative efforts have been made to reshape these policies into new ones which will have a net "constructive" effect—namely, to integrate the resident tribes into the Thai nation by, among other things, turning their attention to the cultivation of socially desirable and marketable crops.[20]

[18] Samapuddhi and Suvanakorn, 1962, p. 1.

[19] On the misuse of police powers in combating insurgency see *New York Times*, May 5, 1968, pp. 1, 3. The border problem is reviewed by Jane Hanks, 1967(?).

[20] Though this discussion is not intended to evaluate the emerging hill tribe policy of the Thai government, it is nevertheless interesting to note in passing that one of the major impediments to success lies

A series of complementary programs has been developed to implement this policy. The Border Patrol Police, formed in 1955 to control the Northern frontiers and seal off the borders, have extended their functions to providing educational, medical, vocational, and agricultural services to the tribes. In 1959 the Ministry of Interior, Department of Public Welfare, formed a Hill Tribes Division, which was given the immediate responsibilities of gathering informaton and establishing a small number of experimental hill tribe land settlements and welfare stations (*nikhom*) in North Thailand, with the aim of working out means of changing the tribes from migratory, opium cultivating "aliens" to sedentary villagers producing products facilitating their integration into the Thai nation. The slow progress of the *nikhom* in attracting tribal villages led the Hill Tribes Division to implement its own mobile development project in 1963; if the tribes wouldn't come to the "developers," the developers would go to the tribes. This was a replication of the Ministry of Defense Mobile Development Unit program, initiated in 1962 as a counterinsurgency device in remote areas of the nation, though primarily in the Northeast. Finally, realizing that great gaps remained in the bureaucracy's understanding of the Northern highlands, the government founded a Tribal Research Center at Chiengmai Town in 1964.

---

in success itself. If the government achieves its goal of relocating a substantial number of tribal villages presently dwelling in Thailand it will have returned extensive swidden territories back to the jungle. Such fertile, fallow lands will serve to invite more villages to migrate into Thailand, perpetuating the very problem the government seeks to eliminate. Of course, in terms of generations of continued effort, the Thai government can in this manner eventually solve the matter by full populating the hills with sedentary tribal villages participating in the Thai economy and nation as full-fledged citizens. In the very long run this policy may thus be of immeasurable benefit. But the goal presently being pursued is of a more short-term nature.

In 1966 it could be said of the *nikhom:* "No spectacular progress has been achieved. . . . the hill stations have not yet made the desired progress." Of the more recent mobile development project it was said that "much more preparation and training of field workers is required." And of the Tribal Research Center the best that could be said was that "A number of research projects are envisaged for the coming years." [21] Obviously, the years since the emergence of a determined public effort to integrate the Northern highlands into the nation have not produced any notable successes. In large measure the lack of success is attributable to the failure to devise a program which is both operational at the tribal level and financially acceptable to the government.

The surge of interest in the Northern highlands in the past decade has brought with it a recognition that the threefold problem of ensuring political stability, conserving the upland ecology, and eliminating the narcotics traffic can be coped with more successfully by seeking to develop the hill tribe economy and induce hill tribe culture to move into closer conformity with the lowland civilization than by forcibly preventing tribal villages from migrating, swiddening, and producing opium. Suppression, it has been recognized, cannot succeed without destroying the hill tribes themselves, because the very conditions which would come under attack form essential components of hill tribe culture. Suppressive action can only compound the problem by increasing the incidence of unrest and lawlessness.

The enlightened approach has, however, raised further important questions concerning the proper path of planned culture change: Must tribal life be wholly disrupted, or can critical variables be isolated? Is cultural assimilation (i.e., the Thai-ification of the hill tribes) required, or is mere inten-

[21] Manndorff, 1967, pp. 544, 546, 549.

sification of economic, political, and social linkages adequate? Is a massive effort necessary so that immediate change will be effected, or will a less intensive effort aiming at gradual change accomplish the desired ends with greater certainty and at lower cost? The typically conservative pragmatism of the Thai, reinforced by severe financial constraints, has determined that policy be geared to the premise that tribal acculturation can best be initiated by evolutionary rather than revolutionary action, that the program will be geared to harmonizing and strengthening Thai-tribal ties rather than outright tribal Thai-ification, and that the effort will focus on the tribal culture's most strategic component, its economy.

Nikhom Chiengdao

The most ambitious project to date has been the establishment of hill tribe land settlements and welfare stations (*nikhom*), an idea deriving from the thirty-six such settlements which have been established since 1940 throughout the nation for the relocation of Thai peasant households on virgin lands. As of 1964 four experimental hill tribe *nikhom* had been organized, encompassing some 180,000 acres of the North's uplands and officially housing a total of 992 representatives of four tribes. The immedate obstacle to the success of the *nikhom* thus is blatantly apparent: they have failed so far to attract many tribal villages. In fact, the villages which populated the *nikhom* in 1964 had all been settled there prior to the government's decision to demarcate their sites as settlement areas.

This was the case when in 1960 the central government selected over 30,000 acres in the hills west of Ban Pong and directly south of the landmark mountain, Doi Chiengdao, as one of its first *nikhom* sites. At the time of its establishment, Nikhom Chiengdao was already inhabited by the tribal villages of Phapucom and Huai Thad; the subsequent splitting off of part of Huai Thad to form Ban Yai Suk extended its jurisdiction to a third hill tribe village. Besides these communities, other tribal villages, occupying inaccessible areas to the western end of the *nikhom* are left alone, and a number of Thai upland and lowland hamlets lining its eastern and southern perimeter are considered by the *nikhom* staff to lie outside its area of authority. Among the Thai communities populating the *nikhom* are the miang-producing hamlets of Village Twelve. Furthermore, the lands allocated to the *nikhom* overlap those cultivated by the Chiengdao Tea Plantation under government concession. Since *nikhom* lands supposedly fall under the special jurisdiction of the Hill Tribes Division of the Department of Public Welfare, the Land Department's plantation concession adds an additional complication into the bureaucratic governance of local territories.

Territorial disputes among tribal villagers, upland Thai peasants, and the tea plantation, for instance, contain an element of jurisdictional ambiguity involving the *nikhom* supervisor, the Thai commune headman, the district officer, Khun Luang, forestry officials, and border patrol police. Because hill tribesmen are technically not Thai citizens, the possibility always remains that problems involving them fall outside local authority entirely. This knotty political issue is resolved locally in terms of the prevailing power structure: all parties defer first to the mediation of Khun Luang; if he feels the issue falls beneath his dignity (or if he wishes to pass the buck), or if disputants are loath to bring it to his attention, it becomes the duty of the *nikhom* supervisor, though the district officer often challenges his authority in local matters (the two occupy parallel positions in the power structure and thus find themselves in frequent conflict);

lastly, minor issues are referred to the headmen of tribal villages and Thai hamlets to thrash out, again a frequently unworkable arrangement because headmen invariably take the side of their constituents.

Though the *nikhom* enters into the local power structure as an additional complicating factor, its primary function rests with the hill tribes alone.

The primary purpose of this project is to settle the hill tribes in locations suited to them by way of establishing land settlement project sites along the hill ridges and high plateaus which are the most favored whereabouts of the hill people, and encourage them to migrate to these sites.[22]

Nikhom Chiengdao has been unable to achieve any results to this end. All the tribal inhabitants it presently considers within its jurisdiction were there in 1960, when it was established. It has not attracted other villages, despite occasional efforts, largely because it has been unable to convince them that they might reap any benefits from such a move. To the tribesmen, migration into closer proximity with the Thai, especially into territories under the close supervision of government officials, carries only the terrors associated with possible future infringements on their freedom, such as constraints against out-migration and prohibition of opium cultivation.

The program at Nikhom Chiengdao has consequently shifted to a series of efforts to discover means of attracting tribal villages. These include experimentation with new crops and improved livestock, marketing of tribal produce and artifacts, erection of demonstration sites for introducing new tools and agricultural methods, distribution of medicines and other needed commodities, provision of education in local Thai schools, and construction of basic modern facilities,

[22] Thailand, 1963a, p. 24.

particularly roads. The impact of these efforts on local tribal villages will be noted in the following chapter. It will suffice here to mention that they have not proved sufficiently attractive to entice additional tribesmen into the *nikhom,* nor do they appear to have been effective in altering the economic conditions of local villages, for Phapucom remains in economic depression, Ban Yai Suk retains a cultural insularity that has scarcely been pierced, and Huai Thad has been influenced by its association with the plantation rather than by the *nikhom.*

Nikhom Chiengdao is not only a territory carved out of the uplands and a project aimed at settling the tribal peoples, it is also a community of minor bureaucrats outposted to a remote hill station. It is in this last perspective that the *nikhom* is ordinarily viewed by local people, including *nikhom* personnel themselves. The *nikhom* headquarters is a cluster of eight bungalows nestled on a mountain spur within ready walking distance of local hill tribe villages and the plantation factory. Its population totals twenty-eight, including twelve civil servants charged with operating the *nikhom* (the director, a medical officer, a clerk, a nurse, three drivers, and five laborers) and their families. Despite the hardship conditions their assignment entails and of which they frequently grumble (social isolation, poor supply and transport facilities, inferior education opportunities for their children, virtual exile from the center of opportunity for advancement) they receive only basic civil service salaries. The community in effect forms a weak entourage: the supervisor (its patron) is in turn the client of his superiors in the Public Welfare Department, and the staff serves not only as their titles would suggest but in the many ways necessary to maintain the community's viability.[23]

[23] The organization of the *nikhom* as an entourage has been observed elsewhere: "I was staying in a remote and sleepy government

In keeping with the functional flexibility that marks entourage relations, the *nikhom*'s superiors within the Public Welfare Department have not delegated to the staff a specific list of responsibilities. The staff's operational frame is, however, limited by three classes of explicit policy guides: general objectives have been sent forth in memoranda discussing the hill tribe program's aims as formulated by the central government at the highest level; specific directives are occasionally transmitted to the staff by various superiors, usually on minor matters having to do with visiting dignitaries or the compilation of reports; the composition and magnitude of various activities are financially controlled by allocating the annual operating budget to specific functions and by restricting the budget as a whole. The 1964 budget amounted to 265,000 baht, of which some 70 per cent went for salaries and general upkeep of facilities and equipment, leaving the small remainder to finance the program which it was formed to implement. Within these limits the operations of the *nikhom* have been developed on a pragmatic basis by the resident and staff.

The lure of promotion is a universal motivation underlying civil servant performance. At Nikhom Chiengdao the hope of reassignment away from this isolated outpost forms an additional stimulus. An example was early set by the first su-

agency [Nikhom Chiengdao] when the leader, after many days of absence, returned at 2 A.M. with the terrifying news of an impending visit by a very important dignitary. Since the leader's reputation was at stake, the entire personnel rose from bed to scrub, polish and ready the place. By 10 A.M., when the distinguished visitor [the director general of the Department of Public Welfare, the *nikhom* supervisor's superior] arrived, all stood smiling in thir pressed uniforms ready to receive him. Without specific contracts to work a given number of hours per day or to receive extra pay for additional work, an entourage is ready at any time for any kind of work" (Lucien Hanks, 1966, p. 58).

pervisor, who received a promotion to an urban post within two years of his initial appointment. Hope of transfer to a higher salaried, more comfortable assignment nearer Bangkok does much to counteract the incentive-sapping discontent with the *nikhom* assignment. The staff recognizes that the key to promotion lies in easily recognizable accomplishment. For this reason they focus attention on conspicuous achievements; operations which entail little tangible evidence are de-emphasized.

Thus, road extension and maintenance, the most conspicuous of accomplishments in this jungle environment, is high on the list of staff responsibilities. Vying in importance is maintenance of the headquarters plant and grounds, which are kept well scrubbed and raked, rose bushes watered and pruned, and badminton court carefully groomed. The visitor's first impression is incredulity at finding a posh resort in the midst of such a primeval setting. High priority is similarly granted the construction of a school house for hill tribe children near the headquarters site (though the school will be over an hour's walk each way from two of the three local tribal villages). Conspicuous, too, are carefully maintained model tea gardens, livestock pens, and fruit trees. A further example of the preoccupation with visible (though substantively negligible) results is the "redevelopment" of the hill tribe village of Huai Thad, a project which has involved bulldozing a road into the center of the village, building fences, and rearranging and reconstructing dwellings. To this list of activities must be added the task of hosting visitors, approximately 100 per year according to a highly prized and closely guarded guest ledger.

Less conspicuous work, and therefore less enthusiastically undertaken by the staff, is dominated by the incessant burden of keeping records and transmitting reports to superiors; this chore involves much of the time of the clerk, supervisor, and medical officer. The medical officer, a dedicated male nurse, has the task of inspecting and reporting on health conditions in tribal villages on a biweekly basis; he also treats local Thai patients. The three tractor drivers maintain a continuous shuttle service between the *nikhom* and Chiengmai Town transporting guests and supplies. In this category of tasks also falls the supervisor's chore of marketing small quantities of hill tribe produce and artifacts in Chiengmai Town. Attempts are constantly made to advertise these activities to superiors by photographing accomplishments and submitting this evidence with staff reports.

Least tangible of all functions is the development of rapport between the staff and local hill tribesmen. Little success is evident. The staff lacks the training required to overcome traditional attitudes of civil servants to the peasantry, of Central Thai to Northern highlanders, of urbanities to rural folk, attitudes which are daily expressed at the *nikhom* through the subtleties of dress, diet, mannerism, and speech. Relations can best be described as friendly but formal and restrained; though tribesmen have not come to confide in the staff and to seek them out for advice, they have at least gained sufficient confidence to spend an evening in a deserted hut at the headquarters to smoke a pipe of opium and to trust the staff with the marketing of a crop of potatoes or coffee beans.

Nikhom Chiengdao has not achieved the results for which it was created. It has not accomplished its major objective, to attract and settle tribal villages, nor has it succeeded in developing and introducing a workable economic substitute for the swidden system and particularly for the opium crop. It has not even gained the full confidence of the tribal villages falling within its administrative bounds. In part, this situation stems from the failure of the government at higher levels to spell out the details of staff operations, a failure which can be interpreted as a generic characteristic of entourage formations. The motivation to rise within the Thai hierarchy has predisposed the staff to undertake activities serving this end rather than the end for which the *nikhom* was nominally established; functional ambiguity permits this shift in emphasis, which in the final analysis serves the selfish interests of the bureaucracy at the cost of operational effectiveness. On the local scene, Nikhom Chiengdao forms but another bureaucratic layer complicating the political situation but not seriously affecting the structures of indigenous economic systems.

Chapter 6

ECONOMIC
DEVELOPMENT ON THE
CULTURAL FRONTIER

Levels of material well-being vary not only within but also among the various economies operating in the Northern Thai uplands. Income levels, the conventional index of material well-being, are stratified in overlapping fashion among the upland economies, as illustrated in the accompanying cross-sectional tabulation of household incomes in the Research Area (Chart 1).

This chart indicates that on a household basis Meo tribes-men of Phapucom compete for low position on the local income scale with landless upland and lowland Thai peasants. Occupying the middle-income range are the Lahu of Huai Thad and Ban Yai Suk, employees of the Chiengdao Tea Plantation, miang gardeners of Village Twelve, lowland rice cultivators of Ban Pong and environs, and the bulk of the staff of Nikhom Chiengdao. The upper income plateaus are inhab-ited by the wealthiest lowland peasants, the *nikhom* director, and, in an exalted place of his own, Khun Luang.

In addition to household income levels, the severity of in-come fluctuations from one harvest to the next and the avail-ability of opportunities to achieve higher income levels over

Chart 1. Household incomes, Research Area, 1963–1964 *

Annual income (baht)	Hill tribes	Tea plantation	Upland Thai	Lowland Thai	*Nikhom*
Above 100,000		Khun Luang (inclusive of income from other ventures)			
Above 10,000				*Pau ijang*	**Director**
10,000			Miang garden and rice land owner		
9,000					
8,000					
7,000	Ban Yai Suk Huai Thad				Staff
6,000		Full-time-supplier	Miang garden owner	Rice land owner	
5,000		Staff			
4,000			Miang garden tenant		
3,000	Phapucom	Laborer			
2,000			Landless laborer	Landless laborer	

* Average income for each village, occupational group, or individual is denoted by the position of the descriptive term relative to the income axis. The range of variation of household incomes around this average is denoted by the length of the vertical line extending from the descriptive term. It should be noted that these statistics are approximations based on sample surveys, census data, and other volunteered information and include monetary imputations for income earned in kind.

one's lifetime also stand as clues to material well-being. In these regards tribesmen are in the least enviable situation, surpassed in increasing degrees of prosperity by plantation employees, upland Thai, lowland Thai, and *nikhom* personnel, in that order. Furthermore, cross-cultural variations in the level of material well-being are even more pronounced in terms of household wealth, rising from left to right among the communities listed in Chart 1.

In their effort to define the structural characteristics of the upland economies, the preceding chapters touched on but did not focus on these systems' interrelations. This chapter takes a cross-sectional view of the upland economic environment. It searches out the reasons underlying cross-cultural economic stratification in the uplands by analyzing the technological and institutional constraints hampering intercultural economic relations and, thus, occupational mobility and industrial diversification within individual upland economies. In closing, it summarizes the connection between the dynamics of upland intercultural relations and the various upland economies' development records and expectations.

Intercultural Economic Relations

None of the economies operating within the Northern Thai uplands is entirely self-sufficient. Each demands consumer and producer goods and services which it is incapable of producing. In order to satisfy these demands each relies on supply contacts in the lowlands whose reliability is ensured by their continuing demands for opium, miang, and tea. The various parallel series of hill-valley economic relations thus formed, in conjunction with the technological barriers and institutional constraints separating the upland systems (to be discussed in subsequent sections), inhibit the development of intercultural economic relations within the hills, and thus the types of economic transactions engaged in among the upland cultures are relatively few and insignificant.

Trade Flows

A small but steady stream of petty transactions in such goods as fruit, vegetables, chickens, pigs, handicraft items, and pipefuls of opium crosses cultural boundaries in the uplands. Typically, trade negotiations are entered into between Thai peasants and hill tribesmen who are mutual strangers; even where the negotiating parties have had prior relations, their acquaintanceship is played down, a procedure which frees the bargaining process from ordinary social constraints and permits it to be entered into by individuals who may otherwise be on unfriendly terms. The bargaining atmosphere substitutes an undercurrent of suspicion if not outright antipathy for the conviviality common to the lowland market place. Valuations in such transactions are invariably in money terms, and payments are normally in cash. The effects of these features are that petty trade among upland dwellers of different cultures permits the overt expression and pursuit of self-interest, that negotiations often break down, and that prices and quantities tend to gyrate with the vagaries of competitive psychology. Thus, this trade flow is not only unpleasant to its participants but inefficient in meeting their material needs.

In terms of aggregate value and volume, such intercultural transactions amount to little. The preponderence of trade is not among upland dwellers but between them and their lowland trading partners. Miang cultivators rely on the continuing relationship with their *pau liang* in their parent villages. Tea processors maintain their commercial contacts with the metropolitan wholesale trade. Hill tribesmen depend on opium runners, who legitimize their presence in the hills (while increasing their profits as well as their usefulness to the tribes) by bringing in a variety of tribal imports.[1] Each upland economy thus possesses cash-crop export channels and consumer- and producer-goods supply links with the valley world which help preserve its independence from its upland neighbors.

These hill-valley trade circuits are not entirely dissociated from one another, however.[2] They are joined by the tea industry's continuing reliance on miang gardens as a raw leaf supply source and by opium smugglers' occasional resort to miang shipments as a means of concealing their contraband.

In an earlier chapter I discussed the Chiengdao Tea Plantation's dependence on raw leaf purchases from nearby miang gardeners; other tea processing operations in North Thailand (all petty affairs compared to the plantation) rely even more heavily on this source of inventory supply.[3] In the competition between the tea industry and the miang trade which results from their common resource base, tea processors

[1] The *nikhom* serves as an additional economic link between the tribes and the lowlands through its services as agent in marketing various minor tribal cash crops and artifacts.

[2] The various distinguishable hill-valley trade circuits are reminiscent of the so-called circuits or spheres of exchange that mark certain African and Oceanic tribal economies. See, for instance, Bohannan, 1968, p. 227-237; and Salisbury, 1962, pp. 187-194. The similarity between the present case and these others is only superficial, however. The notion of circuits of economic activity ordinarily refers to the division of an economic system into discrete sectors, each of which involves different types of goods and services, different technologies, and different exchange institutions. The trade circuits here referred to are distinguishable not as separate sectors within a single economic system but as separate links between different systems; the critical distinguishing characteristic thus becomes the populations rather than the items involved in such transactions, each circuit serving as the link between an upland culture and its lowland trading partners.

[3] Campbell, 1963, pp. 13-36 *passim*.

throughout the North stand at a marked disadvantage. The tea industry is geared to compete for raw leaf on commercial terms, but miang wholesalers have more to offer. The economic and social needs of miang gardeners have traditionally been well served within entourages, which afford them a degree of economic and political security and social status as well as a chance to rise within the peasant hierarchy which commercial relations with tea processors cannot match.

Even if tea processors attempted to extend to raw leaf suppliers some of the services ordinarily provided by *pau liang* they would be hard put to justify them on financial grounds alone.[4] The Chiengdao Tea Plantation, for instance, has taken the forward-looking steps of paying for raw leaf in rice in addition to cash, of supplying local gardeners with rice on credit, of establishing a standard raw leaf buying price, and of contracting with gardeners willing to tie in with the plantation on a long-term basis. But Khun Luang, the entrepreneur, will not and cannot, because of the breadth of his operations and the social gap which separates him from his suppliers, enter into an intimate social relationship with each gardener. Nor has the plantation, as he sees it, benefited from the financial inducements it has offered, for they have not palpably improved the inventory supply situation. The deficit such a policy would generate if consistently followed could only be financed by him by sacrificing the profits of his other, more remunerative ventures. Thus, despite anticipated adverse consequences, he has from time to time been motivated by commercial considerations to curtail his program of weaning local miang gardeners away from their entourage ties.

The tea processor's failure to absorb the functions tradi-

[4] Because patrons of miang entourages weigh considerations of status and power in their determinations of goods and services contributions to their clients, they frequently extend themselves further financially for the benefit of their clients than do commercial tea processors.

tionally performed by the *pau liang* has left the industry susceptible to severe inventory fluctuations, which have raised average costs and thus hampered growth, for its inventory is derived from the surplus remaining in gardeners' hands after other, higher-priority demands have been satisfied. Miang harvests vary by some 10 per cent around the norm, but consumer demand remains relatively stable from one year to the next. The diplomacy of entourage relations suggests that gardeners should not press excess stocks upon their *pau liang* in years of abundance but should cooperate in stabilizing wholesale inventories by holding back on the supply in good years, just as their *pau liang* see them through years of adversity. (Thus, prices in the Thai peasant economy are held steady through the management of supply rather than through the force of untrammeled competition.) The consequent highly variable surplus forms the tea processor's raw leaf supply (in addition, of course, to the harvests of the small number of gardeners without contacts in the miang trade who fall into the tea processor's hands by default).

Adding to the variability of the raw leaf surplus available to tea processors is the intermittent demand for miang among opium smugglers. Opium-running out of the Northern Thai hills is a profitable business. Though it varies with the distance between the tribal village and the point of resale, the quality of the product, the current price in the lowlands, the effectiveness of local policing against the traffic, the cost of bribes to influential officials, the prevalence of banditry, and the quantity being smuggled in from neighboring countries, the rate of return on smuggling rarely runs at less than 50 per cent of the purchase price.[5]

Profitability in this trade is obviously closely related to risk. The rewards must be high to offset the dangers of cap-

[5] Thailand, 1962, pp. 39, 65; and Usher, 1967b, p. 227.

ture by the authorities or interception by rivals or dacoits. Secrecy is of paramount importance; in this regard miang serves a useful purpose. The chance of discovery of a brick of opium hidden within a pack basket of miang in the midst of one of the many ox caravans regularly plying the upland trails is small. Assurance that a careful search will not readily be undertaken derives from the fact that careless unpacking of a miang shipment spoils the product through exposure to air; an official not discovering any contraband through such an inspection will not only make himself a local laughing-stock but will be held personally liable for the loss suffered by the shipper.

A small amount of opium is undoubtedly carried out of the hills on the backs of oxen owned by miang gardeners or their patrons. Professional smugglers, however, resort to this expedient only intermittently, for miang surpluses are not always available to them, nor are they always faced with the risks of detection, risks that make this relatively expensive mode of transport worth the cost.

The intermittent competition of opium smugglers for the variable miang harvest surplus thus complicates the tea industry's supply problem. For instance, 1962 proved to be an unusually profitable year for the opium trade in North Thailand, with prices rising high in the lowlands. It was also a year of increased surveillance of the uplands by the Thai government. The result was an unusual high demand for miang as a smuggler's aid and therefore an unusually low supply of raw leaf available at the Chiengdao Tea Plantation, with disastrous consequences for factory output and sales.

Too much must not be made of the intercultural opium-miang-tea nexus, for it is of only marginal importance to the economics of the opium and miang trades and the upland Thai and tribal peasant communities. The additional income earned by miang gardeners through the sale of surpluses to tea processors and opium dealers is intermittent and undependable; it is treated as a windfall to be dissipated primarily on luxury and prestige goods. Resort to miang by opium traders amounts to nothing more than an occasional expedient; it is certainly not critical to the traffic, and it is thus of no significance to the economic life of the opium-cultivating hill tribes. Only the tea industry finds that the situation sets an effective limit on the scale of its operations so long as it must depend almost exclusively on intercultural trade for its inventory.

Labor Flows

Growth is of major concern to the commercial tea industry in North Thailand, for only through expanded output can individual firms reap the profits emanating from increasing returns to scale and a government-guaranteed price for all they produce. The constraint on growth inherent in continued reliance on intercultural trade dictates that tea processors seek independent supply sources. The pioneering effort of the Chiengdao Tea Plantation to develop its own tea fields has been the natural consequence. As has been pointed out, the plantation has encountered no insurmountable problems in adapting tea horticulture to the climate and soils of the Northern hills, in gaining access to suitable land, in securing adequate capital, in locating managerial talent, or in finding a market; the major bottleneck has been its difficulty in recruiting and retaining a labor force.

Hill tribe and Thai peasant labor is constantly sought far and wide. Active recruiting is undertaken in the valleys; living facilities are provided on the plantation; swidden tracts have been set aside for tribal immigrants; educational and medical services are offered all seekers; wages competitive with those in the lowlands are paid. Yet the average employee remains at the plantation less than three months at a time, and few return for a second engagement.

Both the physical conveniences and the financial rewards offered by the plantation compare favorably with the alternatives facing landless Thai peasants and displaced hill tribesmen. The heart of the labor problem consists in a social climate devoid of the mutuality of interests and an economic climate lacking the mix of incentives motivating Thai and tribal peasants. The ambitions of the landless Thai peasant center on the ultimate acquisition of paddi fields and thereby of a place of relative prosperity, prestige, and authority within his village. The road to success is a long one, to be traveled by hard work and the gradual accumulation of remunerative and liquid assets. Though the typical Thai peasant household laboring on the plantation annually earns surplus income in excess of 900 baht, it lacks the investment opportunities required for economic advancement. Plantation laborers cannot possess oxen, which might wander into freshly terraced, planted, or mulched tea fields to wreak havoc. They consider it dangerous to hoard their earnings in the form of cash, gold, or other negotiable assets, surrounded as they are by impoverished and disreputable strangers. Those who do succeed in collecting a stake leave in search of investment opportunities elsewhere.[6] Those who remain tend to dispose of their surplus income on luxury consumables.

Just as the plantation lacks economic opportunities for

[6] Several plantation laborers have resorted to the compromise of of investing surplus income in nearby miang gardens, which they then harvest for tea. As the gardens mature they continue to work on the plantation. Eventually they reach a position of economic independence and shift their interests to miang.

Thai peasants, so does it lack social stability comparable to that provided by their indigenous milieu. They seek and expect personalized relations with their patrons. From the frame of reference of Thai workers on the plantation the entrepreneur's attitude of depersonalized benevolence represents a distortion of the traditional patron-client relationship. This social climate is alien to the Thai peasant turned plantation employee; it leaves him without the social status and self-respect he gains within the entourage. In conjunction with inadequate economic security and opportunity on the plantation, it leads him to seek relief in escape.

Hill tribesmen, too, generally avoid the plantation. Those who seek continuing employment do so only in exceptional circumstances. Meo and Lahu villages have only been drawn to the vicinity of the Chiengdao Tea Plantation in time of distress by the friendship and tangible assistance offered by the entrepreneur. They have not been attracted by the plantation's labor opportunities; wage labor has only been turned to as a final expedient in coping with near famine conditions (in the case of the Meo) and as a means of earning petty cash and repaying the entrepreneur for his donation of swiddens (in the case of the Lahu).

Despite the material advantages associated with seasonal employment on the plantation, both Lahu and Meo tribesmen have avoided continued involvement. Participation in the plantation carries with it subordination to the dictates of the entrepreneur and his staff, a condition which conflicts dramatically with the tribal village's cherished independence. Analogously, in the Burmese hills some 300 miles to the northwest, Edmund Leach has found that Kachin tribesmen sometimes "have a choice between remaining independent in a small impoverished community or moving into a dependent situation in some more prosperous area." Their decision in the matter leads him to conclude: "It is quite evident that in such contexts Kachins often value political independence more highly than economic advantge." [7] In addition, there is the problem that tribesmen tend to associate wage labor with bondage.

Furthermore, both Meo and Lahu tribesmen have had continuing difficulties in working side by side with Thai peasants in the plantation fields and factory. Tribesmen face constant harassment from their upland Thai neighbors. On the plantation their speech, dress, manners, and unwashed appearance are the butt of humor. Lahu children attending the local school are tormented by their Thai classmates. Tribal livestock is stolen, and swiddens are vandalized. Each season, losses are suffered in the swiddens due to the depredations of wandering Thai-owned cattle. Despite frequent complaints, no action has been taken by local authorities to eliminate these abuses or seek redress for those committed, largely as a result of the ambiguity of jurisdictional authority.

Not unexpectedly in this setting of latent hostilities, tribesmen are not employed in miang gardens, nor do Thai peasants find work in the swiddens. Cases even remotely resembling the reported indenture of Thai opium addicts to Karen tribesmen or the assimilation of Khmu and Kachin tribesmen into lowland peasant society through the acceptance of labor opportunities are not to be found here. Only on the plantation do Thai and tribal peasants associate directly in the production process, and here neither group finds itself in control.

Technological Barriers

The preceding discussion has indicated that the principal economic relations among upland cultures in North Thai-

[7] Leach, 1954, p. 234.

land are of small significance relative to economic relations among producing and consuming units within each system and between them and their lowland contacts: what little intercultural trade is carried on in the uplands is of peripheral interest to all but tea processors, and intercultural labor flows are nonexistent except on the tea plantation, where they are generated only with the greatest difficulty. In sum, it appears that the forces making for mutual withdrawal among upland economies predominate over those promoting interaction. Though this problem is primarily one of institutional rigidities, there exist technological barriers that contribute to the paucity of upland intercultural relations. The following discussion dwells on land and labor barriers and agronomic incompatibilities hampering intercultural relations; problems related to the allocation of capital will be dealt with in passing.

Land

The possibilities of open intercultural conflict in the uplands are greatest where resource scarcities press most severely on socially determined standards of material well-being. In the Research Area, the increasing numbers of swiddens, miang gardens, and plantation fields in concert with increasing restrictions on land use through the intervention of various government agencies means that for Thai and tribal peasants alike land is emerging as a crucial factor of production.

To the present, antagonisms between upland Thai and tribesmen have not been expressed in overt competition for land. A tacit understanding that swiddens and miang gardens will not abut or intrude upon one another, even in cases of abandoned sites, appears to be universally adhered to. As upland populations expand it can be expected, however, that infringements on this understanding will gradually appear.

Already in the Research Area the inadequate swiddens of Huai Thad cannot be extended because of the nearness of the gardens and hamlets of Pang Kud and Pang Wieng Daung. Conversely, these Thai hamlets find themselves restricted in adding to their holdings by the nearness of tribal swiddens.[8]

The plantation's encroachments upon the local terrain have contributed to emerging land pressures. So far, the plantation has carefully limited its tea terraces to hillsides devoid of miang gardens, but Thai peasants fear that it may not continue to do so, and this is one reason for their frequent registration of gardens with the commune headman. Apparently unaware of the tribal convention that abandoned swiddens remain village property until reforested, the plantation took possession of those deserted by the Meo village of Phapucom when it left the area about 1950 and later granted them to the Lahu village of Huai Thad in return for their promise to work in the tea fields when not engaged on the swiddens. When the Meo later returned to find their swiddens appropriated by the Lahu they had no recourse but to vent their anger in clearing less fertile lands some distance west. The Meo have not forgiven the Lahu for their take-over nor Khun Luang for what they consider misrepresentations, adding to their unwillingness to work as tea pickers.[9]

The further limits on upland agriculture introduced by

[8] Cases of Thai vandalism in the swiddens symptomizes emerging pressures of cultural confrontation and may be a preliminary indication of the open hostilities to come.

[9] Technically, it appears, a village which abandons its swiddens on moving to a new locale relinquishes all usufructory rights to them. In the present instance, then, resentments seem to have been generated by a difference of opinion among local groups over the question of the intended permanence of what turned out to be no more than a temporary abandonment of Phapucom's swiddens.

the Thai bureaucracy have been discussed in the preceding chapter. Insecurity of tenure in miang gardens located within the public domain (under the authority of the Land Department) serves as a restraint on the extension of holdings and possibly retards Thai migration into the uplands. Potential enforcement of forestry laws (by the Forest Department) poses a threat to the livelihood of both swiddeners, who depend on the freedom to clear jungle land, and miang gardeners, who require a steady supply of timber to stoke the fires used in miang processing. Suppression of opium cultivation (by the Police Department) creates an even graver potential economic problem for hill tribesmen.[10] These difficulties are compounded in the Research Area by the presence of the *nikhom* (within the Public Welfare Department), whose staff has wide-ranging authority to administer the territory within which both local miang gardens and swiddens are located. Situated on land thus doubly pre-empted (as public domain and as *nikhom*) and supervised by a multiplicity of government agencies, local peasants live in constant danger of the imposition of tenure restrictions or outright dispossession of their land holdings.

Conflicting interests over limited cultivable land are thus generating hostilities which serve to perpetuate the historic divisions among the upland cultures. This barrier to intercultural relations may be expected to intensify as immigration into the Northern Thai uplands continues.

Labor

Though land is emerging as a scarce factor in the uplands, the most important production bottleneck continues to be

[10] Though these problems are recognized and worried over by upland dwellers they are not of overwhelming immediate concern because forestry officials concentrate on the more lucrative teak industry and the police are not overly anxious to eliminate one of their major sources of graft.

labor in each of the agrarian economies under investigation. The rhythm of the demand for labor in each of these systems is highly seasonal, however, with heavy doses being required only during field preparation, sowing, and harvesting periods and with surpluses appearing at other times. Whether such a situation is indicative of conditions of agricultural underemployment, or whether it lowers the marginal product of labor, is an academic question much worried over by development economists; [11] in the present context its answer seems obvious.[12]

Larger labor supplies would certainly permit each of the upland systems to increase output and income through expanding cultivated area or, where land is no longer abundantly available, through improving yields. Alien labor supplies, moreover, appear potentially employable within each system; in other words, there appear to be no technological constraints *on the demand side* hampering the absorption of alien labor forces by any of these labor-hungry economies. Yet, as the preceding discussion of agricultural labor flows has reviewed, the plantation faces a constant struggle in attracting labor from among Thai and tribal peasants, and no labor crossovers whatsoever occur among the other upland economies.

Aside from the institutional rigidities interfering with the flow of labor from each of these economies to its neighbors, the relative rhythms of upland agricultural cycles inhibit such factor exports. Chart 2 indicates that peaks in domestic labor requirements in the various upland systems overlap;

[11] See, for example, Kao *et al.*, 1964; and Myrdal, 1968, pp. 2041–2061.

[12] "It is almost axiomatic in these times, when considering the economy of underdeveloped countries[,] to assume underemployment as a basic characteristic, but in terms of their present technology this cannot be claimed for the Hill Tribes in this region" (Keen, 1963[?], p. 4).

Chart 2. Agricultural calendars, Research Area

	Swiddens		Miang gardens	Lowland fields		Tea fields
	Dry rice	Opium		Dry-season crops	Wet rice	
Jan.			Materials preparation	Sowing		
Feb.		Harvest		Sowing / Weeding and irrigation		Pruning and mulching
March	Field preparation	Field preparation	Harvest	Harvest / Weeding and irrigation	Sowing	
April					Irrigation	
May	Sowing			Harvest	Irrigation	
June *	Weeding and guarding		Harvest		Irrigation	
July *	Weeding and guarding				Harvest / Plowing / Preparing seed beds	Picking
Aug. *	Harvest		Harvest		Planting	Picking
Sept. *	Weeding and guarding	Sowing				Picking
Oct.	Weeding and guarding	Weeding and guarding				Picking
Nov.	Harvest	Weeding and guarding			Harvest	Picking
Dec.			Harvest	Sowing	Harvest	

* Monsoon months.

Note: Solid boxes denote intensive, nearly full-time activity; broken-line boxes denote part-time or intermittent activity.

thus, labor surpluses appear within each system during seasons of low labor demand in neighboring economies. Even where temporary cross-cultural complementarities between supply and demand appear, their short durations, due to the intermittent recurrence of domestic labor requirements, make the resultant pattern of potential intercultural labor flows volatile over the calendar year, reducing the likelihood that such flows can be institutionalized under current technological conditions.

The periods of heavy labor demand over the four-phased agricultural calendar of the upland Thai economy, for instance, coincide with those of the hill tribe economy during swidden preparation, the beginning of the dry-rice season, the early dry-rice harvest, and the weeks of opium sowing. The miang calendar similarly competes with the wet-rice cycle of the lowlands, suggesting that the risks of the move by the Thai into the hills cannot be lessened by dividing attention between miang and wet-rice cultivation. The harmony between the domestic and export crop rhythms of the swidden system and between the dry-season and wet-rice crops of the lowland Thai provides corroborative evidence of the importance of the timing of crop cycles as a labor-saving device in labor-scarce and labor-intensive agriculture. Finally, the smoothness of the labor requirement over the tea plantation's agricultural year, so necessary to the efficient workings of an agriculturally based industrial enterprise, clashes with the fluctuating needs of neighboring systems, suggesting that competitive agricultural cycles contribute to its difficulties in attracting a work force.

Agronomic Incompatibilities

In addition to the impediments to intercultural economic relations emerging directly from noncomplementary factor employments, technological considerations play a part in maintaining a low level of trade even where such complementarities lie latent.

For instance, the land, labor, and seed inputs required for the planting and developing of miang or tea gardens are readily available to local tribesmen; and there is a demand for the harvested product among lowland miang wholesalers and at the tea plantation factory. That the skills required for the cultivation and processing of the crop are within the intellectual capacities of local tribesmen is demonstrated by their educability as tea plantation labor and by the various examples of miang production among hill tribes in Burma and Laos (see Chapter 3).

Tribal cultivators of miang, however, are all Austroasiatics, who do not produce opium and who are generally more dependent on rice imports to meet domestic consumption requirements than are the Sino-Tibetans, represented by the tribal villages of the Research Area. They have, in effect, been afforded the opportunity to develop a miang agronomy because their relatively low level of involvement with crops that call for frequent field site shifting and occasional village relocation permits the exploitation of tree crops—perennials with long gestation periods.

So long as Sino-Tibetan villages, such as those within the Research Area, continue to depend for their livelihood on a technology geared to subsistence rice supplemented by opium exports, they will tend to ignore long-run opportunities available in miang and tea cultivation on a smallholder basis. As soon as the constraints of the swidden technology are lifted, as has happened with the abandonment of opium by local Lahu, an appreciable reduction in resistance to such innovation may be expected.

Similarly, miang gardeners possess all the required factor

inputs to engage in raw leaf sales to the tea plantation or even to undertake independent green-tea manufacture. Yet, the differing details of miang and tea cultivation inhibit ready transferal from one to the other. These differences stem from the purposes to which miang and tea are ultimately put: miang must be fibrous to withstand pulping during mastication whereas tea must be sufficiently delicate to emit its juices immediately upon infusion in boiling water. The best miang is therefore composed of coarse, mature leaf, while superior tea contains only the youngest shoots and buds, the "flush" of the plant. To these ends, miang cultivators permit their gardens to grow in a nearly wild state, whereas tea cultivators prune their shrubs severely in order to maximize the growth of fresh leaf. Adapting a garden from miang to tea entails a severe pruning, a difficult and dangerous job. The change-over endangers not only the health of the plants but the pocketbook of the gardener, who must bear the cost of waiting several years for his plants to return to a high level of leaf regeneration. No gardener in the Research Area has been willing to accept such risks and withstand such costs.[13]

Neither has any effort been made by local hill tribesmen to adjust their techology to compete for the outstanding demand for milled rice among miang gardeners, a demand which is satisfied by wet-rice farmers of the lowlands despite the transport premium involved. One obstacle to adjustment is that the varieties of rice grown by the tribes suit neither the appetites nor the cooking requirements of Northern Thai

[13] Gardeners who supply the plantation with raw leaf do so by selectively harvesting their "wild" shrubs for fresh growth. This is a particularly tedious job, for it requires careful choosing and picking over a large area of foliage. The tendency is to simplify and speed up the job by including some mature leaf, which lowers overall quality. The plantation's negative reaction to this procedure has been reviewed in Chapter 4.

peasants; varieties more appealing to the Northern Thai diet could be introduced but would require troublesome secondary adjustments in the agricultural rhythm and in cultivation and harvesting procedures, for they have different growth rates and threshing characteristics.[14] So long as the tribes continue to grow their traditional varieties for domestic consumption, the superimposition of varieties suitable for export to the lowlands would introduce additional complexities into the dry-rice production cycle, particularly regarding the allocation of field sites among crops and households and the division of labor among crops and over time. Even more troublesome as a barrier to tribal entry into the rice trade, however, is the labor bottleneck (and, within the Research Area, the emerging land squeeze). The concentrated labor inputs required during key phases of the agricultural cycle place an effective limit on output despite the labor surpluses available at other times of the year. Only the introduction of new techniques of production (and of the capital inputs required for their successful application) can reduce this traditional technological constraint on a tribal rice-export surplus.

Institutional Constraints

Each of these barriers to upland intercultural relations is symptomatic of underlying institutional constraints that tend to isolate the upland economies from one another. Participants in each upland economy strive, individually and collectively, knowingly and unknowingly, toward the realization of a distinct, culturally specific ideal: among the tribes the

[14] An analysis of the agronomic characteristics of the varieties of dry rice grown by the hill tribes of the Northern Thai uplands is yet to be undertaken. What little work has been done on the wet-rice varieties favored by the Northern Thai is reviewed in Watabe, 1967; and more briefly in Moerman, 1968, pp. 195–197.

cherished object is village independence from outside economic and political dominance; among the upland Thai it is household ascendance to patronal rank within the peasantry's social, political, and economic order; among all those involved with the tea plantation it is simply material gain, tempered at the management level by a vague paternalistic concern for the welfare of the labor force. To the degree that these incentives differ among the various upland economies, the institutional configurations that prescribe action on their behalf tend to diverge. Thus, each upland system is characterized by a different institutional theme: in the tribal world it is intravillage reciprocity and solidary cooperation; among upland Thai peasants it is reciprocity within hill-valley entourage formations; on the plantation it is redistribution between management and labor.[15]

However, the divergent institutional configurations of the Northern Thai uplands do not all facilitate the pursuit and attainment of their participants' basic aspirations to the same extent. In other words, the upland economies vary in their abilities to harmonize the "real" with the "ideal." This observation suggests that each of these systems many be evaluated on the basis of the internal coherence, or functional integrity, maintained between its institutions and its participants' image of the good life. Though absolute magnitudes of functionalism cannot be determined, the upland systems can be ranked in order of their relative degrees of functional integration.

Each upland Thai peasant household, as we have seen, is afforded opportunities to rise to a position of prominence in the lowland community by reason of its very presence in miang territory and participation in the miang industry. The

[15] On the concepts of reciprocity and redistribution (as opposed to market exchange), see Polanyi, 1957b, pp. 250–256; and Humphreys, 1969, pp. 202–212.

fluidity of entourage relationships, moreover, offers each upland Thai peasant household a relatively broad range of economic options and a substantial degree of social mobility. Success in this cultural milieu depends predominantly on individual diplomacy and initiative. Though few participants actually rise to the top, most see some degree of success within reach; each has only himself (and his *karma*) to blame for his disappointments. Thai peasant institutions thus dovetail with the incentives springing from the Thai peasant ethos to create a *highly functional* economic system in the hills.

The ideal of village independence among the hill tribes is more visionary. Intravillage reciprocity, which furnishes the community a degree of security against poverty and subordination, also inhibits the accumulation of sufficient savings by wealthy households to permit their continuing prosperity. Rice harvest deficits tend to set in motion downward social and economic spirals leading to village disintegration and individual thraldom to outside interests, whereas surpluses ordinarily do not provide the economic strength to shift the village out of its chronically precarious situation. The existence of a separately instituted foreign sector, on the other hand, helps sustain independence by ensuring a continuing supply of essential imports while also serving as a cultural buffer. On balance, then, the institutional configuration characteristic of the tribal economy provides no more than a minimally adequate context for the realization of tribal ideals. The tribal economy must therefore be judged *marginally functional*.

The ultimate object to which the tea plantation is directed by its management wavers between commercial success and the economic improvement of the upland peasant populations.[16] Commercial success is reckoned by the management

[16] This, at least, is the view from the controlling center. Wage laborers, interested in neither the plantation's profitability nor their

in terms of profits and, through them, control of the Thai tea industry; economic improvement is defined in terms of the financial rewards accompanying peasants' assimiliation into the plantation's commercial-industrial environment. The plantation economy has failed to deliver on either score. Profits have been limited primarily by the plantation's inability to control the quantity or quality of its raw materials inflow, a result of its difficulties in attracting an adequate labor force or a faithful coterie of independent suppliers. Correlatively, the local peasantry's material welfare has not been raised because of the plantation's inability to mesh commercial institutions (particularly the labor market) with traditional Thai and tribal peasant economic arrangements. In sum, plantation institutions have provided a context within which neither management nor labor has found it possible to realize its aspirations. In terms of its past performance in the upland environment this economy can only be judged *dysfunctional*.

In terms of their relative degrees of internal coherence the upland economies thus range from "highly functional" through "marginally functional" to "dysfunctional." Restated in the jargon of conventional economics, this summation ranks the upland Thai peasant economy as "optimal," the hill tribe peasant economy as "suboptimal," and the plantation economy as "nonoptimal"—the optimality criterion here being the relative degrees to which individuals acting under different constraints are enabled to maximize their differently perceived satisfactions.[17] In terms of indigenous val-

_____

future on it, seek only cash (or rice) enough to tide them over hard times, to repay outstanding debts to the plantation, or to accumulate grubstakes, after which they hurry to depart. Yet, so long as they work on the plantation they contribute to the common effort to reach the entrepreneur's two goals.

[17] The conventional economist would suggest that the degree of optimality in this context is a function of the presence of institu-

ues, then, the upland institutional configurations differ not only in their substantive details but along functional (or, as the conventional economist might have it, utilitarian) lines.

The varying intensities of relations among the upland economies may be explained in terms of these systems' varying degrees of functional integrity. The most severe mutual withdrawal separates upland Thai and tribal peasants. Despite the opportunities that exist for economic interaction, these communities have little to do with one another. For instance, though miang harvests and swiddening cycles overlap, there are some months during which demand for labor in the miang gardens could be filled by tribesmen temporarily unoccupied in the swiddens—especially during June (the *klang* harvest) and December (the *mui* harvest). Yet no such labor crossovers occur. Even more conspicuously absent is cooperation between tribesmen and upland Thai in the opium trade. The oxen used by miang gardeners to export their harvests to and import consumer goods from the lowlands are underemployed at the usual ten or twelve trips per year. They could undertake to transport opium and consumer goods for tribesmen with little difficulty. Great profits are to be made in this traffic, as the upland Thai peasantry well knows. Yet they rarely enter the trade, leaving it to the Haw and other established traders. Those few who do, hide the fact from their neighbors or are treated as renegades.

---

tional constraints. The implication is that institutions have an inherent negative impact on the operations of an economic system and that, therefore, the optimal (i.e., the "best") system is the one with the smallest number of institutions interfering with "the free workings of the market." What is not adequately considered by proponents of this view is that the market system is itself institutionally integrated; what they imply, in effect, is that one institutional form (the market economy) is superior to others in terms of the ends which *that particular system* is structured to pursue.

Similarly, Thai peasants employed on the plantation are generally drawn only from the dregs of lowland society, among whom the benefits of institutional conformity and the penalties of deviation are smallest. Those upland Thai who drift from miang to the plantation do so under the censure of their fellows and only when economic opportunities elsewhere appear to have been exhausted. Among tribesmen, too, such deviation is discouraged. For the individual tribesman to depart from traditional economic norms virtually guarantees his ostracism. Thus, what deviation does occur requires village consensus and is ordinarily undertaken on a village-wide scale. This has been the case for those tribesmen who have turned to the plantation. In each case the village as a whole has resorted to wage labor as a temporary escape from desperate economic conditions, knowing full well that this has also contributed to its isolation from the mainstream of tribal culture and its failure to realize tribal ideals. As these villages have adjusted to the altered environment, however, their changed situations have generated internal strains which have drawn them into increased intercultural economic relations despite reactionary pressures. Summarily, among the upland Thai the sanctions against social deviation and technological diffusion applied by the established order have to the present succeeded in perpetuating the system's functional integration in the face of pressures emanating from the plantation; among tribal villages associated with the plantation, on the other hand, the dysfunctions that initially prompted resort to wage labor have generated what appears to be a nascent but irreversible trend toward increasing intercultural economic involvements, a trend in which the *nikhom* is becoming peripherally involved.

These varying degrees of functional integration of upland peasant institutional configurations explain in a more consistent fashion than the technological barriers previously discussed the limited intercultural labor flow to the plantation. For instance, though the labor supply problem is regarded as a technological bottleneck on plantation operations when viewed in conventional economic terms, the problem is here seen to emanate primarily from institutional rigidities within the upland peasant economies. Similarly, the experimenting, innovating, and accommodating necessary to permit the peasant economies themselves to attain higher levels of material well-being are fundamentally discouraged not by an assortment of technological barriers but by a common core of indigenous institutional constraints.

Institutional constraints and their consequences are most apparent within the plantation economy itself. Labor and management, products of different cultural influences, pursue divergent ends. Thai labor's search for security and opportunity in entourage formations is frustrated by management's social distance and adherence to a basically pecuniary outlook. Tribal labor's quest for independence is blocked by management's regimentation of factor inputs and by its vaguely paternal attitude toward its work force. The result is social disintegration among the work force and a labor supply problem for management.

Cultural confrontations on the plantation thus exacerbate the very dysfunctions which the relatively more functionally integrated peasant systems seek to avoid by reacting against culture contact. Both cases—functionalism and dysfunctionalism—can thus be seen as self-reinforcing: the functional integrity of the upland Thai peasant economy serves to maintain the established order and, thus, the traditional level of material well-being; the dysfunctions of the tea plantation economy feed upon themselves to promote divisiveness and unrest, deviation and change. The intermediate case of the marginally functional hill tribe peasant economy is balanced on the knife's edge, with some villages temporarily succeeding in maintaining stability and others succumbing to the forces of change implicit in expanding intercultural relations.

The Drift of Events

The Introduction to this study proposed that (1) economic development is a function of technological change under institutional constraint; that (2) in non-Western cultures, lacking institutional configurations permissive of indigenous technologicial innovation, the principal source of economic development resides in culture contact and cross-cultural technological diffusion; and that (3) such diffusion tends to be restricted by the very institutional functionalism inhibiting indigenous technological change.

The present study offers a case in point. In the culturally pluralistic environment of the Northern Thai uplands a direct relationship has been shown to exist between the relative degree of each economic system's functional integrity and the degree of each system's openness to intercultural relations. The various structural restraints upon intercultural economic relations within the uplands thus seriously inhibit technological progress and institutional accommodation within the upland economies, retarding their development.

The severity of these structural restraints has been such, in fact, that the drift of events in the uplands has to the present constituted a study in the persistence of the vicious circle of underdevelopment, even under significant exogenous inducements to change. Despite the institutional frictions inevitably generated in the uplands by (1) the indigenous accretion of technological adjustments in the continuing—though piecemeal, uncoordinated, and largely unrecognized—effort to

237 *

cope with the vagaries of the physical environment and (2) the increasing exposure of economic systems to technological innovations as neighboring cultures come to press on one another under the impact of changing circumstances further removed, the virtuous circle of economic change feeding upon change in an accelerating developmental sequence has not yet come to predominate. It has been argued that this situation may be the general rule in the underdeveloped world:

In sharp contrast to [the] expectation [that economic progress constitutes the universal course of events] are not only the common experience of "low-level equilibrium" in underdeveloped countries and the serious obstacles to development policies, but more generally the astonishing stability of most social systems in history. Balance, far from being the fortuitous result of an unusual and obviously unstable combination of forces, seems to be the rule, not the rare exception. The great bulk of historical, anthropological, and sociological evidence and thought suggests that social stability and equilibrium is the norm and that all societies, and underdeveloped societies in particular, possess institutions of a strongly stabilizing character. In view of these findings the real mystery is how they can escape from equilibrium and can develop. The Western experience of scientific, technological, and economic advance may well be unique: a series of extraordinary circumstances seem to account for the cumulative process of development in Western history—even though the classical economists attempted to explain it by the removal of restraints and thus assumed a spontaneous tendency to develop. In this light the low-level equilibrium and the strong resistances to all attempts to overcome stagnation, characteristic of most underdeveloped countries, no longer appear puzzling. They can be explained by the forces that tend to perpetuate the *status quo* in the face of impulses to change it.[18]

[18] Myrdal, 1968, p. 1871.

However, structural change can be glimpsed on the cultural horizon in the Northern Thai uplands, particularly in the cultural interplay within the Research Area. "The ultimate 'causes' of social change . . . are nearly always to be found in the external political and economic environment"; [19] and so it is here. The conflict between past-binding institutions and progressive technology is producing developmental pressures of increasing severity as the upland economies are driven into closer contact under the indirect influence of the developmental flux radiating from the commercial-industrial hubs into the agrarian lowlands.

Institutional-technological tensions within neighboring cultures are generating a continuing filtration of tribal villages out of China, Burma, and Laos into North Thailand and a continuing flow of Thai peasant households up from the river valleys into the Northern hills, in turn forcing increased central government intervention into upland economic affairs. Contemporaneously, the expansionary thrust of the commercial-industrial economy is being felt in the hills in the form of an expanding inflow of industrially produced goods and services and (as with the plantation economy in the Research Area) in the form of scattered commercially inspired efforts to exploit the uplands' resource endowments. Forces of external origin are thus drawing the upland economies into closer, even if unwanted, proximity with one another and with those of the neighboring lowlands. Each system is thus being increasingly exposed to the conditions making for technological progress amid institutional disruption.

Nevertheless, structural change remains only on the horizon; in the face of mounting developmental stimuli the forces of economic stability continue to prevail. What eco-

[19] Leach, 1954, p. 212.

nomic deviation has been fomented within the upland economies by the heightened tensions of cultural confrontation has
been sporadic and devoid of immediate, structurally significant
implications. In short, the grip of the established order on the
organization of economic affairs has to the present withstood
or aborted the various diffusionist tendencies born of cultural contiguity.[20]

Within the Research Area, opportunities to work as wage
laborers or raw leaf suppliers within the plantation economy
have repelled all but the most destitute or socially dis-
enfranchised Thai peasants of Village Twelve and the neighboring lowlands because of the absence of an institutional
context providing a minimum of security and a range of
opportunities equivalent to those promised by the entourage
network indigenous to the Thai peasant economy.

Similarily, forces are at work to restore the status quo ex
ante in the Meo village of Phapucom, where increasing reliance on wage labor to counter conditions of economic
deterioration has reinforced repugnance against alien domination and has increased domestic dependence on opium,
raising the village preference for swiddening, leading to
abortive attempts to dissociate from further culture contact,
and culminating in chronic depression. Among the Lahu of
Huai Thad a rising reaction against involvement with the
plantation economy has contributed to interhousehold conflicts, culminating in village fragmentation and migration of

[20] Such a state of affairs has often been observed, though the
predilections of the social scientists investigating the circumstances
have ordinarily biased them against this interpretation of the situation. See, for instance, the rejection of the tractor by Tai Lue
peasants, reported in Moerman, 1968, pp. 185–193, and the failure
of New Guinea tribesmen to employ labor-saving steel axes to raise
the level of material well-being, reported in Salisbury, 1962, *passim*
and esp. p. 118.

the new village of Ban Yai Suk away from the cultural frontier as temporary resort to wage labor has drawn the village out of depression.

Only on the Chiengdao Tea Plantation have institutional dysfunctions been sufficiently severe to lead the entrepreneur and his staff to seek a permanent accommodation within the culturally pluralist upland environment by adjusting and readjusting the organization of work within the plantation economy to a form conducive of culture contact and the diffusion of the commercial-industrial ethos. Even here, however, departures from the "common sense" of commercial practices have been constrained by the persistently corrosive effect of the institutionalized quest for profits upon nonpecuniary incentives.

As developmental pressures continue to mount with increasing culture contact in the uplands, it may be expected that a threshold will ultimately by reached beyond which overt hostilities will be unavoidable. The consequences may well be political turmoil, followed by Thai government repression and further cultural polarization, a sequence of events reminiscent of the Burmese pattern over the past generation. Two alternative paths of economic change can be foreseen in such a situation: Indigenous institutional configurations may prove sufficiently resistent to the strains of confrontation to continue indefinitely to fend off technological innovation, exacerbating and extending the conflict, resulting in stagnation of the level of material well-being. On the other hand, they may collapse under external pressure to permit uninhibited accommodaton to the superior technologies to which they are exposed, resulting in institutional dislocations of such severity that they may well lead to economic stagnation equivalent to that deriving from the alternative path of change.

The probabilities, then, are that, left to itself, the economic development of the Northern Thai uplands will parallel the recent unhappy experiences of many other peasant systems exposed to the full blast of the commercial-industrial economy. The solution to this problem lies in enlightened planning, founded on a detailed understanding of the logic of indigenous economic systems and a commitment to building selectively on existing economic structures rather than tearing them down in the unrealistic expectation that the vacuum will inevitably be filled by a thriving economy patterned after the commercial-industrial model.

AN ECONOMIC DEVELOPMENT STRATEGY FOR THE NORTHERN THAI UPLANDS

The press of circumstances far beyond the control of the economies indigenous to the Northern Thai uplands is drawing them into ever closer contact, interaction, and conflict with one another and with intruding elements of the commercial-industrial economy. Structural change will inevitably result as the process of technological diffusion corrodes the functional integrity of indigenous institutional configurations; the precise path of the emerging sequence of events will depend on the institutional incidence of the particular technologies introduced.

The effects of such structural change on local levels of material well-being, and their consequent implications for the economic development of the nation at large, will be determined by the technological and institutional specifics of the development process at work within the various upland economies. That is, the degree to which the material gains potentially arising out of technological progress are realized within the uplands and radiated out into the lowland world will be inversely related to the degree of institutional dislocation and transformation accompanying the process of technological diffusion in the upland setting.

Guidelines

The methodological orientation and empirical findings of this study of economic structure and change may be helpful in devising a strategy facilitating the development of the Northern Thai uplands. Such a strategy should seek to minimize institutional dislocations resulting from the introduction of increasingly sophisticated technology into the upland economies. The particular form, timing, and sequence of technological innovation should also be selected with an eye to easing the institutional adjustment of the upland economies to one another and to the commercial-industrial economy presently beginning to encroach upon them all. A strategy based on these criteria will consider not only the benefits accruing from technological progress but also the costs of institutional disruption accompanying such change.

This statement summarizes the fundamental dilemma encountered by those development planners who seek to promote technological progress while maintaining a degree of institutional order within non-Western economic systems. The most desirable situation undoubtedly would be the complete attainment of both conditions, but, since technological progress and institutional stability are largely competitive in the non-Western setting, hard choices must be made.[1]

During the past two decades, development economists have generally chosen to ignore this problem by emphasizing

[1] This dilemma of choosing between equally attractive but mutually exclusive goals, each of which must be partially sacrificed for the limited attainment of the other, is conceptually akin to the post-Keynesian economic policy problem concerning trade-offs between the attainment of full employment and the elimination of inflation. See, e.g., Samuelson and Solow, 1960; and Holt, 1969.

technological progress to the disregard of its inevitable concomitant, institutional instability. Their rather cavalier explanations, when offered, have been variously that institutional change logically falls outside the economist's field of expertise, that institutional configurations are at any rate generally not seriously disturbed by the process of technological change, or that even if institutional change does occur it is an incalculably small price to pay for the large, lasting, and very tangible benefits of technological progress.

My position, as expounded throughout this study, is that such a perspective on the development process misjudges the economist's role and influence as a development planner, that it underestimates the economic significance of the institutional dimension of the development process, and that it assigns peculiarly Western values to the technological and institutional aspects of economic structure and change in non-Western settings.[2] These radical biases can only be righted by adopting a more holistic and less ethnocentric approach to the subject, one that pays careful regard not only to the play of technology but to the interplay of technology and institutions, and one that evaluates and sets relative priorities on the goals of technological change and institutional stability in the full light of the indigenous ethos of the affected peoples.

These methodological guidelines suggest a perspective on

[2] That I do not stand in total isolation within the economics profession on this point (despite impressions to the contrary when confronted by a "typical" audience of "typical" economists) is reflected in the growing awareness of the play of "noneconomic" factors and non-Western values in the development process throughout much of the world today. This point is noted in Higgins, 1968, p. 224, and developed in, among others, Boeke, 1948; Frankel, 1953; Hagan, 1962; Keyfitz, 1959; Myrdal, 1957 and 1968; Neale, 1968; and Polanyi, 1957b.

the basic development issues which permit planning authorities broad discretion in formulating, implementing, and
evaluating development programs in terms of local economic
realities. Within this frame of reference, the specific development strategy to be employed will depend primarily on the
particular targets and tactics selected by the planning authorities, in conjunction with public resource and administrative commitments.

Vehicle

The development strategy I suggest for the Northern Thai
uplands centers on the selective integration of tea technology into the institutional fabrics of the upland economies.[3]
This agent of development will raise levels of material well-
being in the uplands by generating cumulative technological
progress with the possibility of minimal institutional disruption, an opportunity arising out of the remarkable com-
patibility between tea and the indigenous upland economies.

The suitability of tea as a development vehicle in the
Northern Thai uplands derives from several special factors:
First, tea fits ecologically; it is native to the Northern hills
and, unlike most other economically viable upland crops, is
supportive rather than destructive of the region's balance of
nature. Second, tea has a ready domestic demand, a demand
which can be channeled to the locally produced product
through import restrictions and effective domestic marketing.
Third, tea production is amenable to a variety of technologies

[3] Others have suggested different development vehicles for the
uplands, such as maize, tobacco, coffee, cotton, various fruits, and
livestock. See, for instance, Keen, 1963(?) and 1968; and Brannon,
1963.

covering the gamut from small-scale, labor-intensive, cottage industry through large-scale, capital-intensive, factory-in-the-field operations. And fourth, tea production and distribution are adaptable to a wide range of institutional configurations, including the village-wide and entourage reciprocative forms common among the hill tribes and the Northern Thai, the redistributive form characteristic of the plantation economy, and the market form typical of the peasant and plantation economies in their relations with the commercial-industrial system of the urban hubs.

These characteristics of the tea industry in North Thailand have been touched on in various contexts in the preceding chapters; the threads will be drawn together below for the purpose of summarizing the available preconditions to a workable development strategy in the Northern Thai uplands.

1. That the natural ecology of North Thailand is well suited to tea cultivation (in contrast to intensive upland annuals cropping) has been made evident by the historically extensive, ecologically stable propagation and cultivation of tea shrubs for miang throughout the uplands and by the region's geographical similarities with Assam, northeast India's renowned tea-producing center.

Yet, though some miang cultivators are acquainted with green-tea technology and produce small quantities for home consumption and local trade, and though small, independently owned and operated workshops have been set up in various Northern districts by enterprising Chinese merchants to process and market leaf bought from local smallholders, the Thai have traditionally failed to engage in tea production and trade on a large scale.[4] Furthermore, the possibilities of

[4] Campbell, 1963; and Siampakdi, 1943.

tea as an economic mainstay have been entirely disregarded by the region's Sino-Tibetan hill tribes. In sum, the industry's ecological advantages have yet to be exploited.

2. Despite Thailand's past failure to realize its tea-producing potential, large numbers of its population are avid consumers, or would be if the production were made available to them at reasonable prices. The nation's ethnic Chinese (roughly 10 per cent of the total population) have traditionally been great tea consumers, and in urban areas the taste for tea is rapidly gaining ground among the ethnic Tai, who throughout their history have not consumed it as an infusion. In rural areas tea has long been considered of medicinal value and is today being purchased in increasing volume as inexpensive brands find trade channels into relatively isolated village market places, though unflavored hot water remains the most widely consumed beverage.[5]

The economic feasibility of a domestic tea trade has not gone unnoticed by the Thai government in recent years. *Direct* government efforts to introduce tea production to North Thailand on a commercial scale have to the present consisted primarily of financing the Fang Agricultural Station (a public "demonstration" facility in northern Chiengmai Province which has developed a tea nursery, model tea gardens, and a small manually-operated black-tea factory) [6] and providing a precedent-setting land concession and major capital-expansion loan to the Chiengdao Tea Plantation (discussed in Chapter 4).

[5] The ease with which this habit can be adapted to tea is evident. In requiring the boiling of water, tea consumption also serves as a valuable health measure in combating water-carried parasitic and bacterial diseases common among the Thai peasantry.

[6] Campbell, 1963, pp. 20–22. This author also mentions other tentative efforts to set up tea demonstration sites at various Northern agricultural stations and *nikhom*.

The government's *indirect* actions have perhaps been more effective in promoting the domestc tea trade. In 1957 the government enacted tea import restrictions. Since that year the more than forty firms registered in the tea import business have been required to purchase a specified ad valorem percentage of their stocks from the domestically produced tea held by the Public Warehouse Organization. In 1957 the import requirement was fixed at 10 per cent (meaning that one-tenth the value of imported tea had to be purchased from Public Warehouse stocks of the domestic product); the requirement was raised to 15 per cent in 1963 and 25 per cent in 1968, with notice being given that within the year it would be raised to 30 per cent for some varieties. The stated intent of the import control scheme is to protect and promote the infant industry, with the required rate of importers' Thai tea purchases rising as domestic producing capacity expands.[7]

[7] Domestic tea producers (primarily the Chiengdao Tea Plantation) have been handsomely subsidized by the scheme. Whereas domestic tea sells at wholesale prices averaging less than fifteen baht, per kg., it is sold to importers at prices averaging twenty-two baht per kg. The burden of the implicit tax is borne by both importers and consumers, each group's share of the burden depending on tea price elasticities in the Thai market. Furthermore, the forced wholesaling of domestic tea to importers lends itself to a number of abuses advantageous to Thai producers, the most important being its stimulus to local entrepreneurs to expand output at the expense of quality. (Other abuses include the provision of higher quality domestic grades to importers at lower prices in return for kickbacks to civil servants in charge of public marketing; a black market in domestic tea-purchase vouchers, which permit importers to clear their goods through customs; smuggling of tea into the country in return for kickbacks to customs officials; and smuggling of inferior tea overland from Burma and mainland China so that it may be marketed by the Public Warehouse Organization as the domestic product.) One result is that much that is produced is uncompetitive with foreign brands, importers reluctantly mixing it into their own product and even disposing of some as waste. The effective subsidy

3. No matter how ecologically suitable, readily marketable, and actively promoted tea may be, it will not gain favor as an occupational pursuit in the Northern Thai uplands unless the industry can be adjusted to indigenous economic structures. In this regard, its history reveals that tea technology can be fitted to a wide range of human environments. Perhaps the major cultural feature that tea production requires is a sedentary labor force, but that population may be dispersed or concentrated; motivated by animist, Buddhist, or Christian ethics; closely linked with, indifferent to, or hostile to lowland polity, society, and economy; institutionally reciprocative, redistributive, or market-oriented; and so forth. Furthermore, though the flavor and aroma of the finished product depends on the type of tea technology employed, the international history of the industry and the present Thai demand shows that the type of tea produced is not an important constraint on its marketability.

The experience of the Chiengdao Tea Plantation is instructive on this last point. In his continuing quest to find a *modus vivendi* for his tea venture in the upland cultural milieu, Khun Luang has experimented with tea production processes of varying degrees of sophistication. During the 1940's he relied on green-tea technology, involving in this case manual processing facilities supplied by independent miang gardeners; the small volume turned out by this pilot operation was of a quality readily marketable in North Thailand. As the volume of production expanded during the 1950's he turned to black-tea technology, which entailed mechanization and scientific supervision of processing facilities, though cultivation and inventory control continued along former lines; the product found widespread acceptance in Thailand when

---

to established domestic producers may thus be far larger than the difference in average wholesale price would seem to indicate.

marketed as an import under fictitious labels, despite problems of quality control associated with an undependable raw leaf inventory at the factory. Beginning in 1960, Khun Luang's venture took a further step up the ladder of technological sophistication by integrating tea propogation, cultivation, and inventory operations on a large-scale, scientifically supervised basis into its overall production scheme; again, under government sponsorship the product found an adequate market within Thailand. Thus, each of the production processes employed by the Chiengdao Tea Plantation has yielded a domestically marketable, potentially profitable product, proving that the tea industry is, in all its technological forms, viable within the Northern Thai uplands.

4. Just as the histories of the international tea trade and the Chiengdao Tea Plantation reflect the industry's technological flexibility, so do they demonstrate its institutional adaptability. Different types of tea technology require different capital intensities, different levels of managerial and labor expertise, different forms of production control, and different degrees of entrepreneurial risk. Such variability permits the industry to fit a wide range of institutional configurations.

The tea industry's greatest contribution as an economic development vehicle in North Thailand lies in its institutional adaptability. And it is in this area of concern that the preceding chapters' analyses of indigenous institutional configurations can play their most useful role.

Black-tea technology, with its scale economies and heavy capital and managerial requirements, logically fits market-oriented institutions. The plantation, archetypical of the institutional form facilitating the exploitation of this technology, permits the production of a high-grade, low-cost commodity through the "rationalization" of labor inputs—

that is, labor's integration into industrial operations regardless of repercussions within the indigenous economies from which these labor forces are extracted. This very built-in disregard for the life styles of the peasant population employed on the plantation inevitably generates conflicts among the economies concerned and disruption within each. Since the plantation is the institutional form to which black-tea technology is particularly well suited and since the history of this economic system has shown it to be severely destabilizing of indigenous economic structures in such a preindustrial, noncommercial environment as the Northern Thai uplands, the success of the tea industry as a development vehicle in this setting calls for the application of other technological-institutional correlates.

Of the variety of alternatives, two organizational arrangements traditionally associated with *green-tea technology* appear feasible in the Northern Thai uplands. First, independent smallholder cultivation and processing of green tea, with the finished product being distributed by local patrons of producing households, coincides with the institutional pattern of the upland Thai peasant economy. Second, independent smallholder cultivation, with cooperative processing under the direction of village specialists and with distribution managed by professional lowland traders, dovetails with the institutional configuration of the hill tribe peasant economy. The former arrangement supports and is in turn supported by the web of hierarchically oriented reciprocities characterizing the entourage form of Tai culture; the latter builds on the dual economy, intravillage reciprocative sodality, and limited village-wide functional division of labor characteristic of tribal culture. In both cases, then, green-tea technology can be fitted to indigenous institutional configurations, ensuring minimal disruption of the established socio-politico-economic order and thus speedy diffusion of the technological innovation, permitting the improvement of indigenous levels of material well-being.

Programs

It has obviously not been my intention here to present a full-blown plan for the development of the Northern Thai uplands through the promotion of the tea industry. Such a task would include wide-ranging discussions of matters beyond the scope of this study, such as the development of a national (and perhaps international) Thai tea marketing network, administrative synchronization of involved government agencies, investment in required social and economic infrastructure, protection and subsidization of the infant industry, magnitudes and sources of necessary industrial development finances, interrelations between this development plan and Thailand's overall development effort, and analysis of the plan's aggregate costs and benefits inclusive of externalities. However, I would like to briefly sketch the programs implied by the previously detailed development guidelines and strategy, focusing on their feasibility in terms of their "sensitivity" to the indigenous institutional configurations of the Northern Thai uplands.

Upland Thai peasant households will be introduced to green-tea technology and its material advantages by their *pau liang*, who will themselves assume an innovative role as they are convinced by government propaganda of the long-run decline in miang consumption and the offsetting possibilities in tea. A well-advertised extension of the Public Warehouse Organization's operations into the major towns of the North will assure potential local tea dealers of ready access to a guaranteed market featuring stable and attractive

253

wholesale prices. Furthermore, local interest will be aroused through a public education program (carried out by agricultural extension officers, provincial economic officers, Public Warehouse Organization agents, and the public media) aimed at disseminating information on proper green-tea cultivation and processing techniques, efficient transportation and warehousing practices, and available forms and sources of government assistance to those contemplating entry into the industry.

As upland Thai peasant households are convinced to take up tea cultivation, they will be supplied through their patrons with tea seedlings grown for the purpose at government agricultural stations. Those households already possessing miang gardens can intersperse tea seedlings among mature miang shrubs; this will ensure that seedlings are planted at the finest upland sites and in adequate shade, will obviate the burdensome task of craving additional gardens out of the jungle and maintaining them separately over the years, and will permit households to care for the seedlings without neglecting their traditional livelihood (or vice versa) during the years until the seedlings mature. Landless lowland Thai peasants will also be convinced to enter the industry and to withstand the discomforts of upland life if they are provided technical assistance in garden site selection and in cultivating and processing methods, if they are guaranteed a minimum subsistence income to see them through the early years (*pau liang* acting as government agents in this matter), and if they are granted full and permanent tenure rights to the gardens they clear out of the jungle and maintain. The industry's rate of growth and its ultimate size can be controlled by judicious management of these means of industrial promotion.

Such a program will entail a sizable public commitment of personnel, facilities, and funds, as well as a determined effort on the part of various government agencies to synchronize their functions. However, the program's administrative and financial burdens will be greatly eased by quiet sponsorship and skillful utilization of local *pau liang* as informal intermediaries in the planned process of technological diffusion and as unofficial, unsalaried, and even unknowing government representatives in the infant industry's management at the local level. Beyond the saving involved in reliance on the entourage as the means of organizing this program at the local level, a significant but unquantifiable saving will be realized in the avoidance of conflicts with local vested interests, and thus of institutional bottlenecks, that would otherwise inevitably be encountered. Summarily, in working through the established network of Thai peasant entourages the government will be exploiting indigenous channels of control, communication, and resource allocation rather than duplicating them along relatively inefficient, institutionally disruptive lines.

Involving hill tribesmen in the tea industry will depend primarily on convincing economically distressed tribal villages to migrate to *nikhom* territories in the expectation that they will there receive temporary economic aid (or credit, as tribal villages prefer to see it) without endangering their cherished independence and their traditional livelihood. This has been the means whereby several tribal villages have been attracted to the territory now controlled by Nikhom Chiengdao, and timely propagandizing by government officials (*nikhom* officials, border patrol police, mobile development teams, forestry agents) may succeed in adding to these numbers as additional impoverished villages are encountered, especially if previously aided villages can be pointed to as evidence of good faith and solid results. Since economic conditions in tribal villages tend to fluctuate sharply from year to year it will be of paramount importance to the success of this program that officials keep in close touch with villages considered prospectively movable to the *nikhom* and to tea and that they involve themselves in the situation at the propitious moment.

On the *nikhom*, hill tribesmen will be introduced to the economic opportunities inherent in tea as a supplement to the tribal economy's traditional export sector. *Nikhom* personnel will develop model tea gardens and processing facilities, advertise the advantages of tea cultivation (its low labor requirement, its easy adjustment to the tribal agricultural year, its material rewards), and offer tea seedlings and technical assistance to interested villages. One proposal, made by Nikhom Chiengdao, is of particular interest. Local hill tribe villages are to be promised up to 100,000 tea seedlings if they will terrace depleted swiddens on a phased schedule, each household planting one-fifth of its swidden plot each year, so that the first year's planting will be coming of picking age as the final section is being newly developed. Such phasing will permit tribal villages to adjust gradually from traditional labor commitments to the inclusion of tea cultivation in their economy. Within ten years all gardens will have matured, providing the typical household with a cash income estimated at 7,500 baht (a fifteen *rai* garden producing 250 kilograms of raw leaf per *rai*, selling at two baht per kilogram), an income additional to, rather than in replacement of, its traditional export revenues.

Green-tea processing, requiring a command of production techniques new to the tribal mind, can most efficiently be introduced to each village through a local tribal "expert" in the art, trained by agricultural extension officers, Public Warehouse Organization agents, or *nikhom* personnel. Because it may take time to convince educable villagers to commit themselves to such an innovative role and to submit to

training at the hands of lowlanders, the *nikhom* should itself be prepared to assume responsibility for processing tribal
tea harvests at local workshops (possibly operated by upland
Thai peasants) during the interim period. Ideally, however,
raw leaf harvests will be brought by tribesmen of each village
to a centrally located village workshop, where it will be
processed as a village-wide cooperative undertaking under
the direction of the village tea specialist. Such a collective
undertaking, based on indigenous institutions, will stimulate
active support in the tea development program and will provide a finished product of standard commercial quality.
Village tea specialists will be motivated to excel at their task
in keeping with the status and power deriving from their
new-found role as well as from its material advantages, not
the least of which will be a share in the returns from all
exported tea.

The finished product will be transported to the provincial
public warehouse by the *nikhom* staff, which will reimburse
the tribal tea specialist, as agent for his village, in either cash
or goods, as requested. In its capacity as intermediary between tea-producing villages and the Public Warehouse
Organization and lowland market places, the *nikhom* will be
absorbing the functions traditionally assigned to the itinerant trader and opium smuggler as economic link and cultural
buffer between the tribes and the Thai.

This progam, like that envisioned for the introduction of
tea production into the upland Thai peasant economy, will
be neither cheap nor quickly completed.[8] Early scattered
successes will be critical to the program's long-run effective-

[8] In comparison with the costs of hill tribe counterinsurgency,
border control, narcotics traffic elimination, forest conservation, and
related programs, however, it does not seem unreasonable to suggest
that the promotion of the tea industry among the hill tribes, as
among the upland Thai, may actually entail a sizable saving for the
Thai government in the long run.

ness, for only through prominent tribal examples of the industry's potential will the hoped-for diffusion of tea production to more remote villages (entailing extensions of *nikhom* involvement further into the hills) be realized.

The economic opportunities opened to tribal villages in tea production will, over time and in conjunction with continued pressures against the opium trade, lead tribesmen to substitute tea for opium exports. Reliance on tea will also reduce tribal migration, resulting in the gradual depletion of opium swiddens and contributing to the decline of this export staple. Soil depletion under sedentary swiddening will also reduce dry-rice harvests, of course, and at a much faster rate than with opium; to cope with this problem *nikhom* officials can offer fertilizers and technical assistance to tribal villages, or they can persuade them to raise the volume of tea production and supplementary crops to finance rice imports.[9]

The heart of this program, as in the case of its counterpart for Thai peasants, lies in its adherence to indigenous institutional configurations and its emphasis on minimal direct alien (that is, Thai government) involvement in tribal affairs. Reliance on the tribal tea specialist as intermediary between the village and the *nikhom* here parallels the leadership role assigned to the *pau liang* in the Thai peasant program. In both cases direct government involvement will be

[9] In such matters the question of phasing becomes important. The institutionalization of tea production into the tribal economy will, after all, be largely irreversible once it is well under way. If swiddening difficulties do not arise until then, tribal villages will be strongly motivated to seek assistance in dealing with them; if such problems arise at a very early stage in the process, villages may well find it possible to abandon the tea experiment and revert to the previous economic pattern. Thus, successful program implementation will depend on rapid integration of tea into the tribal economy on the one hand and as long a delay as possible in the depletion of local swidden sites on the other.

limited largely to popularizing the tea industry, providing seedlings and suitable upland sites, and disseminating technical information on production methods.

As their primary target, these tea development programs seek to improve local levels of material well-being through the introduction of a new technology in such a manner as to minimize the disruptive impact on indigenous institutions. They will shift the attention of upland Thai peasant households from their total commitment to a crop with little industrial future to one having significant potential. They will open new opportunities to lowland Thai peasants squeezed off the wet-rice plains by an expanding population. And they will introduce hill tribe peasants to a livelihood economically competitive with and politically more advantageous than opium. In each case, tea can be integrated into the indigenous economy without pervasive institutional transformation. In fact, employment of indigenous institutions as key factors in the programs' implementation will reduce costs in terms of personnel, facilities, and funds while increasing the chances of successful diffusion of the new technology. Success will be recognizable in a significant and enduring improvement in upland levels of material well-being.

BIBLIOGRAPHY

Allen, Francis R., Hornell Hart, Delbert C. Miller, William F. Ogburn, and Meyer F. Minkoff. 1957. *Technology and Social Change*. New York: Appleton-Century-Crofts.

American Economic Association. 1966. "Papers and Proceedings of the Seventy-eighth Annual Meeting of the American Economic Association," *American Economic Review*, LVI, no. 2.

Ayres, Clarence E. 1962. *The Theory of Economic Progress*. New York: Schocken.

Barnett, Homer G. 1953. *Innovation: The Basis of Cultural Change*. New York: McGraw-Hill.

Barringer, Herbert R., George I. Blanksten, and Raymond W. Mack, eds. 1965. *Social Change in Developing Areas: A Reinterpretation of Evolutionary Theory*. Cambridge, Mass.: Schenkman.

Bauer, Peter T., and Basil S. Yamey. 1957. *The Economics of Under-Developed Countries*. Chicago: University of Chicago Press.

Beattie, J. H. M. 1961. "Culture Contact and Social Change," *British Journal of Sociology*, XII, 165–175.

Behrman, Jere R. 1968. *Supply Response in Underdeveloped Agriculture: A Case Study of Four Major Annual Crops in Thailand, 1937–1963*. Amsterdam: North-Holland.

Bennington-Cornell Anthropological Survey of Hill Tribes in Thailand. 1964. *A Report on Tribal Peoples in Chiengrai Province North of the Mae Kok River*. Bangkok: Siam Society, Data Paper no. 1.

Bernatzik, Hugo Adolf. 1963. "Akha and Miao: Problems of Applied Ethnography in Farther India," trans. Alois Nagler. New Haven: Human Relations Area Files (on file cards).

Boeke, J. H. 1948. *The Interests of the Voiceless Far East: Introduction to Oriental Economics.* Leiden, Netherlands: Universitaire Pers.

Bohannan, Paul and Laura. 1968. *Tiv Economy.* Evanston, Ill.: Northwestern University Press.

———, Paul, and Fred Plog, eds. 1967. *Beyond the Frontier: Social Process and Cultural Change.* New York: Natural History Press.

Boserup, Ester. 1965. *The Conditions of Agricultural Growth: The Economics of Agrarian Change under Population Pressure.* Chicago: Aldine.

Boulding, Kenneth E. 1966. "The Economics of Knowledge and the Knowledge of Economics," *American Economic Review,* LVI, No. 2, 1–13.

Brannon, Russell H. 1963. "End of Tour Report." Bangkok: Agency for International Development, Agricultural Division.

Bruton, Henry J. 1965. *Principles of Development Economics.* Englewood Cliffs, N.J.: Prentice-Hall.

Buckley, Walter. 1959. "Structural-Functional Analysis in Modern Sociology," in *Modern Sociological Theory,* ed. Howard Becker and Alvin Boskoff. New York: Harper and Row. pp. 236–259.

Bunyasingh, Khrui. 1962. "Agriculture of the Hill Tribes." Mimeo. Bangkok: Ministry of Agriculture (in Thai).

Bury, J. B. 1932. *The Idea of Progress: An Inquiry into Its Origin and Growth.* London: Macmillan.

Caldwell, J. C. 1967. "The Demographic Structure," in Silcock, ed., 1967, pp. 27–64.

Campbell, P. D. J. 1963. "Report on Survey of Tea Growing Areas of Thailand." Mimeo. Bangkok: Colombo Plan.

Chotsukkharat, S. 1962. *Tour of the North: Culture and Customs of the North.* Bangkok: Odeon Bookstore (in Thai).

Clark, Colin, and Margaret Haswell. 1964. *The Economics of Subsistence Agriculture.* New York: St. Martin's Press.

Conklin, Harold C. 1961. "The Study of Shifting Cultivation," *Current Anthropology,* II, 27–61.

Coser, Lewis. 1956. *The Functions of Social Conflict.* Glencoe, Ill.: Free Press.

Courtenay, P. P. 1965. *Plantation Agriculture.* London: Bell.

Credner, Wilhelm. 1935. *Siam, das Land der Tai: Eine Landeskunde auf Grund eigener Reisen und Forschungen.* Stuttgart: J. Engelhorns Nachfolger.

Curtis, Lillian J. 1903. *The Laos of North Siam.* London: Revell.

Dalton, George. 1969. "Theoretical Issues in Economic Anthropology," "Comments," and "Bibliography," *Current Anthropology,* X, 63–102.

Devakul, Wutilert. 1965. "Headmanship Among the Lahu Na," in Lucien M. Hanks *et al.,* eds. 1965, pp. 31–35.

DeYoung, John E. 1955. *Village Life in Modern Thailand.* Berkeley: University of California Press.

Eden, T. 1958. *Tea.* London: Longmans.

Eggan, Fred. 1963. "Cultural Drift and Social Change," *Current Anthropology,* IV, 347–359.

Ellul, Jacques. 1964. *The Technological Society.* New York: Knopf.

Elwin, Verrier. 1961. *A Philosophy for NEFA.* 3d ed. Shillong, India: North-East Frontier Agency Administration.

——, ed. 1959. *India's North-East Frontier in the Nineteenth Century.* London: Oxford University Press.

Erasmus, Charles J. 1961. *Man Takes Control: Cultural Development and American Aid.* Minneapolis: University of Minnesota Press.

Fairbank, John K. 1969. *Trade and Diplomacy on the China Coast: The Opening of the Treaty Ports, 1848–1854.* Stanford: Stanford University Press.

Fei, John C. H., and Gustav Ranis. 1964. *Development of the Labor Surplus Economy: Theory and Policy.* Homewood, Ill.: Irwin.

Firth, Raymond, ed. 1967. *Themes in Economic Anthropology.* London: Tavistock.

Foster, George M. 1962. *Traditional Cultures and the Impact of Technological Change.* New York: Harper and Row.

——. 1965. "Peasant Society and the Image of Limited Good," *American Anthropologist,* LXVII, 293–315.

Frankel, S. Herbert. 1953. *The Economic Impact on Under-Developed Societies.* Oxford, Eng.: Blackwell.

Geertz, Clifford. 1963. *Agricultural Involution: The Process of Ecological Change in Indonesia.* Berkeley: University of California Press.

Gilfillan, S. 1935. *The Sociology of Invention.* Chicago: Follet.

Gordon, R. A. 1963. "Institutional Elements in Contemporary Economics," in *Institutional Economics: Veblen, Commons, and Mitchell Reconsidered,* by C. E. Ayres, Neil W. Chamberlain, Simon Kuznets, and R. A. Gordon. Berkeley: University of California Press. pp. 123–147.

Gouldner, Alvin W. 1960. "The Norm of Reciprocity: A Preliminary Statement," *American Sociological Review,* XXV, 161–178.

Gourou, Pierre. 1966. *The Tropical World: Its Social and Economic Conditions and Its Future Status.* 4th ed. Trans. S. H. Beaver and E. D. Laborde. London: Longmans.

Graham, W. A. 1924. *Siam.* 3d ed. London: De La More Press.

Greenberg, Michael. 1951. *British Trade and the Opening of China, 1800–42.* Cambridge, Eng.: Cambridge University Press.

Griffiths, Sir Percival. 1967. *The History of the British Tea Industry.* London: Weidenfeld and Nicolson.

Hagen, Everett E. 1962. *On the Theory of Social Change: How Economic Growth Begins.* Homewood, Ill.: Dorsey Press.

Hall, D. G. E. 1964. *A History of South-East Asia.* 2d ed. London: Macmillan.

Halpern, Joel M. 1961. "The Rural and Urban Economies." Los Angeles: University of California, Department of Anthropology, Laos Project Paper no. 19.

Hamilton, James W. 1963. "Effects of the Thai Market on Karen Life," *Applied Anthropology*, X, 209–215.

Hamilton, Walton H. 1930. "Institution," in *Encyclopedia of the Social Sciences*. New York: Macmillan. VIII, 84–89.

Hanks, Jane Richardson. 1960. "Reflections on the Ontology of Rice," in *Culture in History: Essays in Honor of Paul Radin*, ed. Stanley Diamond. New York: Columbia University Press. Pp. 298–301.

——. 1964. Field notes. Mimeo.

——. 1967(?). "National Security in Northern Thailand." Mimeo.

Hanks, Lucien M. 1962. "Merit and Power in the Thai Social Order," *American Anthropologist*, LXIV, 1247–1261.

——. 1963a. Ban Yai Suk census (November). Mimeo.

——. 1963b. Phapucom census (November). Mimeo.

——. 1964. Field notes. Mimeo.

——. 1966. "The Corporation and the Entourage: A Comparison of Thai and American Social Organization," *Catalyst*, no. 2, pp. 55–63.

——, Jane Richardson Hanks, and Lauriston Sharp, eds. 1965. *Ethnographic Notes on Northern Thailand*. Ithaca: Cornell University, Department of Asian Studies, Southeast Asia Program, Data Paper no. 58.

Harler, C. R. 1964. *The Culture and Marketing of Tea*. 3d ed. London: Oxford University Press.

——. 1966. *Tea Growing*. London: Oxford University Press.

Harris, Marvin. 1968. *The Rise of Anthropological Theory: A History of Theories of Culture*. New York: Crowell.

Hempel, Carl G. 1959. "The Logic of Functional Analysis," in *Symposium on Sociological Theory*, ed. Llewellyn Gross. New York: Harper and Row. Pp. 271–307.

Higgins, Benjamin. 1968. *Economic Development: Principles, Problems, and Policies*. Rev. ed. New York: Norton.

Hill, Polly. 1966. "A Plea for Indigenous Economics: The West African Example," *Economic Development and Cultural Change*, XV, 10–20.

Hirschman, Albert O. 1959. *The Strategy of Economic Development*. New Haven: Yale University Press.

Holt, Charles C. 1969. "Improving the Labor Market Trade-off Between Inflation and Unemployment," *American Economic Review*, LIX, no. 2, 135–146.

Hoselitz, Bert F. 1963. "Main Concepts in the Analysis of the Social Implications of Technical Change," in *Industrialization and Society*, ed. Bert F. Hoselitz and Wilbert E. Moore. Paris: UNESCO. Pp. 11–31.

Humphreys, S. C. 1969. "History, Economics, and Anthropology: The Work of Karl Polanyi," *History and Theory*, VIII, 165–212.

Ingram, James C. 1964. "Thailand's Rice Trade and the Allocation of Resources," in *The Economic Development of Southeast Asia*, ed. C. D. Cowan. New York: Praeger. Pp. 102–126.

Jones, Delmos J. 1967. "Cultural Variation among Six Lahu Villages, Northern Thailand." Ph.D. thesis. Ithaca: Cornell University.

——. 1969. "The Multivillage Community: Village Segmentation and Coalescence in Northern Thailand," *Behavior Science Notes*, III, 149–174.

Judd, L. C. 1964. *Dry Rice Agriculture in Northern Thailand*. Ithaca: Cornell University, Department of Asian Studies, Southeast Asia Program, Data Paper no. 52.

Kandre, Peter K. 1967. "Autonomy and Integration of Social Systems: The Iu Mien ('Yao' or 'Man') Mountain Population and Their Neighbors," in Kunstadter, ed., 1967, pp. 583–638.

——, and Lej Tsan Kuej. 1965. "Aspects of Wealth-Accumulation, Ancestor Worship and Household Stability among the Iu Mien-Yao," in *Felicitation Volumes of Southeast-Asian Studies Presented to His Highness Prince Dhaninivat*. Bangkok: Siam Society. Pp. 129–148.

Kao, Charles H. C., Kurt R. Anschel, and Carl K. Eicher. 1964. "Disguised Unemployment in Agriculture: A Survey,"

Mason, Edward S., ed. 1959. *The Corporation in Modern Society*. Cambridge: Harvard University Press.

McCarthy, James. 1900. *Surveying and Exploring in Siam*. London: Murray.

McClelland, David C. 1963. "The Achievement Motive in Economic Growth," in *Industrialization and Society*, ed. Bert F. Hoselitz and Wilbert E. Moore. Paris: UNESCO. Pp. 74–96.

Milne, Mrs. Leslie. 1924. *The Home of an Eastern Clan: A Study of the Palaungs of the Shan State*. Oxford, Eng.: Clarendon Press.

Mishan, Ezra J. 1967. *The Costs of Economic Growth*. New York: Praeger.

Moerman, Michael. 1961. "The Village World and the Larger World: Aspects of Village Life in Northern Thailand and Village Response to Modern Social Forces." Mimeo. Bangkok: United States Information Service, Regional Research Report no. 8.

——. 1964. "Western Culture and the Thai Way of Life," *Asia*, no. 1, pp. 31–50.

——. 1965. "Ethnic Identification in a Complex Civilization: Who Are the Lue?" *American Anthropologist*, LXVII, 1215–1230.

——. 1966. "Kinship and Commerce in a Thai-Lue Village," *Ethnology*, V, 360–364.

——. 1967. "A Minority and Its Government: The Thai-Lue of Northern Thailand," in Kunstadter, ed., 1967, pp. 401–424.

——. 1968. *Agricultural Change and Peasant Choice in a Thai Village*. Berkeley: University of California Press.

Mote, F. W. 1967. "The Rural 'Haw' (Yunnanese Chinese) of Northern Thailand," in Kunstadter, ed., 1967, pp. 487–524.

Murdock, George P. 1956. "How Culture Changes," in *Man, Culture, and Society*, ed. Harry Shapiro. New York: Oxford University Press. Pp. 247–260.

Myint, Hla. 1964. *The Economics of the Developing Countries*. London: Hutchinson.

Myrdal, Gunnar. 1957. *Economic Theory and Under-Developed Regions*. London: Duckworth.

——. 1968. *Asian Drama: An Inquiry into the Poverty of Nations*. New York: Twentieth Century Fund.

Nash, Manning. 1964. "The Organization of Economic Life," in *Horizons of Anthropology*, ed. Sol Tax. Chicago: Aldine. Pp. 171–180.

——. 1966. *Primitive and Peasant Economic Systems*. San Francisco: Chandler.

Neale, Walter C. 1959. "Economic Accounting and Family Farming in India," *Economic Development and Cultural Change*, VII, 286–301.

——. 1968. "On Peasant Motivation and Economic Behavior: Preparatory Notes for the Workshop on Peasant Motivation and Economic Behavior." Mimeo. New York: Agricultural Development Council.

Nimmanahaeminda, Kraisri. 1965. "The Irrigation Laws of King Mengrai," in Lucien M. Hanks *et al.*, eds., 1965, pp. 1–5.

Parsons, Talcott, and Neil J. Smelser. 1956. *Economy and Society*. Glencoe, Ill.: Free Press.

Pelzer, Karl J. 1945. *Pioneer Settlement in the Asiatic Tropics*. New York: American Geographical Society.

Pendleton, Robert L. 1962. *Thailand: Aspects of Landscape and Life*. New York: Duell, Sloan and Pearce.

Polanyi, Karl. 1957a. "Aristotle Discovers the Economy," in Polanyi *et al.*, eds., 1957, pp. 64–94.

——. 1957b. "The Economy as Instituted Process," in Polanyi *et al.*, eds., 1957, pp. 243–270.

——, Conrad M. Arensberg, and Harry W. Pearson, eds. 1957. *Trade and Market in the Early Empires: Economies in History and Theory*. Glencoe, Ill.: Free Press

Premarasami, Thanom. 1963. *The Laws of the Department of Forests*. 2d ed. Bangkok: Ministry of Agriculture (in Thai).

The Record. 1922. "Report of the Botanical Section." II, no. 6, 8–16.

———. 1923. "Report on the Cultivation of 'Miang.'" III, no. 1, 16–20.

Riggs, Fred W. 1966. *Thailand: The Modernization of a Bureaucratic Polity.* Honolulu: East-West Center Press.

Robinson, W. 1841. *Descriptive Account of Assam.* London: N. pub.

Rogers, Everett M. 1962. *Diffusion of Innovations.* New York: Free Press.

Ruttan, V. W., A. Soothipan, and E. C. Venegas. 1966. "Changes in Rice Growing in the Philippines and Thailand," *World Crops,* March no., pp. 1–16.

Sahlins, Marshall D. 1965. "On the Sociology of Primitive Exchange," in *The Relevance of Models for Social Anthropology,* ed. M. Banton. London: Tavistock. Pp. 139–236.

Saihoo, Patya. 1963. "The Hill Tribes of Northern Thailand and the Opium Problem," *Bulletin of Narcotics,* XV, no. 2, 35–45.

Salisbury, R. F. 1962. *From Stone to Steel: Economic Consequences of a Technological Change in New Guinea.* London: Cambridge University Press.

Samapuddhi, K., and P. Suvanakorn. 1962. "A Study of the Effects of Shifting Cultivation on Forest Soils." Bangkok: Ministry of Agriculture, Department of Forests, Royal Forest Department Publication no. R. 51.

Samuelson, Paul A., and Robert M. Solow. 1960. "Analytical Aspects of Anti-Inflation Policy," *American Economic Review,* L, no. 2, 177–194.

Satow, E. 1892. "The Laos States," *Journal of the Society of Arts,* XL, 182–196.

Schmookler, Jacob. 1966. *Invention and Economic Growth.* Cambridge: Harvard University Press.

Schultz, Theodore W. 1964. *Transforming Traditional Agriculture.* New Haven: Yale University Press.

Sealy, J. R. 1958. *A Revision of the Genus Camellia.* London: Royal Horticultural Society.

Seidenfaden, Erik. 1958. *The Thai Peoples: The Origins and Habitats*. Bangkok: Siam Society.

Seth, A. N. 1968. "Report on Land Reforms in Thailand." Mimo. Bangkok: FAO Regional Office.

Sharp, Lauriston. 1965. "Philadelphia among the Lahu," in Lucien M. Hanks *et al.*, eds., 1965, pp. 84–90.

———, and Pramote Nakorntheb. 1963. Huai Thad census (December).

Sharp, Ruth B. 1965. "It's Expensive to Be a Yao," in Lucien M. Hanks *et al.*, eds., 1965, pp. 36–39.

———, Ruth B., and Lauriston. 1964. "Some Archaelogical Sites in North Thailand," *Journal of the Siam Society*, LII, 233–239.

Shway Yoe (James George Scott). 1910. *The Burman: His Life and Notions*. London: Macmillan.

Siampakdi, Siang. 1943. "Miang Tea Trade in Changwat Chiengmai," *Commercial Magazine*, IX, no. 2 (in Thai).

Siffin, William J. 1966. *The Thai Bureaucracy: Institutional Change and Development*. Honolulu: East-West Center Press.

Silcock, T. H., ed. 1967. *Thailand: Social and Economic Studies in Development*. Canberra: Australian National University Press.

Spencer, J. E. 1966. *Shifting Cultivation in Southeastern Asia*. Berkeley: University of California Press.

Srirachaburutra, Luang. 1963. *Explanation of the Laws of the Land*. 2d ed. Bangkok: Thamasarn (in Thai).

Stevenson, H. N. C. 1943. *The Economics of the Central Chin Tribes*. Bombay: The Times of India Press.

Steward, Julian. 1955. *Theory of Culture Change*. Urbana: University of Illinois Press.

Stolper, Wolfgang. 1966. *Planning without Facts: Lessons in Resource Allocation from Nigeria's Development*. Cambridge: Harvard University Press.

Supple, Barry E., ed. 1963. *The Experience of Economic Growth: Case Studies in Economic History*. New York: Random House.

Suwathapantha, Kasin, 1947. "The Process of Making Tea from Miang Leaves," *The Farmer*, pp. 15–22 (in Thai).

Symes, Michael. 1800. *Embassy to Ava in 1795*. London: N. pub.

Thailand, Government of. 1960. *Self-Help Land Settlement in Thailand*. Bangkok: Ministry of Interior, Department of Public Welfare.

——. 1962. "Report on the Socio-Economic Survey of Hill Tribes in Thailand." Mimeo. Bangkok: Ministry of Interior, Department of Public Welfare.

——. 1963a. *Hill Tribe Development and Welfare in Thailand*. Bangkok: Ministry of Interior, Department of Public Welfare, Central Hill Tribe Welfare Committee (in Thai and English).

——. 1963b. "Nikhom Agricultural Survey of Lahu Villages, 2506." Ministry of Interior, Department of Public Welfare, Nikhom Chiengdao (in Thai).

——. 1965. *Thailand Official Yearbook, 1964*. Bangkok: Government Printing Office.

——. Various dates. *Agricultural Statistics of Thailand*. Bangkok: Ministry of Agriculture, Division of Agricultural Economics.

——. Various dates. "Annual Statement of Foreign Trade of Thailand." Mimeo. Bangkok: Ministry of Economic Affairs, Department of Customs.

Thisyamondol, Pantum, Virach Arromdee, and Millard F. Long. 1965. *Agricultural Credit in Thailand: Theory, Data, Administration*. Bangkok: Kasetsart University, Faculty of Economics and Business Administration.

Thompson, Carey C., ed. 1967. *Institutional Adjustment: A Challenge to a Changing Economy*. Austin: University of Texas Press.

Uchendu, Victor C. 1967. "Some Principles of Haggling in Peasant Markets," *Economic Development and Cultural Change*, XVI, 37–50.

Udy, Stanley H. 1959. *Organization of Work: A Comparative Analysis of Production among Nonindustrial Peoples*. New Haven: Human Relations Area Files Press.

Ukers, William H. 1936. *The Romance of Tea*. New York: Knopf.

Usher, Dan. 1967a. "Thai Interest Rates," *Journal of Development Studies*, III, 267–279.

——. 1967b. "The Thai Rice Trade," in Silcock, ed., 1967, pp. 206–230.

Van Roy, Edward. 1965. "Structure of the Miang Economy," in Lucien M. Hanks *et al.*, eds., 1965, pp. 21–30.

——. 1966. "Economic Dualism and Economic Change among the Hill Tribes of Thailand," *Pacific Viewpoint*, VII, no. 2, 151–168.

——. 1967. "An Interpretation of Northern Thai Peasant Economy," *Journal of Asian Studies*, XXVI, 421–432.

——. 1968. "The Introduction of Plantation Economy to North Thailand," *Explorations in Entrepreneurial History*, 2d ser., V, 36–57.

——. 1970. "On the Theory of Corruption," *Economic Development and Cultural Change*, XIX, 86–110.

——, and James V. Cornehls. 1969. "Economic Development in Mexico and Thailand: An Institutional Analysis (Part Two)," *Journal of Economic Issues*, III, 21–38.

Vella, Walter F. 1955. *The Impact of the West on Government in Thailand*. Berkeley: University of California Press.

——. 1957. *Siam under Rama III, 1824–1851*. Locust Valley, N.Y.: Augustin.

Wales, H. G. Q. 1934. *Ancient Siamese Government and Administration*. London: Quaritch.

Watabe, Tadayo. 1967. *Glutinous Rice in Northern Thailand*. Kyoto, Japan: Kyoto University, Center for Southeast Asian Studies.

Watters, R. F. 1960. "The Nature of Shifting Agriculture," *Pacific Viewpoint*, I, No. 1, 59–99.

White, Leslie. 1959. *The Evolution of Culture*. New York: McGraw-Hill.

White, Lynn. 1962. *Medieval Technology and Social Change*. London: Oxford University Press.

Wicitrajantra, Narongrit. 1962. "Tea Growing in the North," *The Farmer*, pp. 531–537 (in Thai).

Wickizer, V. D. 1944. *Tea under International Regulation*. Stanford: Stanford University Food Research Institute.

Wiens, Herold J. 1954. *China's March toward the Tropics*. Hamden, Conn.: Shoe String Press.

Wijeyewardene, Gehan. 1965. "A Note on Irrigation and Agriculture in a North Thai Village," in *Felicitation Volumes of Southeast-Asian Studies Presented to His Highness Prince Dhaninivat*. Bangkok: Siam Society. Pp. 255–259.

——. 1967. "Some Aspects of Rural Life in Thailand," in Silcock, ed., 1967, pp. 65–83.

Williams, Harry. 1956. *Ceylon, Pearl of the East*. 5th ed. London: Hale.

Wolf, Charles. 1955. "Institutions and Economic Development," *American Economic Review*, XLV, 867–883.

Yano, Toru. 1968. "Land Tenure in Thailand," *Asian Survey*, VII, 853–858.

Young, Gordon. 1962. *The Hill Tribes of Northern Thailand*. 2d ed. Bangkok: Siam Society.

INDEX

acculturation, tribal, 202
addiction, drug, 66, 71, 73, 76, 100;
    see also narcotics
administrative agencies and centers,
    35-36, 194-201; see also *nikhom*
Africa: economy of, 214n; slave
    trade, 65; tea production in, 142;
    tea research institutes in, 146
agricultural: calendars, 43-44, 104,
    107, 173, 224-230, 256; proletariat,
    143, 157, 188; stations, 200, 254;
    surveys, 88
agriculture, *see* swiddening *and in-
    dividual crops*
Agriculture, Ministry of, 194, 198
ahsia, 120n
aid: foreign, 74-75, 155; public, 72,
    76, 180, 255
Akha tribe, 27, 48n, 65n, 76n
Allen, Francis R., cited, 4n
American Economic Association, 4
Amphur Mae Thaeng, 36
ancestral villages and homelands,
    113, 127-128, 182
animal husbandry, 33n, 41, 47; *see
    also* livestock *and specific animals*
animism, 24, 250
*Annual Statement of Foreign Trade
    of Thailand*, 177
antagonisms, between upland Thai
    and tribesmen, 221-223
anthropology, 1, 2n, 6n, 8n, 10n, 50n,
    68, 147, 238
Argentine tea, 156n
artisans and artifacts, 3, 33, 47-48,
    52-53, 55, 62, 75n, 80-81, 104, 208,
    213, 214n

aspirin, as preservative, 54, 72
Assam, and tea industry, 139, 150,
    158-160, 247
Austroasiatic tribes and traditions,
    26-27, 87-88, 228
authority: ambiguous, 183-184; juris-
    dictional, 221; realms of, 191, 195;
    village, 219
autonomy, regional, *see* regionalism,
    Northern
Ayres, Clarence E., cited, 10n
Ayutthaya, 28

"balance of nature," 41
Ban Pong, 36-39, 128, 135, 136n, 160,
    202, 210
Ban Pong Valley, 36-39
Ban Yai Suk, 76, 78-83, 203, 205,
    210, 241
banditry, 216
Bangkok, 17, 21, 25, 28-35, 38, 99-100,
    163, 196, 207
Baptist missionaries, 77
bargaining atmosphere, 99, 189n, 213
Barnett, Homer G., cited, 4n
Bauer, Peter T., cited, 14n
Behrman, Jere R., cited, 157n
benevolence, 178-180, 190, 220
Bennington-Cornell Anthropological
    Survey of Hill Tribes in Thailand,
    26n, 34n, 44n, 49n, 52n, 66n
Bernatzek, Hugo, cited, 34n, 44n,
    48n, 50n, 59n, 62n, 65
betel consumption, 85
black market, 249
black-tea production and trade,

black-tea production & trade (*cont.*) 139-147, 164, 166, 248, 250-252; *see also* tea

Boeke, J. H., cited, 245

Bohannan, Paul and Laura, cited, 214n

bondage, wage labor associated with, 65, 221; *see also* slaves

Border Patrol Police, 200, 203, 255, 257n

Boulding, Kenneth E., cited, 4n

boundaries and borders, 18n, 19, 23, 28-29, 49n, 257n

Brannon, Russell H., cited, 246

bribery, 216, 249n

"bride price," 63, 75n

British East India Company, 138

British Empire tea industry, 139, 141, 145n, 159

British India, 138

British-American Tobacco Company, 158-159

Bruton, Henry J., 14n

Buckley, Walter, cited, 6n

Buddhism, 24, 84, 106n, 127, 178, 250

buffalo, 33, 136n

Bukkavesa, Sombodhi, 100n

bureaucracy: levels of, 31, 101-102, 185-186, 209; local, 191-197; national, 16, 203, 224

Burma, 19, 187, 241, 249; ethnic groups in, 23-24, 199; frontier of, 27-28, 35; hill tribes of, 79n, 84, 87, 96, 140n, 228, 239; and miang, 84, 85, 88; military forces of, 77, 220; refugees from, 173; trade with, 66n; Upper, 84

Bury, J. B., cited, 11n

caffeine, in miang leaves, 100

Caldwell, J. C., cited, 105n

Campbell, P. D. J., cited, 88n, 90n, 160n, 214n, 247-248n

capital: allocation of, 222; definition, 60-61; forms of, 60-61; intensity on the plantation, 150-152; and technology, 14, 32, 54

caravans, 97-98, 106, 110, 122, 124, 217

cartels, industrial, 141, 152

cash: crops, 50n, 59n, 90n, 214; earning products, 57, 80, 213; for farm labor, 119; income, 74, 81, 220; transactions, 49, 55, 117

causality, concept of, 155

census officers, 101

central government, 32, 38, 197; *see also* Thailand, government of

Central Plain, 18n, 21, 25

Central Thailand, 25, 31, 42, 116, 193, 197; *see also* Central Plain

centralism, trend to, 30n; *see also* regionalism, Northern

Ceylon, 140n, 141, 153

Chanthaburi hills, 19

Chao Phraya River and delta, 19, 21, 28, 92

cheap labor policy, 152-153, 157

Chiengdao District, 35, 99, 128

Chiengdao Tea Plantation, 143, 161, 166, 168, 175, 177, 180, 203, 210, 214-220, 241, 249-251

Chiengmai, province of, 1n, 18n, 28n, 50n, 69, 77, 91n, 116, 128, 161n, 173

Chiengmai Town, 22, 24, 33n, 35-38, 84, 98, 108n, 128, 165, 208; government officials in, 90n, 91; railway to, 31; seminaries in, 80; Tribal Research Center at, 200; University of the North at, 31n

children: buying and selling of, 64-66; raising of, 62, 64; school-age, 186; wage labor of, 63, 75, 107, 175

China and the Chinese, 19, 77, 87n, 150; ethnic minority in Thailand, 25, 248; mainland relations with Thailand, 27-28, 86, 199, 249n; tea smallholders, 84, 139-140, 143, 171; traders, 25, 58, 120n, 138-139, 163n, 247; *see also* Haw

chitemene, 42

Chotsukkharat, S., cited, 89n, 94n

Christianity, influence of, 38, 77-80, 184, 250

civil servants: attitudes of, 192-193, 208, 249n; salaries of, 205

clients, role of, 115, 118, 121-122, 176, 186-187, 220; *see also* entourages

climate, 43, 99, 198, 218

Education, Ministry of, 125
elite, Thai, 25, 30, 68, 164, 179, 188, 190, 193
Ellul, Jacques, cited, 11n
Elwin, Verrier, cited, 144n
"embedded," use of as economic term, 7n, 8n
enclaves, cultural, 8n, 149, 154-155, 181; *see also* dualism, economic and social
entourages, 123, 133-134, 159-160, 162-163, 189-191, 209; conflict with market systems, 178-179; definition and formation of, 113-121; network of, 192, 240; political role of, 186-187, 247; relationships within and among, 136, 169-170, 188, 194n, 215, 231-232; reliance on, 125, 255; social status in, 220, 252
entrepreneurs: village and local, 119, 249n; Western, 12, 116, 179; *see also* Khun Luang *and* merchants
environment: changes in, 8, 83, 235; control of, 3, 5, 11, 52; indigenous, 151, 154; pluralistic, 10, 237-238; upland, 10, 137, 184, 188, 212; *see also* ecology
Erasmus, Charles J., cited, 4n, 11n
established order, preservation and role of, 6-7, 10-12, 15
estates, tea, 152-153, 180
ethnic groups and classifications, 21n, 24, 26n, 60n, 70, 140n, 175, 248
ethnocentricity, 9n, 158, 245
ethnolinguistic categories, 26
Europe, 8n; *see also* West, the
exchange: media of, 55; rates of, 49n
expenditures and expenses, 71, 108-110, 130-131, 164, 172-173
exports: crops, 38, 91; earnings, 82n; of livestock, 57; surplus, 76, 230; trade, 34, 57, 80, 141, 155

factionalism, 103, 185
factories, 77, 128, 160, 162, 221, 228, 248; operating expenses of, 164-165, 170; storage capacity of, 169
Fairbank, John K., cited, 139n
Fang, 128

Fang Agricultural Station, 35, 77, 160, 248
Fei, John C. H., cited, 9n
fermentation process, 144n; miang, 89; tea, 145-146, 168
field sites, 41-45, 53, 56, 164, 230
field-site distribution, 3, 7, 184
firearms and ammunition, 54, 72
firms, *see* West, the: firms
Firth, Raymond, cited, 1n
fiscal procedures, 30, 121-123, 155; *see also* aid, credit, *and* taxes
floods and flooding, 19, 87, 198
foraging, 45, 47, 73, 75n, 81n
foreign: aid, 72, 74; financing, 155; ownership, 150, 151n, 155; sector, 25, 43, 49n, 53, 55-56, 59, 74-75, 82-83, 232; trade, 55, 56n, 57
forests: clearing of, 43, 199; deciduous, 22-23; laws of, 224; and public domain, 194-195; regeneration of, 43; tea, 85
Forests, Department of, 194, 198, 224; officers of, 195-196, 198, 203, 255
Foster, George M., cited, 10n
Frankel, S. Herbert, 9n, 245
frontier: cultural, 210, 241; political and geographical, 29, 139n, 199-200
functional integrity, 231-237
functionalism, definition of, 6n, 8n

Geertz, Clifford, cited, 42n
Gilfillan, S., cited, 4n
Gordon, R. A., cited, 1n
Gouldner, Alvin W., cited, 115n, 121n
Gourou, Pierre, cited, 154n, 156n
government: actions of, 68, 81, 125, 198, 208-209, 248-249; agencies, 222, 224, 253; central, 31-32, 38, 39, 191; investment, 32; officials, 25, 31n, 101, 195-196, 204; propaganda, 253; rules and regulations, 192-193, 196
graft, 224n, 249; *see also* bribery
Graham, W. A., cited, 30n
Great Britain, 87n; colonization by, 28, 139; *see also entries under* British

institutional (*cont.*)
225, 235; constraints, 183, 212, 230-237; *see also* economics: institutional
institutions, 6, 73, 76, 147-148; economic, 1n, 3, 5, 9, 14-15; political 182, 184-185; social, 16, 78, 185
integration: normative, 8n; political, 183; vertical, 141
intercultural: economics, 15-16, 212-213; labor flow, 236; relations, 10-11, 13, 224, 230, 237; trade, 218, 222; transactions, 213, 217
interdependence, functional, 8n
interest rates, 111n, 177
interhousehold economic relations, 49, 50, 53
Interior, Ministry of, 194, 200
international affairs, 5, 31-32, 141-143, 151
intervillage economic transactions, 34, 52, 55, 64
intravillage economic transactions, 51, 67, 78, 232, 252
inventions and innovations, consequences, 4, 10n
inventory: controls, 250-251; fluctuations, 216; supplies, 214-215
investment, 32, 61, 109-111, 151, 219
Irrawaddy watershed, 86n
irrigation projects and programs, 21, 32-33, 39, 109, 195n
itinerant laborers and traders, 38, 110n, 134; *see also* Haw

Japan, 142, 159
jhum, 42
Jones, Delmos J., cited, 50n, 60n, 77n, 78n, 79n, 80n, 82n
Judd, L. C., cited, 22n, 34n
jungle: fertility, 22, 43, 53, 69, 83, 105; growth, 45, 92; land, 33, 59, 86, 139, 187, 200n, 224, 254

Kachin tribe, 79n, 139, 220-221
kaingin, 42
Kampaengphet, province of, 18n
Kandre, Peter K., cited, 55n, 62n, 63n, 65n, 66n
Kao, Charles H. C., cited, 225n
Kaplan, David, cited, 1n

Kapp, K. William, cited, 1n
Karen tribe, 27, 39, 66n, 221
karma, belief in, 106n, 232
Keen, F. G. B., cited, 225n, 246n
Ketu-Sinh, Ouay, cited, 100n
Keyes, Charles F., cited, 31n
Keyfitz, Nathan, cited, 245n
Keynesian economic policy, 244n
Khaun Myang, 21, 25
Khmer, 24
Khmu tribe, 26, 87, 221
Khorat escarpment, 19
Khun Luang, 158, 160, 162-164, 167, 169-172, 177-180, 189, 192-193, 196, 203, 210, 215, 223, 250-251
Kingshill, Konrad, cited, 24n, 32n, 33n, 36n
kinship, 50n, 60n, 64, 68-69, 78, 80, 97, 102-103, 106, 113, 116, 118-119, 127, 184, 187
klang harvest, 94, 97, 135n, 234
Kunstadter, Peter, cited, 23n, 26n, 59n, 70n, 191n, 195n

labor: division and specialization of, 5, 41, 130, 132, 133, 175, 230, 252; household, 56n, 63, 218, 227; mobility, 49n, 55, 62, 110n, 118, 156, 234-236; obligations, 43-44, 51, 119n, 183; plantation, 128-129, 140, 152-158, 161, 163, 170-176, 188-189; productivity, 43, 61, 63, 74, 130n, 186; relations, 113, 140, 150, 180; supply, 48, 52, 59-66, 90, 145n, 157, 218-219, 225, 227; turnover rate 108, 171, 174; unions, 189n; *see also* wages
Lahu tribe and villages, 27, 39, 60n, 63-65, 69-70, 76-83, 162, 173-175, 183, 210, 220-221, 223, 228, 240; *see also* Ban Yai Suk *and* Huai Thad
lam, 120n
Lamet tribe of Laos, 87, 120n
Lampang, province of, 18n, 29
Lamphun, province of, 18n, 29
land, 59, 72, 183, 223, 225, 230; concessions, 162, 190, 203, 248; deforested, 187, 198-199; development, 60-61, 162; holdings, 38, 118; public, 61, 196; tax, 70n, 108n, 186;

land (*cont.*)
use, 56, 73, 154, 182-183, 194-195;
see also *nikhom* and tenure, land
Land Code (1954), 194
Land Department of the Ministry
of Interior, 162, 194-196, 203, 224
landlessness, 105-106, 111-112, 180,
210, 219, 254
landlords and ownership, 110, 112,
116, 120
Lannathai, 29
Lao, 21n, 23-25, 85
Laos, 19, 21n, 23-25, 28, 72, 84-87,
120n, 128, 187, 228, 239
Lasker, Bruno, cited, 65n
Lave, Lester, cited, 4n
law: ambiguity of, 197; legal codes,
30; upland, 161; *see also* Land
Code
Lawa tribe, 26
LeBar, Frank M., cited, 21n, 23n,
26n, 44n, 78n, 87, 88n, 90n, 96n,
101n, 108n, 135n
LeMay, Reginald, cited, 22n, 28n,
29n, 31n, 84n, 85n
Leach, Edmund R., cited, 26n, 220
leadership: abilities, 115-116; political, 80; secular, 172, 184n; tribal,
195; *see also* bureaucracy
legal codes, 30
Lehman, F. K., cited, 26n
let pet, 84
liquid assets, 64, 112, 219
Lisu tribe and villages, 27, 39, 65n,
76n, 79n
livestock, 47, 54, 57, 60, 63-64, 72, 80-
81n, 98, 204, 207, 221, 246
loans: government, 162, 190; repayment of, 123; rice, 50; *see also*
credit
Loei, province of, 18n
Lowe, Adolph, cited, 10n
lowland: agriculture, 27, 104-105,
198, 227; culture, 23-25, 187, 192;
economy, 33, 76, 80, 82, 104-105,
231-232; geography, 19-22, 33, 39,
49, 151, 196, 212; peasantry, 30-35,
83, 86, 101, 127, 134, 158, 210, 221,
229, 254; society, 106, 221, 235;
trade, 54, 57, 214
Luang Prabang, 128

Lue, *see* Tai Lue
luxury articles, 54, 72, 109, 218;
consumables, 58, 87-88, 172, 219

Machlup, Fritz, cited, 2n
Mae Kok river basin, 50n
Mae Rim district, 35
Mae Thaeng district, 35-36, 99, 128
Maehongsorn, province of, 18n
maize, 45-46, 57, 81, 246n
Malaysia, 140n
management: plantation, 153, 159,
209, 231-232; scientific, 151, 236
Manndorff, Hans, cited, 195n, 201n
Mansfield, Edwin, cited, 4n
market places and marketing, 58,
98-100, 110, 120, 163, 208, 249n,
257; towns, 38, 122; world, 32, 34,
149, 151, 182
market system, 14, 141, 152, 231
marriage, 50, 60n, 63-64, 68, 106
Martindale, Don, cited, 6n
Mason, Edward S., cited, 179n
material well-being, *see* welfare
matriarchal and matrifocal tendencies, 24, 64
McCarthy, James, cited, 85n
McClelland, David C., cited, 7n
mechanization, 32, 140, 150-154, 156,
250; *see also* technology
medical officers, 53, 205, 208
medical services, 157, 190, 219, 248
Meo tribe and villages, 27, 39, 48n,
62-65, 68-76, 82-83, 168, 172-174,
184, 210, 220-223, 240; *see also*
Phapucom
mepacrin, 152
merchants, 25, 38, 58, 80, 120, 122,
134, 142, 160, 163, 173
"merit making," 109, 127
miang: bundle sizes, 99; consumption of, 85, 98-101, 253; cultivation of, 88-90, 91n, 92-97, 106, 108,
114, 125-126, 129n, 130, 135-136,
213, 247; economics of, 84, 86-87,
89, 91, 130; gardens and gardeners,
84, 92-97, 106-109, 112-113, 120,
124, 128, 161-162, 166-169, 187, 196,
199, 210, 214, 219n, 221, 224, 229;
harvests, 94-97, 107, 216-217; industry, 104, 107, 114n, 129; and

miang (*cont.*)
labor relations, 130, 132-133, 144n, 160; storage and dispersal of, 97-98, 102; trade, 89, 97-101, 214; transportation of, 122, 135
migration, 26, 69, 105, 126, 140n, 204, 240; to the hills, 88, 92, 102n, 104; Thai, 88, 104-106, 200n, 224; tribal, 44-45, 51, 79, 87n, 88, 184, 201, 228, 255, 258
Milne, Mary Lewis, cited, 84, 94n, 96n
milpa, 42
mineral deficiencies, 54
minority groups, 25, 58n, 171, 195, 248; *see also* hill tribes
Mishan, Ezra J., cited, 11n
missionaries, influence of, 38, 77, 79-80, 84n
Mobile Development Unit, Ministry of Defense, 200
model-building in economics, 2
Moerman, Michael, cited, 24n, 30n, 32n, 33n, 36n, 103n, 108n, 116-117, 155, 193n, 196n, 230n, 240n
money and moneylenders, 55, 59, 120, 122, 188, 269
monks, 38, 127, 128n
monsoon season, 33, 46, 93, 198
Mote, F. W., cited, 58n
mountain ranges and trails, 21, 23, 35, 39, 125
mui harvest, 94, 96-97, 135n, 234
multivillage communities, 60n, 77-79, 183
Murdock, George P., cited, 10n
Myint, Hla, cited, 151n, 153n, 156n, 157n
Myrdal, Gunnar, cited, 10n, 43n, 61n, 109n, 151n, 153n, 154n, 155n, 225n, 238n, 245n

nai, 120n
Nakorntheb, Pramote, cited, 79n
Nan: province, 18n, 29; river, 21
narcotics, 56-57, 73n, 197-198, 257n; *see also* addiction, drug
Nash, Manning, cited, 8n, 9n
nation-building, 18, 159, 192, 197
nation-state, 36, 182, 185-186, 191, 197

Neale, Walter C., cited, 109n, 245
Netherland Indies, 158
New Guinea, 240n
New York Times, 199n
nikhom, 200-209, 235, 248, 258; economics of, 214; personnel, 203, 205-206, 212, 224, 257; remoteness of, 205; territories, 255; tribesmen, 256-257
Nikhom Chiengdao, 202-209, 255-256
Nimmanahaeminda, Kraisri, cited, 22n
nonconformity, pressures against, 9, 11, 13; *see also* ostracism
non-Western: cultures, 7, 8n, 10, 148, 158, 237; economic systems, 9, 14, 244-245; values, 16, 155, 244-245
North America, 8n
North Vietnam, 28
Northern Thailand: culture, 23-28; definition, 18; economics, 32-35; geography, 19-23; immigrant groups, 76; lowlands, 39; peasantry, 25, 34; political systems, 28-31; society, 20, 24-25, 84-85; uplands, 1-3, 16, 22-23, 139n, 182, 199, 201, 243-244, 248
nutrition, standards of, 73, 75, 157

occupational: hierarchy, 130-131; mobility, 137, 212; specialization, 130-133; *see also* labor
Oceanic tribal economy, 214n
Omkoi district, 69-73
opium: abandonment by Christianized tribes, 79-80, 228; consumption, 66, 73-74, 79, 198, 208; cultivation, 33, 45-47, 56, 59n, 66, 87n, 201, 204, 224, 227, 240; harvesting, 46, 49, 51n, 52, 71; labor requirements of, 48, 55, 56, 198, 258-259; prices, 58; processing, 46-47; trade in, 56-59, 136, 138, 139n, 197-199, 216, 218, 234, 257-258; *see also* smuggling and smugglers
ornaments, 47, 55; silver, 54, 63, 71-72
ostracism, 14, 234, 240
oxen, use of, 69, 93, 97-98, 104, 109-

oxen (*cont.*)
110, 120, 122, 129, 132-133, 135-136, 217, 219, 234

pa mieng, 85
paddi, 81; fields, 219
Palaung tribe, 84, 87
Pang Hok, 126-129, 134
Pang Huai Thad, 126, 129, 160, 162, 171
Pang Iak, 126, 128-129, 133
Pang Id, 126, 128-129
Pang Kud, 126-129, 135, 162, 223
Pang Wieng Daung, 126-127, 129, 134, 223
Parsons, Talcott, cited, 6n
patron-client relationship, 34, 115-116, 123, 176, 220; *see also* entourages
patrons and patronage, 52, 112, 115-116, 118, 120-121, 128n, 130, 133-134, 137, 164, 186-187, 190, 193, 205, 220, 231, 236, 254
pau liang, 120-123, 134-137, 161, 169, 213, 215-216, 253-255; *see also* entourages *and* patrons and patronage
peasants: economy, 15, 35, 95, 101, 114, 124, 169-170n, 172, 193, 216; households, 102, 202, 232, 253-254, 259; in the lowlands, 32-35, 83, 101, 112-113, 127, 158, 210, 254; population, 24-25, 104-106, 156, 232, 252; society, 87, 101, 111n, 112, 136, 215; tribal communities, 36, 40, 171, 196; in the uplands, 90-91, 103, 112-113, 124-126, 232, 253-254, 259; Western influences on, 38
peddlers, itinerant, 38, 80
Pelzer, Karl J., cited, 41n
Pendleton, Robert L., cited, 19n, 22n, 33n
personnel, 151, 203, 205-206, 210, 212, 224, 256-257, 259; *see also* staff
Phapucom, 68-76, 202-203, 205, 210, 223, 240; impoverishment of, 73, 76, 80, 83; swidden harvests, 71-72; tribesmen of, 77, 82, 172-174, 184
Phitsanulok, province of, 18n

pigs, 47, 55, 62, 80-81, 110, 213
Ping River, 21, 35, 73, 108n
plantation: economy, 15, 74-75, 129, 137, 140-143, 147-158, 167, 170, 176, 233, 236; labor force, 152-158, 170-176, 189; management, 150, 153, 159, 232; tea, 81, 150, 165, 203, 232; Western hemisphere, 156
pluralism, ethnic, 140n; *see also* culture, pluralism
Polanyi, Karl, cited, 6n, 8n, 9n, 231n, 245
Police Department and police officers, 101, 198, 199n, 217, 224
political: entity, 25, 49n, 101, 185, 191; independence, 29, 30n, 31, 221, 231; integration, 15, 30, 120, 183; propaganda, 11, 27-28; security, 115, 197, 215; structure, 77, 80, 123, 125, 186, 188, 190, 194n, 201; systems, 34, 68, 123, 182-190, 191, 241; ties, 24, 128
polygyny, 63
population: centers, 17, 22-23, 44n, 125, 250; Central Plain, 21; growth, 105, 195, 259; lowland, 30, 56, 75; peasant, 25, 156, 232, 252; pressures, 83, 87-88, 90n, 104-105; tribal, 25n, 26, 30, 71n, 79, 174, 183, 205; upland, 222; Village Twelve, 126
poverty, 52, 65-66, 69, 71, 76, 80, 83, 103, 153n, 232; *see also* income *and* welfare
Prae, province of, 18n, 29
Premarasami, Thanom, cited, 194n
prestige durables, 109, 172, 218
price-earnings ratio, 111n
price-fixing, 99, 152, 160
prices, *see* trade *and individual goods and services*
private enterprise, 40
private property, 188
profit motive, 140, 149, 152, 154-155, 178, 181, 189-190, 215, 233-234
progress, concept of, 6, 11-12
proletariat, agricultural, 143, 157, 188; *see also* labor
property concepts and rights, 59-60, 108-110, 183, 188
public: domain, 108n, 164, 187, 194-

285 *

welfare: material, 2, 4-5, 8, 12, 80, 83, 148, 233; stations, 39, 70, 72, 75n, 81, 125, 202

West, the: culture, 8n, 115; entrepreneurs, 116, 179; firms, 32, 141, 148-150, 158, 178, 180; history, 238; idea of progress, 11; imports from, 38, 91; technology, 52, 141; visitors from, 84-85, 91

wet rice: agricultural cycle, 227, 230n; cultivation, 24, 33, 90, 229; economy, 112; fields, 104-105, 112n, 120, 136n, 187, 196, 259; technology, 32, 59; see also rice

White, Leslie, cited, 4n

White, Lynn, cited, 4n

wholesaling and wholesalers, 120, 142, 151, 213, 228, 250

Wicitrajantra, Narongrit, cited, 89n

Wickizer, V. D., cited, 141n

Wiens, Herold J., cited, 72n

Wijeyewardene, Gehan, cited, 36n, 102n, 103n, 105n, 108n, 116n

Williams, Harry, cited, 153n

wives: infertile, 64; sale of, 64-66

women, status of, 63, 75, 175

woodsmanship and woodworking, 33, 47, 106

World War II, 142

Yamey, Basil S., cited, 14n

Yang River, 21

Yano, Toru, cited, 194n, 196n

Yao tribe, 27, 59n, 61, 63n, 65n, 76n

Yen tzu ch'un ch'ui, 86

Yoe, Shway, cited, 84n

Yom River, 21

Young, Gordon, cited, 26, 44n, 62n, 66n

Yumbri tribe, 26

Yunnanese Chinese, 27, 58n, 72, 77, 86, 234

*Economic Systems of
Northern Thailand*

Designed by R. E. Rosenbaum.
Composed by Vail-Ballou Press, Inc.,
in 11 pt. linotype Janson, 3 points leaded,
with display lines in monotype Deepdene.
Printed letterpress from type by Vail-Ballou Press
on Warren's No. 66 text, 60 lb. basis,
with the Cornell University Press watermark.
Bound by Vail-Ballou Press
in Interlaken Pallium bookcloth
and stamped in All Purpose foil.